EXPERIMENTS OF THE MIND

Experiments of the Mind

FROM THE COGNITIVE PSYCHOLOGY
LAB TO THE WORLD OF FACEBOOK
AND TWITTER

EMILY MARTIN

PRINCETON UNIVERSITY PRESS
PRINCETON & OXFORD

Published by Princeton University Press
41 William Street, Princeton, New Jersey 08540
6 Oxford Street, Woodstock, Oxfordshire OX20 1TR

press.princeton.edu

Library of Congress Cataloging-in-Publication Data

Names: Martin, Emily, author.
Title: Experiments of the mind : from the cognitive psychology lab to the world of Facebook and Twitter / Emily Martin.
Description: Princeton : Princeton University Press, [2021] | Includes bibliographical references and index.
Identifiers: LCCN 2021013535 (print) | LCCN 2021013536 (ebook) | ISBN 9780691230719 (hardback ; alk. paper) | ISBN 9780691177311 (paperback ; alk. paper | ISBN 9780691232072 (ebook)
Subjects: LCSH: Psychology, Experimental. | Psychology—Experiments. | Cognitive psychology—Experiments. | Human experimentation in psychology. | Experimental psychologists.
Classification: LCC BF181 .M3155 2021 (print) | LCC BF181 (ebook) | DDC 150.72/4—dc23
LC record available at https://lccn.loc.gov/2021013535
LC ebook record available at https://lccn.loc.gov/2021013536

British Library Cataloging-in-Publication Data is available

Editorial: Fred Appel and James Collier
Production Editorial: Natalie Baan
Jacket Design: Layla Mac Rory
Production: Erin Suydam
Publicity: Kate Hensley and Kathryn Stevens
Copyeditor: Michele Rosen

This book has been composed in Arno

Printed on acid-free paper. ∞

Printed in the United States of America

10 9 8 7 6 5 4 3 2 1

Dedicated to the four experimental cognitive psychologists
who opened their laboratory doors to me

CONTENTS

LIST OF ILLUSTRATIONS

Figures

Table and Box

PREFACE

AS I WAS finishing writing this book, New York City, where I live, was beginning to emerge from the first wave of the COVID-19 pandemic. I had experienced many months of strict isolation in my apartment because of my husband's and my age-related vulnerability. We lived a version of what many people around the world lived through: emergency sirens running day and night, scenes of macabre horror reported from many city hospitals, descriptions of serious illness and death that rivaled Dante's lowest circles of hell, essential health workers risking their lives, medical tents in parks and ICUs on ships in the harbor, burial pits on offshore islands, inequities of resources, health care, and housing coming glaringly into daylight. Estimates claimed that one in five New York City residents were infected.[1] I questioned whether the universities, the presses, the workforce, and retail outlets would ever be functioning again to produce and market a book, any book, and, if so, whether this book would be relevant to anyone in a post-coronavirus world.

This book is about the historical and contemporary infrastructure that has been developed by experimental psychologists, which I argue underlies social and digital media platforms. These platforms work alongside a burgeoning array of devices positioned on streets and doorways, worn on the body, or installed in homes and office buildings. The pandemic has brought an array of new wearable devices to monitor COVID-19 status, such as BioButton™ or SafeZone. Many scholars and organizations are already tracking these means of gathering data, which are now, in the wake of the pandemic, needed to inform public health decisions. These means of gathering data are also responsible for producing voluminous quantities of information about the whereabouts and activities of individuals and populations. It is my hope that the story of how we got to this moment when enormous quantities of numerical data suddenly became beneficial to many technologies, including those needed to help control a pandemic, will help the general public understand and evaluate the practices that underpin all of them.

ACKNOWLEDGMENTS

I EXTEND heartfelt gratitude to the psychologists who introduced me to this field. Four generous senior faculty launched me on this project, opened many ports of call, and guided me through numerous rocky harbors. They also read the final draft of this book with meticulous care and gave me detailed editorial feedback that saved me from many blunders and omissions. There is no way to adequately thank people who are so welcoming and open-minded but who wish to remain anonymous, so instead I am dedicating this book to the four of them. I extend the same gratitude to the late Charles Gross, whose course on cognitive psychology at Princeton University was my original introduction to the field. To acknowledge all the psychologists I learned from at any length and in any firsthand capacity over the years of my research, I list them here without further identifiers: Tobias Bosch, Marisa Carrasco, Michelle Fine, Steven Glickman, Tom Griffiths, Will Griscom, Todd Gureckis, Eve Isham, Setha Low, Jennifer Mangels, Mike McCloskey, Line Lerche Mørck, Morten Nissen, Yuliya Ochakovskaya, Steven Palmer, Elizabeth Phelps, Bill Prinzmetal, Jeremy Purcell, Brenda Rapp, Donald Riley, David Rothlein, Nava Rubin, Louis Sass, Jennifer Shea, Dan Slobin, Luca Tateo, Robert White, Ron White- man, Bob Wiley, and the late Steven Yantis.

My thanks to the many historians of science, historians of psychology, and anthropologists whose current work greatly enlightened me: Jane Anderson, Warwick Anderson, David Bond, Angela Creager, Joe Dumit, Heidi Geismar, Stefanos Geroulanos, Susan Harding, Stefan Helmreich, Anita Herle, Klaus Hoeyer, Don Kulick, Ruth Leys, Elizabeth Lunbeck, Lisa Malich, Andreas Meyer, Todd Meyers, Jill Morawski, Adriana Petryna, Mary Louise Pratt, Graham Richards, Renato Rosaldo, Nikolas Rose, Richard Rottenburg, Erica Schoenberger, Amy Smiley, Michael Sokal, Noelle Stout, and Karen-Sue Taussig. From the pioneering laboratory studies by Bruno Latour and Steven Woolgar, Sharon Traweek, and Michael Lynch, to the current, fine-grained ethnographic and historical work on science and technology studies in many monographs and a growing number of journals, I was guided by a rich heritage.[1]

Special thanks to Ceridwen Dovey, who, writing for *The New Yorker's* website, interviewed me in depth at just at the right time to help me make sense of it all. I am particularly indebted to Leith Mullings, who gave me courage that this project was worthwhile and contributed many specific insights over wine at dinners and on walks in the parks on the Upper West Side of New York City. For their virtual and in-person company, which lifted my spirits during the pandemic, I thank my apartment building neighbors, Jos Dudgeon, Michelle Landau, Lucy Bolton, and Allan Guggenheim.

It goes without saying that, as ever, I have learned a great deal from my former or current graduate students in the Department of Anthropology at NYU who are working in the anthropology of science, and I thank them from my heart: Dwai Banerjee, Lucas Bessire, Anisha Chadha, Wenrui Chen, Alison Cool, Grace Gu, Joseph Livesey, Schuyler Marquez, Laura Murray, Vijayanka Nair, Alyse Parker, Sujit Thomas, Jennifer Trowbridge, Shannon Ward, Summer Woods, Emily Yates-Doerr, and Tyler Zoanni.

I appreciate the important feedback I received from colleagues at the university departments and conferences where I gave talks on topics related to this book: UC Davis, UC San Diego, the University of Pennsylvania, the University of Toronto, the American Anthropological Association, Aarhus University, Lübeck University, UC Berkeley, New York University, the Wenner-Gren Symposium on Potentiality, CUNY Grad Center, University College London, and the University of Colorado at Boulder.

I spent many years doing this ethnography of the world of experimental psychology in university labs. That world I came to know from the inside, in a limited way. The world of digital life I only know as a participant, like anyone else with a computer and access to the internet. So, my links between the lab and the digital world are based on a substantial reading of secondary material and the help of my colleagues who have worked on digital matters for many years and provided detailed guidance. In particular, I am indebted to Lucy Suchman, Joan Greenbaum, Sareeta Amrute, Andrew Clement, and all the researchers at AI Now and Data & Society Research.

I am grateful for the helpful efforts of numerous curators and librarians for access to archives I consulted about the early history of anthropology and psychology: Anita Herle at the Museum of Archaeology and Anthropology in Cambridge; Peter Meadows at the University of Cambridge Manuscripts Reading Room; Hilary Dorsch Wong at the Hemenway papers in the Division of Rare and Manuscript Collections, Cornell University Library; staff for the Franz Boas correspondence at the American Philosophical Society Library; and Melanie Locay at the New York Public Library's Allen Room.

My gratitude goes to Ralph Guggenheim for working his magic in preparing digital files for the illustrations and to Kara Healey for her expert drawings.

I owe special thanks to Fred Appel, my editor at Princeton University Press, for sticking with me over the long haul of the research and writing for this book. His editorial acumen was on the mark as always, and his belief that the project was worthwhile sustained me many times. In addition, I thank James Collier for his assistance in moving the manuscript through the final stages at the press. I am enormously grateful for the experienced hand of Natalie Baan, who proficiently guided the manuscript through its production, and the skillful and meticulous oversight of my copyeditor, Michele Rosen.

For generous funding support, I thank the Wenner-Gren Foundation, the National Science Foundation's Cultural Anthropology, Science, Technology, and Society, and Social Psychology programs; and the Perception, Action, and Cognition Program. I am grateful for sustained administrative, editorial, and computer help from Roma Aryl, Cristine Khan, Carmen Diaz, and Uli Fernandez. I greatly appreciate the editorial work of Peter Wissoker, who undertook a review of the manuscript at a late stage and helped to lend much more organizational coherence to the overall story.

And most of all, thanks to the patience and forbearance of my family, Richard, Jenny, Ariel, Yohance, Morgan, Soleil, Winona, and Chester, without whose support and company on daily adventures and fun vacations I could have written nothing. My husband Richard read an untold number of drafts with a keen editor's eye and a scientist's expectation of clarity and fairness. The research for this book began in 2012, nine years before its publication. Only with Richard's clear explanations of underlying biophysical processes, his indefatigable editorial readings, and his confident belief that the project was worthwhile could I have persisted. I am thankful for his patience and his generous and inspiring help.

DRAMATIS PERSONAE

DR. B was the very first psychologist I found who was open to the idea that I could be an ethnographer who observed psychologists doing experimental work. I was sitting on an old couch in a basement hallway waiting to be a subject in a research project run by another faculty member in his department. Although the basement level had no natural light, I was aware that office and lab space there were not considered subpar: they were quiet, solid, stable, and often roomy. The campus, a long flight of stairs above, would be wreathed in bright sunlight year round. Dr. B looked out of his office and, seeing me sitting there alone, said, "Hello, can I help you?" I explained about waiting for the experiment to start and gave my quick version of the research project I wanted to launch: something about the history of psychology and anthropology when they were young and cooperating disciplines and then how things got going in a different way in the early twentieth century. "Hmm," he said, "come on in." In his office he pulled an old book off his shelf, a large tome by Robert Woodworth. He had been interested in Woodworth, he said, because "ideas were being explored in the early 1900s that got forgotten about later." I lit up because I was aware that Woodworth was part of the early-twentieth-century period when psychology was parting ways from what was called "introspection" and heading toward behaviorism. Dr. B opened all the doors I needed for this research project, lending his openness, generosity, and insight to my path through the discipline. He had retired from his research lab but was busy collaborating with former graduate students and attending conferences and department events. He was certainly a good example of what anthropologists call key informants, because of his extraordinary willingness to imagine a different kind of psychology and entertain the way an anthropologist thinks about the world. I spent many hours sitting with him at events, talking about everything on my mind in the campus outdoor café or in his office. If our disciplines are still like closed boxes that confine our minds, Dr. B takes delight in breaking those boxes open.

Dr. S had his office in a distant part of Dr. B's building, also in the basement. The door to his office was covered with many different doorbells, so that subjects for different experiments could signal the right graduate student. Inside was a warren of rooms, booths for experiments, offices, and one larger conference room filled with a random assortment of chairs and desks arranged around the perimeter. Dr. S stood out from all the other psychologists I met for several reasons. He generated sociality around him like an electric current. He often extended dinner invitations to the whole lab. Dinner would be a potluck at his house in a nearby neighborhood followed by a movie on the TV. Absent lab members could join by Skype as they watched the same movie. The lab meetings and larger events he organized always had food and or drink—as if we were of course present as minds and bodies both. Dr. S's research stood outside the usual lines of topics in psychology. He was unafraid of "subjectivity," and in fact his research sought it and depended on it. He was unafraid of topics like aesthetics, music, or art that might seem challenging to study quantitatively and therefore scientifically. He was an explorer personally, artistically, and scientifically. He didn't hesitate to tell me off when I allowed an orthodox story of psychology to dominate my thinking—he was forthright about correcting my false impressions, for which I was always enormously grateful.

I met Dr. J through the network of a fellow anthropologist in New York City who sent out a plea on email to dozens of colleagues in psychology. Dr. J was the only person who replied, saying the project sounded interesting to her and inviting me to her office. I was nervous. I read all her publications. I brought my last book as a gift. She was a gracious person, impeccably honest and dedicated to her work and her students. Accordingly, she was cautious with me. What would I do exactly? What were the risks and protections? Would we sign a contract? This was perhaps the rockiest initial interview I had.

Finally, she agreed that I could attend lab meetings and talk to graduate students with their permission on a trial basis. But maybe her understandable caution led to fuller acceptance in the end. After some months of attending lab meetings, joining teams of experimenters when I could be useful, and having long interviews with selected grad students, Dr. J wrote my name on the white board as a lab member, designated "anthropologist." I was given an ID card for the building and the lab and links to the lab website and Google schedule.

Dr. J's lab was brimming with social interactions. The lab space was crowded, and people worked close by each other, real estate being at a premium in the surrounding city. The topics studied were social: how people learn, how they forget, how they lose track of tasks, how they are motivated.

She often stated the lab mantra: we help each other. We volunteer when another set of hands or eyes are needed. We teach each other. And this was matched by an endless series of rituals and celebrations. Everyone's birthday was marked with a cake and other treats; graduations, publications, grants, jobs, all were marked with some interesting and delicious food, as often as not prepared at home and brought in to share.

The lab's cooperative ethos meant that I could join a group of students and staff who left the city at a very early hour to travel to a neighboring state's public schools to conduct an experiment in a large class. It meant that I could lend a hand to Randall, a grad student whose experiment needed a large number of student-volunteers. Signing them in, giving them screening tests, recording which person was matched to which computer, logging the results, and debriefing them during and after a two-hour experiment: all this needed more than one person. I usually felt like an academic younger sister to Dr. J. She was immensely kind to her students. She cared about her university and took on administrative tasks willingly. She struggled with childcare problems that I remembered well—running late, leaving early, scheduling sitters. She was adaptable, whether moving from a private to a public university, adjusting to the increasing demand for neuropsychological research findings, or finding sources of support outside academia.

Engaging Dr. R in my fieldwork crossed many lines. I was a colleague of hers in a different department of the same university for years. She was literally my next-door neighbor for some years. Dr. B wrote her a letter of introduction in which he reminded her that he had shared materials she used for her dissertation. All this gradually opened her lab's doors. I could attend lab meetings, interview grad students, and be a subject when appropriate in ongoing studies. I could also be a "control" subject when the lab needed someone of my age in order to match a real subject who was willing to be tested in an fMRI machine. The research projects ongoing in this lab were intense. Their aims were to determine which parts of the brain are involved in cognitive activities like spelling and reading. Partly because of the prestige of this private university, lab members were ambitious. They were well funded, attended many conferences, published many papers, and expected to make careers in the field. Collaborations tended to be with other specialists outside the lab or the department. Each individual lab member was single minded and focused, while also being willing to help others reach their research goals. People would bring lunch or snacks to lab meetings, but it was clear that participating in intense discussion of ongoing research was the priority. The lab was spacious: there was office space for post docs, grad students, as well as a dedicated conference room. There were windows open to the gardens outdoors and a feeling of freedom to move around the office, which was well appointed with furniture and equipment.

Graduate Students

I followed two PhD graduate students in each of the three labs, one early in his or her program, one far along. By happenstance they included one woman and five men, one from Eastern Europe, one Black American, and four White Americans. They came from a variety of public and private universities across the United States.

Dr. R's Lab

Rob was an advanced student who had some important publications to his name. He was widely accomplished in the field and was conducting the final experiments needed for his dissertation. He was poised and gentle, confident in his abilities, detail-oriented and devoted to his work. He warmly invited me into his fMRI study in progress and patiently explained the technology and its limitations.

Wade was a first-year student when I met him. He was deeply committed to understanding how we learn non-Indo-European scripts. His hope was to gain graduate training in cognitive neuroscience and then apply his findings to classroom teaching. His eyes were wide open about the world he was entering. He was generously frank with me about what puzzled him early on and the many challenging steps he would need to take in the field. His bright intelligence was in play. His work soon took off like a shot, and he published a major paper in his third year.

Dr. J's Lab

As an advanced student, Randall was an exceptionally articulate teacher of concepts in cognitive psychology. He never condescended, and always took even the most naive of my questions seriously. He kindly granted me extensive access to his planning and training, as well as participation in all of his ongoing experiments. He was gracious and enabling. In answer to a question from a journalist—what is it like to be studied by Emily?—he said, "Emily was not studying me, we were studying experiments together." He was publishing innovative papers and speeding toward the completion of his degree.

Ulla was a beginning student when I met her. We had many amiable and warm-hearted conversations in the lab and over coffee. She openly shared with me her fears and doubts about entering a new technical scientific field. None of those doubts mattered because her quick intelligence led to her proficient mastery of the field in short order. Her mind was so full of brilliant thoughts that sometimes her speech could not keep up with them. She had a mischievous streak that I enjoyed a great deal. In frustration over "cleaning" noisy brain wave data, it was Ulla who said wryly, "this is life inside psychology."

Dr. S's Lab

Sam was nearly finished with his PhD when I arrived. He had mastered all the tools of the trade and was often in a position to significantly help other graduate students learn how to develop their experiments or design a poster. His manner was calm, and he communicated a modest but well-earned confidence about his future and the future of the field.

Jim was a first-year student when I met him. He was beyond delighted to be in a graduate program in cognitive psychology and in the particular lab where he was working. As an undergraduate at another university, he had been at the forefront of efforts to promote programs for the study of the mind and the brain. The PhD he was beginning was his passion. He was casual, relaxed, and amiable. He would have been at home on a nearby beach or mountain trail, but his devotion to cognitive psychology was clearly his priority.

EXPERIMENTS OF THE MIND

Introduction

There is something disturbingly paradoxical about a science that has for its
subject the agent that creates the science.

—ROGER SMITH, *THE NORTON HISTORY OF*
THE HUMAN SCIENCES, 1997

THE DISCIPLINE of experimental cognitive psychology contains a powerful
set of concepts and practices that play an active role both in research laboratories and in the daily lives of many people.[1] The discipline of experimental
psychology propels our concepts of the mind and the person in particular
directions. This book follows a series of ethnographic clues that show where
the discipline came from and how it is implicated in digital media like Facebook and Twitter and corporate internet platforms like Amazon or Google.

At its beginning, my ethnographic research in psychology labs felt a bit
misguided. I struggled to maintain my sense of purpose because my anthropology colleagues and friends were frequently mystified by my choice of subject. They found the topic of experimental psychology frankly boring, and
when it evoked memories of introductory courses in psychology in college,
they also found it old-fashioned and passé. Their reaction was not novel: more
than one hundred years ago, William James spotted the beginning of experimental psychology in Germany and thought its large-scale, statistical methods
would tax anyone's patience to the utmost. Scornfully, he imagined these
psychological experiments would create tedium that could only be borne by
Germans, since they were incapable of being bored.[2]

I was never bored, however, but rather gripped by a conviction that experimental psychology might be a powerful and sometimes unseen force in daily

1

life, one that is hidden beneath the latest digital technologies. My interest was validated when psychological experiments were, remarkably enough, the subject of a play at the Lincoln Center Festival in New York City. In 2017, I went to see the play *Opening Skinner's Box*, which was based on the book of that name by Lauren Slater. In the book and the play, Slater investigated each of ten "extraordinary" psychological experiments, as *Playbill* described them; it went on to refer to these experiments as "one way of telling the story of the twentieth century and the struggle to understand who we are and what we are really like as a species."[3] Slater interviewed some of the psychologists who conducted the experiments and people who were subjects in them, and she incorporated some of the interviews into the play script so they could be portrayed on stage.[4] The play asks the audience to contemplate the Zimbardo Stanford prison experiment (during which undergraduate subjects who were randomly assigned to the prison guard role became domineering and cruel to undergraduates who were randomly assigned the role of prisoner). Next, we learned about the Milgram shock experiment (many people followed orders from an insistent experimenter to inflict apparently dangerous electric shocks on someone else, even when doing so conflicted with their personal conscience). Finally, we came to the Festinger cognitive dissonance experiments. For these, subjects who agreed to express an opinion they actually did not hold would experience uncomfortable cognitive dissonance between their true opinion and the false one. They were given a monetary reward for tolerating this discomfort. But those subjects who thought the monetary reward for expressing a false opinion was insufficient compensation for their cognitive discomfort reduced their discomfort in another way: they adopted the formerly false opinion and came to believe it more strongly than their previous opinion. The conclusions were depressing enough: the human species is prey to delusion and false beliefs, and easily adopts cruel and even sadistic behaviors. In the play, however, the depiction of the original experiments themselves was more complex. Slater's interviews allowed us to hear subjects talking about what it was like to enact cruel or sadistic behavior or to find they had shown themselves to be illogical fools.

My Research Questions

Slater's play validated my research questions: What is it like to be a subject in a psychology experiment? What do experimenters assume about subjects? What is required of a good subject? What makes psychologists' descriptions of the human psyche appealing to many Americans? I wondered whether answers to all these questions might place limits on the conclusion that the experiments reveal universal truths about humankind. The paradox that lies at the heart of experimental psychology is this: How can human experimenters produce objective results using data produced by other humans? If objective results must be stripped of any subjectivity, how can objective results be obtained when both experimenters and subjects are human beings, ordinarily awash in their own subjective perceptions and beliefs? What kind of constraints, rules, regulations, or training would be necessary for experimenters and their subjects to ensure that objective data could be produced by experiments with human subjects? Historians have shown in great detail that during the post–Second World War period, the cultural reception of research in psychology differed from today. Jill Morawski shows vividly how the penumbra of experimentation in the German concentration camps cast a troubling pall over post-war psychology experiments involving human subjects. There was anxiety that the authority of the scientist in the laboratory might share the grim features of a totalitarian state. There was also anxiety over whether the subjects in lab experiments were, as researchers hoped, "stable and interchangeable" participants in an enterprise in which they would earnestly play an honest role. There was worry that unruly subjects might trip up the experimenters by deliberately or unintentionally failing to follow instructions. Now, seventy years later, these anxieties have receded, with the help of technical refinements that allowed researchers to see subjects as "mostly rational and autonomous beings whose thoughts could be measured through appropriate experimental controls."[5]

But even in the absence of post–World War II anxieties, the experimenter-subject system is best considered part and parcel of a much wider social context. Graham Richards describes vividly how the psychological experiment is not only an isolated experimenter-subject system in the laboratory that emits results. Rather, the system is embedded in "circuitry" that connects the self-knowledge of the experimenter, the self-knowledge of the subject, and the social context in which psychological knowledge is produced and through which it circulates.[6] This is an opening for an anthropologist of science, if ever there was one! The psychological laboratory appears to be an isolated place, ensconced in a university research building, inhabited only by trained researchers or researchers-in-training, joined by subjects who are asked to perform specific tasks under carefully controlled conditions. But what if the apparent isolation of the lab is a mirage?

In *Cognition in Practice*, anthropologist Jean Lave showed that labs studying cognition, in particular the cognition involved in mathematical calculations, presumed they were located outside of society. From their isolated setting they sought to be the arbiters of how rational mathematical calculations were done. Lave investigated how people worked math problems outside of the lab and the school, while shopping in grocery stores or managing their money, and she found that they worked effectively with practical cognitive competencies that were not quite the same as the rational calculations studied in labs and taught in school. She argued that the isolation of the lab from everyday life impoverished both the lab's and the school's conception of how cognition works in ordinary social settings.[7] In my research, I did not often follow the subjects in experiments into their everyday lives, but I took seriously the possibility that the boundary between the experimental psychology lab and the wider society is porous and permeable, and I asked whether that permeability might even be necessary for the experimenter-subject system to operate.

Working with neuroscientists who use neuroimaging to understand how the human brain works, anthropologist Simon Cohn has shown the extent to which scientists need to develop personal, even intimate, relationships with their subjects in order to secure their cooperation. Only by enlisting subjects in a social relationship, even if briefly, do the researchers feel they can depend on the subjects to follow directions to the best of their ability. Strapped down uncomfortably in a dark, noisy scanner, subjects must nonetheless pay attention and follow directions in order to produce data the researchers can use. Before the subjects ever enter the scanner, researchers provide them with reassurance and sympathy and share personal experiences, creating a subjective alliance between researcher and subject. Although these tactics might influence the specific subjective experiences revealed in the scanner, they are carefully expunged from the experimental write-ups so that only the signals from subjects' brains in response to stimuli in the scanner come to light. This is thought to preserve the goal of objective results uncontaminated by subjectivity.[8]

Cohn and a number of other scholars who have focused on neuroscientific studies in cognitive science suggest that subjective experiences of participants are valuable in their own right and that they could be harvested with the right techniques and triangulated with data from brain scans and lab reports. They also describe the elaborate methods cognitive scientists use to cross-check what subjects report, methods that give them confidence that they can rely on non-scientist participants to produce trustworthy data.[9]

In the coming chapters, I will explore these questions in the laboratories of a different set of scientists; namely, experimental cognitive psychologists. Although I will build on insights gained from observers of research in neuroscience and cognitive science, there are several reasons I thought experimental cognitive psychology needed a closer look. First, it is part of a discipline, psychology, that traces its origin to the late nineteenth century, when it was closely allied with early anthropology. This invites the question of how psychology became a distinct discipline from anthropology. Second, unlike anthropology, this discipline generally aims to determine what "normal" and "universal" human psychology looks like.[10] Although one of the labs in my research draws on subjects who have had brain injuries, and whose cognitive responses are therefore different from the norm, the point of experiments even there is to shed light on what constitutes normal cognitive processes, taking advantage of a kind of "natural experiment." One of the reasons that the underpinnings of this science have spread so far from the laboratory, into many domains of daily life, is that lab science is devoted to describing what are considered to be normal cognitive processes, not abnormal ones. Third, these labs are not predominately interested in medical problems. So, although I am indebted to studies of the use of brain imaging technologies for medical purposes, such as Barry Saunders' *CT Suite*, this book opens an inquiry into what goes on when the goal is to describe the cognition that most humans share when they are functioning normally.[11]

Delving into the basic methods of a venerable old science allows me to explore the deep grammar of the experimental method as it is applied to human psychology. Readers will see how this knowledge has permeated many spheres of ordinary life, and how, with the rise of social and digital media, large numbers of people are participating in psychology experiments—whether they realize it or not—in the course of daily life. Nicholas Rose once commented that psychology is a "generous" discipline, offering its methods for ready use by governments, corporations, medicine, the military, and others.[12] What readers will learn from this book is how the key elements of the experimental method in psychology have been set free from both the discipline and the laboratory and are now walking about gathering data from many people in their ordinary lives. More often than not the data thus gathered enable the formation of new kinds of commodities, for better or worse: apps we can buy to monitor our health, algorithms corporations can buy to predict our purchases. The experiment-subject system is no longer limited to the laboratory; it goes about its business collecting data in broad daylight, reports its findings in the news media, and informs the design of instruments to collect more data. This is an instance of new wine in old bottles. To understand the potential and the limitations of the new wine, we need to understand the constraints provided by the old bottles.

There is a compelling need to understand the quotidian basics of psychological research: "data," "experiment," the "normal," "statistical significance," the "subject." Only in this way can you and I learn the full implications of what we are being asked to do when we complete a fun questionnaire on Facebook or Google, or report our level of satisfaction with the job performance of a waiter, a delivery person, a doctor, a hairdresser, or a teacher. Only in this way can we understand how the "data" that are collected in this way do not disappear but return in other forms to profoundly affect our daily lives. It is these fundamental concepts and practices that need to be illuminated, since the data, the norms, and the statistical operations in these contexts do not depend on the latest brain scanning technologies but nonetheless have a potent effect on our lives. My goal is to show how they work in the laboratory setting, with all their strengths and limitations, so we can better assess what we *can* learn from them and what we *cannot*. Experimental cognitive psychology is a kind of engine for producing psychological knowledge. The workings of that engine ride abroad among us.

Consider one small example of how the techniques used in psychology research laboratories have escaped the lab and are now out in the public, beckoning people to participate. Suppose you read an article online about how we think about aging.[13] In the article you discover that there is something called "implicit bias" that psychologists study. If you were to Google the term, you would find an inviting website offering findings from studies of implicit bias: not surprisingly, there is an implicit bias against older people compared to younger people. In an effort to decrease the stigma of aging, a group of older adults were told that their performance on a memory test was above average for their age group. This intervention, called a "prime" or induction, actually led the older adults to perform better, according to data gathered from subsequent memory tests. All the elements of a standard experimental setup in psychology are present here: the *recruitment* of volunteers to participate as *subjects*, a *sample* of participants sharing a characteristic (being older), a "*prime*" devised to produce a certain effect, measurement of reaction time as the criteria of cognitive activity, and collection of *data* in numeric form. As consumers of this news story, we are encouraged to accept that the findings of this experiment are enlightening with respect to human cognition and social attitudes. We are *not* encouraged to question whether the method is a good way to reach conclusions about human behavior, or whether we should rely on data of this kind as an accurate description of what people think. Even more alarmingly, we are invited to join the enterprise of producing this kind of data. Any number of links from the article lead to the "implicit bias" site, where you can add your own data to the project.[14] This is a circle in which the terms of knowledge are set by standard techniques in psychology, and then the base of knowledge is increased by participants who accept those terms without questioning them. This book aims to interrupt that circle, not by claiming the techniques are wrong, but by identifying them and putting them in a broader context.

The Deep Penetration of Experimental Psychology into Daily Life

Immersion in the field of psychology has made me curious, and a little envious, about the extent to which the results of research in experimental psychology occupy a prominent place in the media compared to my own field of cultural anthropology. A Google Trends report of worldwide searches during the past year (November 2019 to November 2020) found there were more than eight times as many searches on psychology as there were on anthropology. Major scientific journals and news media frequently publish articles based on experimental psychology, claiming, for example, that storytelling is a "human universal" that played an important role in human evolution.[15] This latter idea was put forth by Daniel Kahneman and Amos Tversky, who described the "heuristics" of human decision making with simple but elegant experiments and won a Nobel prize.[16] Major media journalists like *The New York Times'* David Brooks quote psychological research, claiming that "our minds evolved for tribal warfare and us/them thinking."[17] Almost any cultural anthropologist would cringe at these claims because they are uncomfortably close to a simplistic version of Darwinian evolution. I always thought "storytelling" and "tribal warfare" were specialties of cultural anthropology! Of course, the obvious reasons for psychology's popularity are that it is a large field with a long history, and that it holds a firmly established role in high school and college education, not least because of its conformity with standard experimental scientific practices. In the United States it also has the federal funding to support this prominent role. Practically speaking, psychology was more useful to

US government interests during the world wars and the Cold War than anthropology could have ever dreamed of being. In the same vein, surely some of the continuing popularity of psychology in the media might be its ability to give practical advice on a host of everyday problems and dilemmas: how to give a good gift or how to build a healthy relationship.[18]

Of course, popularity in media does not tell the whole story. One critic, Amanda Anderson, a scholar of literature, notes that while current experimental cognitive psychological research is "gleefully embraced in the media," the field carries with it an impoverished view of human moral capacities, of how people reflect on which ideals and values are worth caring about and aiming for, which actions are meaningful and why, and which actions cause regret and sorrow. Cognitive psychology "falls short precisely when it comes to the more existential or meaning-laden realms of life."[19] Anderson argues that because the experiment in psychology is confined to a "punctual" kind of time, it cannot "adequately capture basic elements of human experience that condition the textures and forms of our moral lives and our commitments to moral reflection."[20] Such meaning-laden processes require "slow time," which is precisely what "most experiment formats simply cannot capture."[21] In this book we will meet the "punctual" time of the experiment, which in my fieldwork was called "brief reaction time," and we will come to understand its essential place in the experimental regimen. But we will also come to recognize that *laboratory* life in psychology does indeed involve slow time, time that allows social obligations and moral values to come to the fore.

Before I began this research, there was already a large secondary literature about psychology, both American and European. That literature ranges over the many subfields of psychology: clinical, applied, social, developmental, forensic, industrial, and so on. I want to stress that my fieldwork focused only on one subfield: American experimental cognitive psychology. I did dip my toe into experimental social psychology by volunteering as a subject in studies of emotion, but this was an introductory phase, before I was able to establish long-term field sites in experimental cognitive psychology labs. These labs focus on the study of cognitive activities like learning, remembering, or paying attention, using experimental methods with human subjects. Thus, my primary claims in this book are about experimental cognitive psychology in the United States, rather than any other subfields of the discipline or any other countries where psychological research is done.[22] This caveat is important because of the distinctiveness of psychology's subfields. Their distinctiveness was brought home to me when I asked about the "replication crisis." Over recent years there has been a storm of claims and counterclaims about whether experiments in social psychology in particular are statistically robust enough to be scientifically valid. A key concern in this debate is whether experimental findings can be confirmed when experiments are repeated. This matters because replicability is an essential criterion for the validity of a scientific finding.[23] I was aware of this controversy during my fieldwork, but none of my interlocutors were concerned by it, and they assured me that experimental psychology, unlike social psychology, had been shown to have acceptable replication rates.[24]

Invidious Practices

This book is constructed as a conversation between me, as a cultural anthropologist using the method of participant-observation, and my psychologist interlocutors, using their method of the experiment. Both of our disciplines have inherited a legacy of racism, classism, and sexism, not least because the founders of both fields were white, Euro-American men from the educated classes. More broadly, they were also imbued with the value of rationality inherited from the Enlightenment and with the notions of superiority that form the basis of colonialism. In previous centuries, some practitioners in both disciplines adopted overtly racist and sexist paradigms that were common in their time.[25] In the more recent past, both of our fields have been responsible for egregious harm, conducting research or sharing the results of research in ways that contravened accepted professional ethical standards.

Both fields have benefited from the introduction of the Institutional Review Board, which is required to vet research proposals in any institution that receives federal funds. The IRB, as it is known, is a committee of faculty, administrators, and community members that applies federal standards of ethics meant to preserve the well-being of research participants and subjects. Researchers (including anthropologists) must gain the approval of their research projects from the IRB before beginning research. The oversight of the IRB, which began in 1974, has had the effect of reducing the kind of harm that some earlier experiments may have caused to participants.[26]

Today, both disciplines are part of the academic world, which is still dominated by white Euro-American men, however much progress has been made to diversify the academy and these disciplines in particular.[27] Invidious distinctions are not necessarily the choice of anyone in these fields, but nonetheless they are in the air we breathe and cannot be ignored. Graham Richards put it well: "Psychology as a discipline is a product of the 'psychologies' of those within it. The psychological knowledge it produces directly articulates and expresses the psychological character of the psychologists producing it—their ways of thinking, their priorities, attitudes, values, and so on."[28] The same could be said of anthropology and anthropologists.

To counteract the dominance of white, Euro-American men in these disciplines, scholars can do several things. They can attend to ongoing work in both disciplines that focuses on the mechanisms behind discrimination based on race, gender, or sexuality.[29] They can look to responses from post-colonial writers, who see things in distinctly different ways; they can also look toward a day when the makeup of academic disciplines will be more diverse in terms of race, gender, and class.[30] Many of us would welcome that new world. Even if such changes were to be immediate and thorough, newcomers would find these disciplines built on methods and technologies they did not invent. What would happen then is unknown, but we can say for sure that if the world were otherwise and the practitioners of psychology or anthropology had been mostly women, or mostly Black Americans, for example, they would have asked different questions and developed methods that are different from the ones we have now.

In the past, practitioners in both fields have also run afoul of their own discipline's current ethical guidelines. Both anthropology and psychology played a part in nineteenth- and early twentieth-century eugenics.[31] Both have played unsavory roles in global wars and conflicts. For anthropology's part, during the Cold War, ethnographic research was deeply implicated in projects undertaken by the CIA and the Pentagon, and after 9/11 some anthropologists participated in the US military's Human Terrain project. The military intended to place ethnographers in areas where they would understand the local language and customs and could further the efforts of anti-terrorist military action.[32] For psychology's part, some experiments conducted before the guidelines of the IRB, such as those depicted in Slater's play, may have caused more harm than benefit to their subjects. More recently, the American Psychological Association reiterated its position restricting psychologists from participating in detainee interrogations, such as those that led to the torture of prisoners in Guantanamo Bay.[33]

Both disciplines include watchful scholars who identify sites of unethical research. In anthropology, critical studies are pervasive, covering the discipline's involvement in Cold War military engagements and its involvement in structural racism, colonialism, and gender discrimination.[34] Within psychology, "critical psychology" is virtually its own subfield, and some-times forms a separate program in psychology departments.[35] Critical psychology examines the political aspects of the field's assumptions with the goal of illuminating and challenging its effects on groups who are relatively marginalized by virtue of their race, gender, disability, or access to material resources.

Road Map

In the following chapters, we will hear from the key psychologists in the labs I studied, and from their graduate students. Personal sketches of these key interlocutors appear in the section entitled Dramatis Personae. To anticipate a terminological issue, in recent years, out of concern for giving people who participate in psychology experiments more respect, the term research "participant" has been used instead of "subject." Indeed, some journals now require the term "participant." Since tradition lies with the term "subject," and both terms are acceptable according to the *Publication Manual of the American Psychological Association*, I will use them interchangeably.

All of my fieldwork was conversational, taking place during face-to-face meetings between me and the psychologists or subjects, or in the course of an experiment they had designed. I was motivated by anthropologist Stefan Helmreich's question: "How different are contemporary cultural anthropologists' notions of culture and those of practicing scientists? And what happens when these notions encounter one another?"[36] My interlocutors were usually way ahead of me in describing the significance of their goals and methods. I have chosen to lay out the path of their instruction and my learning (or failing to learn) with only occasional guidance from me as all-seeing narrator. My interlocutors are by far the most reliable narrators of what graduate student Ulla called "life in psychology." To honor the large role they had in my research, I have formatted quotes from interviews and conversations as dialogues with quotation marks, when they are part of a conversation where multiple speakers are being quoted.

In a preliminary chapter 1, I describe how I began this project and some of the hurdles I faced. In a historical chapter 2, I turn back in time to the late nineteenth and early twentieth century, to explore how, during the dawning years of the discipline of experimental psychology, anthropologists also used psychology's methods and technologies, relying on archival material and the work of historians. Readers who are experimental psychologists are hereby

forgiven for skipping this historical chapter and moving directly to the ethnographic material in chapters 3–9.

In the ethnographic chapters, I will draw from my long-term observations
of experimental psychologists at work in their labs, by paying attention to the
exact words they said and specific actions they took, which allowed them to
carry out experiments. Since these labs were all composed of both a senior
faculty member and his or her graduate and undergraduate students, everyone
was endeavoring to teach at every moment. Senior faculty were instructing
students; advanced students were instructing beginning students. I inserted
myself in these labs as an unusual kind of student, a senior in faculty status but
a novice in knowledge of experimental cognitive psychology. In the coming
narrative, I occupy the role of a student who is being instructed by mentors.
Since the answers to my research questions were often given explicitly by my
mentors, I have stayed close to their words and actions. This way of narrating
the story has an important advantage: since my interlocutors allowed me to
observe their work only on the condition that I would not "make them look
bad," putting myself in the position of a bumbling and insecure novice (which
I was), allowed *me* rather than *them* to "look bad." As a result, the manuscript
itself became a written record of what the psychologists taught me and what
I learned. To my surprise, all of my main interlocutors read the manuscript in
draft form and returned it to me with many pages of editorial changes to consider, paragraphs to insert, new resources to consult, and mistakes to correct.
Since one of the main answers to my research questions involves the striking
finding that although the field of experimental cognitive psychology focuses
on the *individual*, and presumably autonomous, subject and produces results
that shed light on *individual* psychology, the process of this research is intensely social. I experienced the generous responses my interlocutors gave
to my manuscript as further proof of the socially engaged and collaborative
nature of the field.

Finally, I consider social and digital media in chapters 10 and 11. In Chapter 10, I discuss other sciences that are also dependent on psychology—
ergonomics and user friendly design—as background to the connections
between experimental psychology and social/digital media I present in chapter 11. The results from these scientific fields infiltrate our daily lives in large
and small ways, affecting many objects from the keys on computer keyboards
to the arrangements of seats on jumbo aircraft. I introduce the "playbook" of
practices from experimental psychology that underlies such designs.

In chapter 11, I show how the methods of experimental psychology have recently been redeployed in social and digital media. Amplified and enhanced in power by vast troves of data and the powerful new statistical tools of machine learning, a model of human psychology abounds, one in which numerical data is paired with trained algorithms that can be asked to manipulate and predict. This new wine in old bottles needs all the scrutiny we can provide!

Psychological research was used to design Facebook and Twitter: the way it is deployed there to manipulate users has spread to other internet platforms including Amazon and Google. Ironically, the big data fueling the algorithms that predict and influence behavior has been provided by—users! How did it become so normal, even pleasurable, for millions of people across the globe to fill out questionnaires about their personal likes and dislikes, hopes and wishes? What makes people tolerate or even enjoy answering questions that anonymous others have created, fueling an internet with data that can be readily exploited and used to surveil us and to predict our behavior? In other words, as Tom Boellsdorff asks: Why do "so many find surveillance acceptable and even pleasurable"?[37] Importantly, the minds and bodies of the public have been trained and disciplined in accord with one specific disciplinary tool kit: the pervasive templates based on the experimental model created by experimental psychology.

1

Doing This Ethnography

Throughout history, the red thread [Ariadne's Thread, which she gave to Theseus to help him escape the labyrinth after he killed the Minotaur] has come to represent a pattern, or underlying current, that connects seemingly disparate thoughts to reveal a larger narrative woven just beneath the surface.

—STEPHANIE CRISTELLO, *THE SEEN*, 2018

MY FIRST attempts at observing experimental psychologists as an ethnographer met with failure. I emailed numerous colleagues in psychology at New York University, where I was a professor in the anthropology department, in which I explained what an ethnographic study of a science lab was like. I stressed that as an ethnographer I would be unobtrusive in the process of trying to understand what their work was about and what it meant to them. I would want to hang out at lab meetings and conferences, as well as interview faculty and students in the lab. I would be seeking to grasp ordinary, normal practices and conceptions in their work: what anthropologist Tim Ingold called "a way of knowing *from the inside*."[1] I would ask to "learn to learn" as Gregory Bateson put it, to be taught how to look at the psychology of human cognition through their eyes and how to do the technical experiments that would reveal new aspects of human cognition. The email I sent read:

> Would you be willing to allow me to look in on or follow any studies you might be doing in the lab during the next couple of summers? Anything you might be working on would be of great interest to me. Alternatively, or in addition, do you think there is anyone else in the psychology department who would be amenable to my following any ongoing experimental work?

Perhaps a student's project in a lab? Of course, I would strictly follow confidentiality guidelines and try to be unobtrusive. I would greatly appreciate any advice or suggestions.

Although I knew most of these colleagues from academic committees and meetings, I never got a reply from any of them.

This aroused my interest, especially since not long before, I had rather easily gotten permission to talk with people who had medical—even psychiatric—diagnoses and the clinicians or research scientists interacting with them. As I have mentioned, initially I wanted to do this new ethnography to understand whether it matters that reports based on experimental psychology are broadcast loudly in the news, whereas reports based on anthropological research barely make a sound. The same could be said for research funding. Why was a field that sought to understand the human mind through experiments so able to benefit from major sources of funding? Was a part of this field's appeal that it sought to describe universal aspects of the human mind in objective, scientific ways? This central assumption was certainly part of my fascination with the field and the source of my uneasy feeling about it. Trained in cultural anthropology, I was dubious about any purported human universals. I had been taught to assume that cultural ideas and practices vary tremendously and play a part in any supposedly universal human characteristic, even physical traits like height, weight, vision, or hearing. Eventually, over the course of this research, I came to appreciate that my understanding of what psychologists mean by universal traits of the human mind was far too simple. I also came to appreciate that my interlocutors in psychology were well aware of the problems with the universal claims that made me uneasy. They had long been aware of them, in fact, and they had already come to sophisticated ways of contending with them. Occasionally they expressed concerns about the ways their research was being used by internet companies to manipulate human behavior. But getting to these insights first required access to the daily life of their labs.

Stymied

I felt stymied but also intrigued after my initial futile efforts. So, I burrowed down in several oblique directions. I began to look into the history of anthropology and experimental psychology in relation to each other, I sought out general conversations with psychologists without bringing up any request for fieldwork, and I began to volunteer as a subject (a participant) in psychology experiments. Early on, a casual conversation with Dr. N, a neuroscientist from another country, shed light on my difficulty. She was proud of her country's ethos of openness and democracy. She had no trouble explaining why I was being given the cold shoulder.

> When I was a postdoc at Harvard, the psychology undergraduates protested the requirement to participate in psych experiments. And so, facing the difficulties of getting subjects from the general public, psychologists just started using each other—in other words, they became their own subjects. You can only tell this from the published papers because the subjects' responses have the initials of *lab* members next to them.

Having dipped my toe into the history of experiments in psychology, I exclaimed that this was just like the earliest days of experimental psychology, when students alternated between the roles of experimenter and subject.

Dr. N continued,

> That's so. Subjects from the general population can be terrible. They might be a secretary from an academic department, for example. The ideal subject is an undergraduate student who's taking classes and used to tests, who is basically willing to be disciplined, to sit still for a certain time and place and do a designated task, who understands the importance of clarity and consistency. And the general population may not. It is very frustrating to begin a series of tests with such a subject who is going to be a dud. Useless. They're inconsistent, contradict themselves, and you end up wasting a whole series of experiments to get data which you can't use. This is basically why people prefer to use each other for subjects in their own lab. And this is psychology's dirty little secret.

She called the secret "dirty" because if known, it could undercut public confidence: the public might wonder whether subjects who knew a lot about the purpose and design of the experiment might unwittingly bias the results. Was it possible that because of protests from students and general concerns about the ethics of using human subjects, the field was undergoing a seismic shift in the nature of the human subjects it employed just at the moment of my field project? Could it be that being observed during such a time would be so uncomfortable that my proposed research would be anathema? This turned out not to be true. One subfield within experimental psychology, psychophysics, has long used lab members as subjects. Their experiments, aimed at understanding the relationships between sensations and the physical stimuli that produce them, are so lengthy and tedious that they require more discipline and motivation than an ordinary volunteer would have. This accommodation to the nature of their experimental tasks is not regarded as controversial. Other psychologists told me informally that they simply pay subjects, whether they are students or otherwise. Students who are required to participate for course credit tend to be less motivated and attentive than paid participants, so token payments ensure that all subjects behave appropriately. So much for Dr. N's idea that a "dirty little secret" was the cause of my troubles.

Shortly after my talk with Dr. N, I was waiting to volunteer for an experiment in a psychology department on the West Coast. Dr. B popped out of his office a few doors down and struck up a conversation with me about the history of our respective fields. He was interested in the archival research I was doing about the 1898 Cambridge Anthropological Expedition to the Torres Straits, a scientific endeavor that combined both early ethnography and experimental psychology. In the lab of Wilhelm Wundt, in Leipzig, Germany, some of the most enduring concepts in contemporary psychology had been born, and the Cambridge anthropologists took Wundt's psychological instruments with them on the expedition. Over the next weeks, Dr. B and I traded early-twentieth-century books and articles about our fields, and in time he helped me find possible sites for my ethnographic research. He sent helpful emails to his colleagues (including the hyperbole typical of letters of reference):

> A very nice and smart woman, Emily Martin is an anthropologist who is interested in the history of psychology in the 19–20th century. Her faculty position is at NYU. She is also interested in the development of psychological ideas. She hopes to follow two labs at another university but wants to follow a lab here. She would just show up at a few lab meetings, and not say anything. She has come to two cognitive psych conferences. She will not write anything that would embarrass us. I think your lab would be perfect. If you think this is OK, I will have her email you. You might want to have coffee with her first or something, but she is charming and smart. (About my age.)

His generosity and forthright recommendation opened a door into one lab on the West Coast. Such are the accidental lucky contacts that ethnographers depend upon!

In the meantime, an anthropologist with a joint appointment in psychology, Setha Low, offered to send a plea to her large network in New York City.

I got only one reply. This psychologist interviewed me and, after expressing a lot of doubt ("Will there be a contract?") and hesitation ("What exactly will you do?"), allowed me to begin attending lab meetings on a trial basis. Finally, I approached a former neighbor in another East Coast city who ran a psychology lab at a university where I had taught for almost twenty years. She was worried ("What if lab members don't want to talk in front of you about things they could be criticized for?") and apprehensive ("How will you keep our identity confidential given that our research is highly specific?"), but she too agreed to let me begin on a trial basis.

As I mentioned, the condition set on my research was that I would not "make them look bad." I think they were legitimately worried about whether I would be looking for misconduct of some kind. Was I on the track of faked data or sloppy methodology that I could publicize and use to create yet another scandal for the field, one that could threaten their ability to continue getting grants and publications? This was never my goal at all, and I suspect that soon enough they realized that I did not know enough to be able to identify any such misconduct, even if I had wanted to. I realized that I would have to moderate my own initial critical take on the field. However, what was muted instead was my rather knee-jerk reaction to the idea of treating human beings as if their cognitive experiences could be studied by means of the experimental method. To my surprise, through long exposure and detailed observation, I did become convinced that important things could be learned with this method. And, also to my surprise, I found that my interlocutors actually shared many of my doubts and hesitations.

What began as a hard-won trial stretched into years. Between 2011 and 2017, I circulated among the two West Coast and the two East Coast sites doing fieldwork in the midst of other academic responsibilities. On the East Coast, I lived in my own apartment in New York City and made frequent trips to the other East Coast site, where I could stay with family; a sabbatical leave in 2016–17 enabled me to live near the West Coast sites with the help of Sabbaticalhomes.com and the like. As is often the way with anthropology of science projects, anthropologists become familiar to their interlocutors—not exactly colleagues and not exactly friends but a very appealing combination of the two. Like many other anthropologists, I had the status of a student in the lab and was often given jobs to do: running subjects through tasks at computers, serving as a "normal" experimental subject who provided data that could be compared to other subjects, or bringing food to contribute to innumerable social occasions in the labs.

Sociality

Since I envisioned that an important part of the project would be tracing not only the joint beginnings of anthropology and psychology, but also how they eventually definitively divided into separate disciplines, I expected most of my life inside psychology to be unfamiliar. I was struck by how many of my initial assumptions were mowed down. I had read that experimental psychology celebrated and promoted individualistic ideas, operated on the belief that people could be treated as isolated, autonomous units, and in fact perpetuated a distinctly asocial idea of the human mind. In the 1960s, George Miller had identified the strain in empiricist British thought that entered into early experimental psychology: "It is a theory about the *individual* mind; social implications are not considered. All minds are created free and equal. An individual mind is a private, personal thing, completely independent of all other private, personal minds and free to enter into any contracts or agreements with others that suit its own purposes."[2] To think through the implications of such a focus on the individual, I relied on the work of sociologists and historians such as Nikolas Rose. Rose urges us to see how the growth of psychology since the nineteenth century was "intrinsically linked with transformations in the practices for 'the conduct of conduct' that have been assembled in contemporary liberal democracies." The "conduct of conduct" refers to social guidelines for the management of subjectivity, which have become "psychologized."[3] For instance, because experimental psychological research about the human mind has been conducted with human subjects in seemingly isolated experimental settings where subjective or interpersonal elements are meant to be eliminated or controlled, the field can be said to have encouraged conceptions of human nature that fit and even amplify the demands of global capitalism, with its market-based rubrics that assume it is *individuals* who make choices. Habits and beliefs have been instilled that encourage people to consider themselves as individuals: individuals who are willing to calculate their well-being according to psychological traits, individuals who are willing, even eager, to devote time and energy to improving psychologically—to become happier, more flexible, and more risk tolerant.

In contrast, I knew that some research in a related field, social psychology, contests the role of the individual. Primatologist Frans DeWaal, writing about emotions among animals and humans, has welcomed the insights of the social neuroscientist Jim Coan. As DeWaal put it, "most psychologists believe that our species' typical responses occur while we are alone. They regard the

FIGURE 1.1. Experimental psychology lab potluck. Photo by author, 2020.

solitary human as the default condition. Coan, however, believes the exact opposite: how we feel while we are embedded with others is the actual norm. Few of us deal with life's stresses on our own—we always rely on others."[4] To my amazement, the life of my fieldwork labs was vastly more social than the life of the anthropology departments I had experienced. I observed that every possible social occasion was celebrated: birthdays, new members joining, old members leaving, holidays and on and on. People brought food—family recipes for meatballs, special homemade desserts, dumplings, fruit, sushi—and the sharing of this food went along with serious discussions of ongoing research.

More striking, lab members were told explicitly that lab research was collaborative. Dr. J was eloquent: "We depend on each other, we help each other. When someone asks you for help running subjects or analyzing data, remember that you may need that exact kind of help some day. There is sweat equity, so if somebody does help somebody else they can expect that other person to chip in when needed." In one study during my fieldwork, more than a dozen lab members were needed to manage a study involving a middle school classroom. The school was in a neighboring state, and everyone had to get up at the crack of dawn to catch a regional train. Dr. J noted that all of the lab members showed up on time even though this was not their project: "I think they got something out of it. I talk a lot about helping each other, I care about that." I cannot think of a single time in more than forty years of university teaching in anthropology that professors explicitly encouraged graduate students to work together on their ethnographic PhD research projects. Anthropology's common practice of solitary fieldwork in unexplored settings makes research collaboration rare: each researcher is a lone pioneer.

I soon found out how true it is that psychologists collaborate. Subjects are unruly. They may show up late or at the wrong place; they may not understand directions or fail to follow them exactly. There are many aspects of an experiment that require careful organization of both subjects and equipment. This labor often requires more than one person to work together to pull off any single experimental trial: sharing the labor of answering subjects' questions, correcting their misunderstanding of instructions, handing out materials, collecting screenings, starting up computers, entering passwords, testing earphones, plugging earphones back in, keeping records straight. Sometimes the sites of experiments are not close to the lab, and members are expected to travel on public transport, endure the lack of meals or comfortable facilities, and stay on their feet until the event is finished. At one lab, the yearly open house to encourage new undergraduate majors fell on a date the professor was out of town. She delegated many tasks to students: design and print a brochure describing the work of the lab, make a video demonstration of the lab's usual scanning techniques, make sure there is food and drink for the visiting students. I volunteered to bring "brain food" like berries and nuts.

The most intense sociality happened when labs formed small groups working on similar projects. Often there were rather permeable work-life boundaries: groups of coworkers would meet for potluck dinners and then watch a movie on TV, joined by absent members watching the same movie via Skype. During major conferences, lab members often shared hotel rooms. More than once, I was offered a place to sleep in a hotel room shared with other lab members. When Dr. B read my account of lab sociality, he said I should add this caveat:

> Although compared to many academic disciplines, cognitive and experimental psychology has a great deal of esprit de corps and mutual aid, not all labs are like this. It's a general culture [norm] to be collaborative and supportive of one's colleagues, but it's not 100% universal. Furthermore, almost every graduate student has moments of angst even in the best of labs. Graduate students might doubt whether they are appreciated by the head of the lab, whether their work is good enough, whether they can "make the grade." Certainly, a supportive, collaborative lab, the birthdays, potlucks, etc., help one through this passage, but for few people is graduate

school a "complete bed of roses." It is the nature of the enterprise. There is a lot of uncertainty, as there is a lot of uncertainty in all science. One never knows whether one's contribution will be important or not. Faculty advisors do not know whether one's finding is important. Sometimes it takes years before one's contributions are recognized, and this uncertainty causes moments of self-doubt and conflict, in even the most supportive of labs.

Even with this caveat, I was struck by the frequently cozy and often mutually supportive relationships in these labs. An even more striking revelation will emerge in later chapters: the actual process of doing experiments with subjects was also much more deeply social than one would expect, given the field's emphasis on the individual mind. Unexpectedly, I found that experimental psychologists are solicitous of the needs of subjects and thoughtful about how their experimental protocols shape the data they gather. As we will discover, subjects in psychology experiments are brought into the social world of the experimenter, "socialized" in a way by being trained to be good subjects who can produce useable data.[5]

In my own field, researchers also have solicitous and thoughtful relationships with their interlocutors. But, in contrast, since ethnography is usually done by a solitary researcher, there is not often an equivalent to collaborations among researchers. Advisors help advisees one on one, and peers help each other. But anthropology networks in a department are as much based on individual friendships and individual professional obligations as anything else. Being among the psychologists felt by comparison like being in a warm kitchen with any number of fellow cooks.

If anthropology is like solitary exploration into the unknown by a lone ethnographer, psychology is like joining a large crowd living in a well-built dwelling with many sturdy and well-walked corridors. The number of students in the United States who take psychology courses or major in psychology, as well as the number of professional psychologists and the funding they obtain from federal and other sources, makes an anthropologist's eyes bug out. Psychology's numbers exceed anthropology's at least by a hundredfold. Moving from my field to this one was like moving from a small hamlet to a large city teeming with people. The speed of production in psychology was also mind-boggling to me. A rough estimate is that psychology researchers produce their scientific findings on the order of ten times faster than anthropologists. Anthropologists, working alone and for several years or more on a single project look like tortoises compared to the jackrabbit teams of psychologists who finish and publish several projects a year.

Terms

I promised my interlocutors that I would keep their identities confidential and that I would not embarrass them by making them look bad.[6] All of the labs were eventually welcoming beyond my imagination. One lab included me on their webpage and on the whiteboard list of lab members. I was introduced in lab meetings as "our very own resident cultural anthropologist coming to study these strange creatures" and so doing the science of science. Nonetheless, their fear that I might embarrass them was overt throughout my research. A student would say something humorously sarcastic, and the Principal Investigator (PI) of the lab would say, "Don't say that kind of thing, Emily is taking notes." A student would describe how a portion of research didn't go as hoped, and the PI would say, "Look at Emily, she is really taking notes now." Despite my assurances that I was after common and taken-for-granted assumptions rather than mistakes, the nervousness never entirely went away. Two years into the project, Dr. J told her lab during a meeting, "Here she is at the end of two years of lab meetings. She has been trained how to run subjects. We see her taking notes, but we are still wondering: when will she publish in the *National Enquirer!*"

Let me provide more detail about how I will deal with the confidentiality I promised, admitting that these are imperfect solutions. All my main interlocutors will be given pseudonymous initials: Dr. S, Dr. B, Dr. J, and so on. This is how many lab members address their lab's PI. Graduate students, both beginning and advanced in each lab, will be given first name pseudonyms: Randall, Ulla, Rob, and so on. When I describe my ethnography of research in progress, I focus on the general aspects of their work. What makes a good experiment? How do protocols evolve over time? What presence do subjects have in the research? But because this general level cannot capture the fine points of a finished publication, I have included some published papers in the reference list, which relate to, but are not necessarily identical to, work in the labs I followed.

The protocols and vocabulary of psychology threw me. Every experiment in which I had responsibility sent waves of anxiety through me. Their methods were precise and accurate. There would be real live human beings sitting in front of me producing data. More often than not I felt I could not follow the instructions well enough. From my field notes about an upcoming study of middle school students in Dr. J's lab:

> The whole two hours of training is devoted to detailed, step-by-step instructions on what we are to do to set up the computers for the kids. They are giving us detailed written protocols many pages long. When am I going

to master all this material? I find everything quite hard to follow. I can't see the small print in the power point presentation, I can't see the white board either, and fear not getting every detail straight. I keep standing up to see better and asking the lab manager in a whisper what is going on.

Later, the lab manager joked that I was probably paying more attention than anyone else.

At other times I felt sure I was in a different country where another language was being spoken. In a lab meeting about an ongoing fMRI (functional magnetic resonance imaging) study, I wrote down: multivoxel pattern analysis; encoding variability hypotheses; collapsed data; average pattern; Harvard Atlas of Brains; mean activation; GLM; beta; Z score; faces vs. houses; pseudo word; behavioral accuracy; fixation baseline; and experimental baseline. Some of the words were familiar, but I could make little sense of the whole picture, let alone help the graduate student in charge of the study. Although I read a textbook on fMRI and showed up to perform the task I had been allotted, I felt (and was) like a person drowning in deep water. My task was to design a "stimulus graphic form" with the correct shape for the experiment. I sat at the lab's Windows computer in dismay. I had no idea how to start. The grad student, Rob, answered my questions patiently, but I did not dare tell him that not only did I not understand what he needed, but, as a long-time Mac user, I had no idea even how to open a Windows file or application! After pretending to work for an hour or so, I saved nothing, made my excuses, and fled. The labs worried I would embarrass them, but that time I was the one who was embarrassed.

The Kitchen Table of Science

The account that follows is both empirical and personal, with the help of audio recordings I made, with permission, from meetings, interviews, and conversations during my own participation in experiments. It aspires to simply "say what happened," with me as the observer in the narrative. I focus on a style of thinking (the experiment) that is not new but stretches back to the scientific revolution. I rely on remembering the questions I asked, listening carefully to what people actually said and what they didn't say, and carefully tracking their relationships with other people and the tools of their scientific practice. I emphasize periods of time or moments in daily lab life where common assumptions were in conflict or under question, the better to understand what was at stake.

I take the question of what is at stake to be a very broad one, encompassing what psychologists think is in the world, what should be in the world, what their research goals are, and what material and ideological constraints affect them.

Toward the end of the book, in chapter 11, I will move to a broader view and argue that findings from experimental psychology are fundamental to how social and digital media are structured. By "social and digital media" I mean the canonical platforms, like Facebook and Twitter. I also include other forms of digital media, like Google or Amazon, which use some of the same techniques, enabling them to track, monitor, and aggregate online behavior, in order to influence our behavior in profitable or politically advantageous directions.

During my fieldwork, my stance tended to be quizzical rather than critical. I often thought about how many of the activities I observed could be called classic language games. I remembered Rush Rhees, who cited a comment of Wittgenstein's about language games: "The advantage of looking at language games is that they let us look step by step at what we otherwise could only see as a tangled ball of yarn."[7] I learned that Dr. B, who is interested in subjectivity, was trying to untangle different kinds of "attention" rolled up in the ball of yarn that have been the subject of experiments on "attention" in psychology. He could be said to be trying to untangle psychology's ball of yarn step by step. I was trying to do the same.

Early on I learned the crucial importance of accuracy and numerical measures in psychology experiments. But accuracy and measuring are also language games in the sense that they are built up from a tangle of uses and practices over time. In due course I will untangle the specific balls of yarn containing accuracy, precise measurement, and control, which are the core assumed values in cognitive psychology. Untangling such hopeless knots led me to notice mundane ways in which these core values were realized— something as simple as a participant sitting at a table on a chair looking at a computer screen displaying a fixation point. Some of my interlocutors found that these simple insights opened a door to imagining a different kind of psychological experiment. Untangling the yarn gave me a kind of Ariadne's thread that helped me find my way from the laboratory to digital media and back again.

But first, I turn to the history of the early psychology labs in Germany, where it all began.

2

Sensing the World

Psychology must not only strive to become a useful basis for the other mental sciences, but it must also turn again and again to the historical sciences, in order to obtain an understanding for the more highly developed mental processes.

—WILHELM WUNDT, *AN INTRODUCTION TO PSYCHOLOGY*, 1912

I STARTED research for this book during the present moment in experimental psychology, but in the back of my mind there was always a historical question: What was happening in psychology in Europe and America at the beginning of experimental psychology, when anthropologists also used some of the same methods? This chapter is different from the coming ethnographic chapters because, instead of in-person observations, I can only rely on written letters and publications that have survived from an earlier time. However, my key finding from the nineteenth-century psychology labs anchors what I will describe about today's labs: the early labs established the thoroughly social way students were required to bring their life habits into sync with each other so they would be able to produce comparable data.

Early Fieldwork

One of the earliest anthropologists in America, Lewis Henry Morgan, wrote treatises on the American Indians of the northeast. There were sprouts of what became ethnography in that work. There were also sprouts of ethnography in his parallel work on natural history. For example, when he studied the American beaver, he paid attention to an exact description of their artifacts, their behavior, their tools, and their houses. There was a certain style of engagement between him as an observer and the beavers he observed that took the intentions of the observed into account, even though they were only beavers! In *The American Beaver*, Morgan described watching for them all night and hiding in a blind to try to observe them unnoticed. He carefully interviewed people, but only those who had observed the beavers' behavior firsthand over many years: trappers, traders, Indians, missionaries, and railroad workers. Most tellingly, he closely scrutinized the beavers' architecture, their lodges, dams, and canals. Measuring the ebb and flow of water, he determined that their canals and dams were—far from natural results of erosion—intentionally designed for efficient access to the trees they needed for food and for a viable water route to haul those trees back to the lodge. He was not beyond prodding the beavers to come out and be observed. He would break the top of a dam and watch them emerge to patch it back up. He called them "mutes," not because they could not communicate, but because they communicated by means of their engineering.[1] As anthropologist Gillian Feeley-Harnik points out, he called this "a minute exposition of their artificial works, where such are constructed; of their habits, their mode of life, and their mutual relations." She notes perceptively, "Words, put together in letters, journals, books, and libraries, had their structural analogues in sticks, stones, and earth, put together in houses, tombs, lodges, dams, and channels."[2] Morgan looked at the world as the beavers would see it to understand the principles behind their constructions.

Other well-known early anthropologists also began in a natural history tradition. In 1881 at the University of Kiel, Franz Boas did his famous PhD thesis in physical geography on the color of sea water. Later he went on to do ethnographic studies of the Inuit of Baffin Island in Canada and elsewhere. He founded the academic discipline of anthropology in America as a field that embraced the natural history of humankind. On the British side, it is less well known that A. C. Haddon studied marine biology before he organized the path-breaking anthropological expedition to the Torres Straits Islands (between Papua New Guinea and Australia) in 1898. He studied the marine reefs near the Torres Straits until he got to know some of the islanders and realized they were more interesting to study than the marine animals in the reefs. Like Morgan's, Haddon's natural history consisted of intricate description of how living beings exist in their natural setting, and his drawings demonstrate that principle.[3]

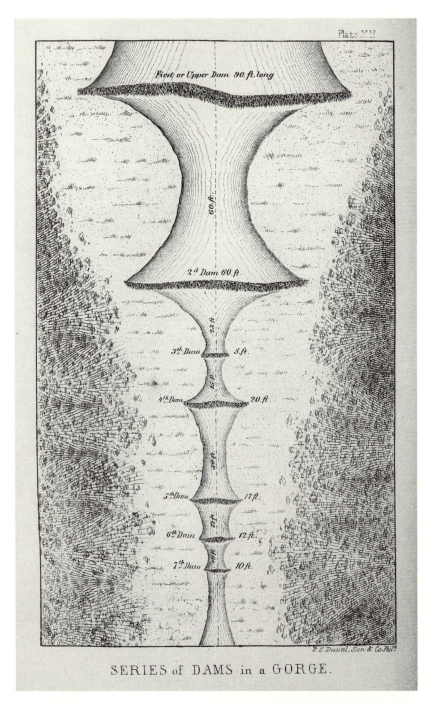

Plate XII

First or Upper Dam 90 ft. long

60 ft.

2ᵈ Dam 60 ft.

23 ft.

3ᵗʰ Dam   8 ft.

16 ft.

4ᵗʰ Dam   20 ft.

10 ft.

5ᵗʰ Dam   17 ft.

12 ft.

6ᵗʰ Dam   12 ft.

10 ft.

7ᵗʰ Dam   10 ft.

P.S. Duval, Son & Co. Phil.ᵃ

SERIES of DAMS in a GORGE.

FIGURE 2.1. Sketch of beaver dam from *The American Beaver and His Works*,
Lewis Henry Morgan, 1868, p. 168, Lippincott.

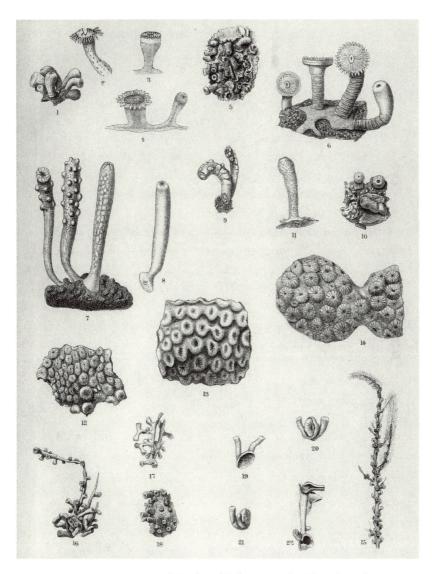

FIGURE 2.2. *Reports on the Zoological Collections Made in Torres Straits* by Professor A. C. Haddon, 1888–1889, Royal Dublin Society, 1891, plate LXI.

Wundt's Introspective Methods

These ancestors of my field began their careers in natural history. They were committed to the ideals and goals of the sciences of their time. What happened when their objects of study began to include human beings? That story requires me to turn to the beginnings of experimental psychology in Wilhelm Wundt's psychological laboratory in Leipzig, Germany, with its "introspective" methods. Foreshadowing contemporary psychology, the experiments in Wundt's laboratory all depended on the precise measurement of time intervals. Historians Ruth Benschop and Deborah Coon have written in detail about the technologies that enabled time to be measured in a standardized way and recorded accurately. As Coon explains, laboratory hardware standardized and regulated the physical stimuli to which the subject would respond, and "it also gave quantified, standardized output to the introspective method."[4] Perhaps even more important, the subject *himself* (at the beginning of psychology's history, all subjects were male) had to be standardized. Even though, "In the early stages of psychology's development, typical experimental subjects were professors and graduate students, not experimentally naive college sophomores and white rats," there was still "too much individual variation among these flesh-and-bone introspecting instruments. In order to standardize themselves as experimental observers, therefore, psychologists resorted to long and rigorous introspective training periods. [. . .] Only if *introspectors themselves were standardized* could they become interchangeable parts in the production of scientific psychological knowledge."[5] Edwin Boring, a historian of psychology, reports that Wundt insisted, "[N]o observer who had performed less than 10,000 of these introspectively controlled reactions was suitable to provide data for published research."[6]

A shared routine enabled common skills in introspection to be achieved more easily. Historian Ruth Benschop tells us that standardization also extended to regular exercises *outside* the context of the experiment itself. An American student of Wundt, James Cattell, relates how he followed a strict scheme of physical exercise, and he remarks in a letter to his parents that he and the other experimenters were required to walk three to six miles a day.[7] In sum, as the psychologist Edward Titchener explained in 1912, it was not that "the subject should be hooked up to machines," it was that the subject had "virtually become the machine, capable of automatic introspection."[8] In this experimental setup, the subject would be presented with a stimulus (a word or a color) and his response time would be carefully recorded. With training, the subject could register his response: the exact time at which he had *recognized* the stimulus (understood the word's meaning or recognized the color's name). The difference between the two times was the Wundtian reaction time: the delay between the appearance of the stimulus and the mind's psychological, *introspective* recognition of the stimulus.

Wundt and his collaborators aimed at measuring processes in what has been called "the generalized mind," those parts of mental life shared by all human adults alike. As Benschop explains, "Being practised in appearing in experiments helped to make sure that the results were representative of the 'universal features of adult human mental life.'"[9] Imagining that the subject's mind was like all other minds meant that experimenter and observer could switch roles between trials without affecting the format of the experiments. A person could run the experimental apparatus one day and be a subject in the same experiment the next.

What did they mean by introspection? As George Miller explained in the 1960s, Wundt held that the only way a living system can be studied from the inside (the goal of psychology) is by self-observation or introspection.[10] But casual, unsystematic self-observation would tell us nothing scientific. Instead, observations must be made by trained observers under carefully specified and controlled conditions. In an experimental situation, the questions observers attend to should be well-defined and conditions so well controlled that they could be replicated. In a handbook from 1913, observers were trained to give a "detailed description of your consciousness during the experiment."[11] In an example of an experiment on attention, observers listened to sounds from a metronome while doing mental arithmetic. An observer gave a description of his consciousness:

> The sounds of the metronomes, as a series of discontinuous clicks, were clear in consciousness only four or five times during the experiment, and they were especially bothersome at first. They were accompanied by strain sensations and unpleasantness. The rest of the experiment my attention was on the adding, which was composed of auditory images of the numbers, visual images of the numbers, sometimes on a dark grey scale which was directly ahead and about three feet in front of me. This was accompanied by kinaesthesis of eyes and strains in chest and arms. When these processes were clear in consciousness the sounds of the metronomes were very vague or obscure.[12]

The intricate detail subjects provided as they introspected about their auditory, visual, and general bodily sensations shows why extensive practice was necessary.

To a cultural anthropologist, Wundt's notion that experimenters had to synchronize their everyday practices is appealing. Even more appealing—at first glance—is his insistence that not all of human life is amenable to understanding through the experimental method. The vast majority of human activities—language, art, myth, and customs—he relegated to "folk psychology" (*Völkerpsychologie*) and reserved for a ten-volume book published in 1900. In his view, folk psychology was best studied by a method other than experimental psychology. Alas, these volumes reveal that Wundt, unsurprisingly, shared the assumptions of his time about human evolution. He thought that modern man had progressed through a number of stages, from primitive man through the totemic era, the age of heroes and gods, and finally to full humanity.

As man progressed through these stages, he moved farther away from wild animals and nature, and became more capable of higher processes of thought.[13] Wundt divided psychology into a number of subfields, including "individual psychology, animal psychology, psycho-physics, and *Völkerpsychologie*." Only the first three could be studied by the experimental method.[14] Despite his adherence to now outmoded theories of human evolution, Wundt wisely set clear limits around what experimental methods could illuminate. Psychologist Jerome Bruner judged Wundt to be "virtually opaque" and "quaintly antique," and wished as a psychologist that "God spare us another Wilhelm Wundt!"[15] Of course I agree that Wundt's ideas about evolution are odious, but I want to resurrect his laboratory practices to compare them, shortly, to contemporary psychology.

James Cattell and the Lip Key

Into Wundt's system came an earthquake. James Cattell, while pursuing his PhD in Wundt's Leipzig lab, realized at a certain point that he was unable to carry out Wundt's directions. As he explained,

> When I was a student in the Leipzig laboratory, attempts were being made to measure the time of perception by letting the subject react as soon as he knew from introspection that an object had been perceived. . . . [16] I attempted to continue these experiments, but feeling no confidence in the validity of my introspection in such a case, took up strictly objective methods in which a movement followed a stimulus without the slightest dependence on introspection."[17]

What did this mean? Wundt's method was to let the subject react as quickly as possible in the first trial, and then in the second trial to wait until he "distinguished the impression" (like recognizing a color or understanding a word). The difference between the two times gave the "perception-time."[18] Cattell explained his problem:

> I have not been able myself to get results by this method; I apparently either distinguished the impression and made the motion simultaneously, or if I tried to avoid this by waiting until I had formed a distinct impression before I make the motion, I added to the simple reaction, not only a perception [i.e. a discrimination], but also a volition [i.e. a choice].[19]

What was Cattell's solution to this problem? He added an instrument to the experiment, namely the lip switch or lip key. This was an electric switch the subject held between his lips. When he was in the act of perceiving a color or a word, it was assumed that he would move his lips unconsciously, as if silently naming the object of his perception. Hence the lip key would register the time of the perception without the need for any problematic conscious introspection on the part of the subject.

Why does such a minute-seeming change as the lip key loom so large? It was at this moment that Cattell joined the mind to the brain. As soon as he finished his experiments using the lip key, he adopted a relentlessly physicalist perspective, and questioned whether purely mental qualities existed. This was in 1886! As he explained this transition, *it takes time* for light waves to work on the retina and to generate in cells a nervous impulse corresponding to the light. *It takes time* for a nervous impulse to be conveyed along the optic nerve to the brain. *It takes time* for a nervous impulse to be conveyed through the brain to the visual center. *It takes time* for a nervous impulse to bring about changes in the visual center "corresponding to its own nature, and to the nature of the external stimulus." When all this has happened, the subject sees a red light. Between these changes and the sensation or perception of red "does not take any time." Once the brain is in the necessary state, the subject's sensation of a red light occurs simultaneously. This immediacy is parallel to the chemical changes in a galvanic battery: the chemical changes take time, but once they have happened the current does not take any additional time. "The current is the immediate representative of these changes."[20] He concluded, "Mental states correspond to physical changes in the brain." Henceforth his goal was "to inquire into the time needed to bring about changes in the brain, and thus to determine the rapidity of thought."[21] The times he recorded with the lip key were only to capture cerebral processes without the intrusion of introspection. Cattell's innovation paved the way for what historian Kurt Danziger would later conclude was the relentless *discounting* of the subject's experience in experimental psychology by the 1950s.

James Cattell and William James

After James Cattell came to the United States permanently in the late 1880s, he tangled with the de facto dean of American psychology, William James, who held an august position at Harvard University. William James was not an experimentalist: he was interested in detailed descriptions of everyday psychological states, from conscious states like attention to unconscious states like dreaming. Nor was he limited to the everyday. James was deeply involved in research on psychic phenomena, and as writer George Prochnik put it, he played a key role in the "phenomenal popularity of Spiritism in turn-of-the-century United States."[22] James organized a nationwide survey asking whether Americans had experienced a psychic event, such as having a vision or other sensory impression of a human person when that person was far away. Using postmasters as his assistants, he gathered more than five thousand questionnaires and estimated that more than 13 percent of respondents had experienced authentic hallucinations. The results of this research into psychic phenomena were published in thirteen volumes of scholarly monographs by the *Journal of the Society for Psychical Research*. James published a report in that journal in 1909, reviewing all the séances of the noted psychic Mrs. Piper. He allowed that "the stream of veridicality" might get lost in a "marsh of feebleness," but that the "veridical current" in the stream was real.[23]

Fresh from his experimental accomplishments in Germany, Cattell directly criticized James' psychic research in the weighty journal *Science*, impugning with a pun the validity of Mrs. Piper's psychic reports. "We have piped unto you, but ye have not danced." [24] In a subsequent issue of *Science*, after being sternly upbraided by James, Cattell says that James' research threatened to lead others into "quagmires"! [25] Historian Deborah Coon has shown that the emerging desire of some psychologists to establish psychology as a science led them to try to leverage the great public interest in Spiritism to show that psychologists were the only adequate judges of whether psychical phenomena were genuine or fraudulent. "They would offer alternative naturalistic explanations and they would be the self-appointed guardians of the scientific light."[26]

This quarrel shows us plainly a fork in the road in American psychology. On one path, James' approach allowed him to swing wide the door to reported states of mind. James relied on the kind of introspective descriptions that Wundt tried to harness in his laboratory, but he left them in the form of descriptions. His view allowed perception by all the senses, even those that could have paranormal origins. On the other path, Wundt, and Cattell after him, moved away from participants' descriptions of their psychic states, instead adopting quantitative measures of responses to stimuli.

Torres Straits Islands—The "Generalized Mind"

Where was anthropology in all this? During the late nineteenth century, the founders of this field pushed beyond the natural history of beavers, sea water, and coral reefs, but there was still no academic discipline of anthropology until the very end of the century. An important theme for anthropology in the academy was borrowed from the psychologists. Scientists on the Cambridge Anthropological Expedition to the Torres Straits Islands in 1898 depended on understandings, practices, and instruments they took directly from Wundt's introspective methods. The shared life practices required for research in Wundt's lab made lab members' introspections comparable because a shared environment determined the way the mind perceived the world. So, the Cambridge expedition's scientists assumed that after immersion in the daily life of villagers on the islands, they could themselves serve as appropriate experimental subjects comparable to the native inhabitants. Their introspective reports of the time they took to react to a stimulus could be measured and compared to the reports of native Torres Straits Islanders. The notion of a generalized mind (now extended to these islanders) entailed that the context in which such minds were trained determined their specific characteristics and made them commensurable. For this reason, as in the Wundt lab, experimenters and subjects could trade places. In the centennial volume of papers commemorating the expedition, Henrika Kuklick and Graham Richards analyze a photo of W.H.R. Rivers with the color wheel. Rivers and his companion (his name is Tom) are on the same side of the table: Rivers is not studying Tom here; he is showing him how to use the color wheel so that he could operate it and gather information on Rivers and other expedition scientists.[27]

Rivers articulated these practices especially well. According to Kuklick, Rivers explicitly trained himself to participate with the "minds" of Torres

Islanders: he imagined he could immerse himself in the lives of Torres Straits Islanders as a "sympathetic observer, who could reproduce in himself the emotions of the person he wished to understand by imitating that person's postures, gestures, and facial expressions . . . If the anthropologist conducted himself as his subjects did, he would become an embodied instrument, literally thinking and feeling as they did."[28] Clearly there was *resonance* between these practices and the ideas behind Wundt's laboratory training, both of which aimed to make subjects comparable through the experience of the same daily regimen. In the Cambridge Expedition, the regimen entailed immersion in the environment and social life of the islanders.

The Cambridge Expedition scientists realized that this immersion had its limits: they could not embody the islanders' past experiences. So, for example, when they saw that hearing was strikingly diminished in some villagers, expedition leader Alfred Cort Haddon attributed this to their previous injury from diving for pearl shells among coral reefs.[29] Their less acute hearing was put down to an activity they had been forced into by European (and increasingly Japanese) traders. They described this labor as the result of "ruthless exploitation" by traders, until the 1881 Pearl-Shell and Beche-de-Mer Fishery Act was passed "regulating the engagement and employment of natives."[30] Pearl shell companies wanted divers to work in ever deeper water as shallower waters were fished out: this required divers to board company boats and stay in more distant reef waters for days at a time, often under arduous and brutal conditions. This meant that they could not work their gardens during the week and so became dependent on buying goods for cash at the company store. Haddon describes the invidious cycle:

> Some natives own their own boats and make up crews on a system of sharing; others hire themselves out to white men. They generally start out on Monday and return on Friday or Saturday. All the time they are away they feed on tinned meat, biscuits, flour, and other white man's food. They get accustomed to this food, and as they are away from home so much, they cannot "make" their gardens. Thus, it comes about that agriculture, as well as fishing, is greatly neglected, and a considerable portion—and in some instances the bulk—of their food has to be bought from the stores. Should the supply of pearl-shell fall off, or the price be lowered, the natives would suffer greatly; and if the storekeepers left the island, the people would practically starve. As it is, many are considerably in debt to the

traders, and often the traders have to advance supplies of flour and food to ward off starvation. With all their apparent prosperity, the people are really in a false economic condition, and their future may yet be temporarily deplorable.[31]

On the poorer auditory performance of the male islanders they said, "there can be no doubt that in the majority of the islanders diving had caused a considerable amount of deafness."[32]

At the time of the Torres Straits expedition, the psychologists on the team (W.H.R. Rivers and C. S. Myers) were troubled by the widely accepted evolutionary theories of Herbert Spencer that "primitives" surpassed "civilised" people in psychophysical performance because more energy remained devoted to this level in the former instead of being diverted to "higher functions."[33] In this theory, a central tenet of late Victorian "scientific racism," "primitive" people were closer to the animal world than "civilized" people: their dependence on hunting, for example, would require animal-like acuity of sight, hearing, and smell. But despite this orthodoxy, the expedition experiments did not find significant differences in the predicted direction. In the *Reports*, they called the Spencerian view the "prevailing view," and directly contradicted it: summarizing their tests of the ability to smell, they said, "Of nine adult islanders . . . four were worse than, three were equal to two members of the expedition (W.H.R. R. and A. C. H.) [Rivers and Haddon], whose acuity was investigated at the same time."[34]

Perhaps the expedition scientists were on the cusp of a profound challenge to the assumptions of Wundtian experimental psychology: they pushed the meaning of the "generalized mind" far beyond where the Leipzig experimenters intended, by including subjects of different cultures. They also took the idea of being an embodied instrument farther than the Wundtians, by taking the experimental system and its training regimen to different environments altogether. Pursuing their version of the generalized mind, they replicated their Torres Straits experiments in British villages near Cambridge and in Aberdeenshire, Scotland. Their comparative charts between the Torres Straits Islands and British villages assumed that one could set "reaction times" from experiments in these different places alongside one another. They were willing to take the quantitative measure of reaction time as the basis for comparing perception across cultures. Once again, contrary to Spencerian assumptions, they did not find striking differences between the putatively more "civilized" university town of Cambridge and the putatively less "civilized" rural villages.[35]

To be sure, the Cambridge scientists did not rid themselves entirely of prevailing views about racial hierarchies. They freely used terms such as "savage," "barbarous," and "primitive." Such terms were commonly used even by the next generation of anthropologists, including the esteemed Bronislaw Malinowski. Historians concede that it is difficult to pin down exactly the limits of their challenges to the prevailing views. Haddon, who also disapproved of private property and customs that hampered the status of women, comes off the best of the group. Historian Graham Richards found "sufficient grounds for seeing Haddon as having moved somewhat beyond classic scientific racism, even while retaining some of its perspectives."[36] Along the same lines, historian Elazar Barkan acknowledged that although Haddon held many of the prejudices of his time, he, far more than his peers, related so-called racial differences to environmental factors. Alongside his prejudices, he also expressed esteem and empathy for the islanders. Barkan compliments him as "the cradle of egalitarianism."[37]

Bringing Back Context

Anthropologists have sometimes cited the expedition members' interest in photography as evidence of their desire for a kind of distant and uninvolved objective scientific knowledge. This point is well taken for the stark examples of photographs of physical types, which they certainly collected. Measuring heads and arranging populations on scales of primitive to modern, which they did, is the epitome of an objectifying practice. But the expedition was run through with other strands. I mention only a few of the photographs that convey a different kind of relationship between scientist and subject. First take a look at the group of them, as shown in figure 2.3: they stand there, slouching, barefoot, wearing grubby clothes and miscellaneous felt hats. In a phrase from even earlier expeditions, some of whom actually also visited the Torres Straits and were quoted widely by the Cambridge expedition Reports, they were "living rough," engaged in "rough living."[38]

Next consider the interactions depicted in photos such as figure 2.4, which shows the Torres Straits Expedition researchers and is included in Stocking's important history *After Tylor*. Stocking, never a fan of the expedition, claimed in his photo caption that their assistant was "unnamed." In fact, as we know from anthropologist Anita Herle's account, all their assistants and associates

FIGURE 2.3. Cambridge Anthropological Expedition members: Haddon (seated) with (l-r) Rivers, Seligman, Ray, and Wilkin. Mabuiag, 1898. Reproduced by permission of the University of Cambridge Museum of Archaeology and Anthropology (N.23035.ACH2).

were individually named. I would think the most remarkable thing about this photograph is that Haddon is allowing himself (during a timed photograph) to look at and speak with another member of the group, namely the islander Jimmy Rice.

Michael Taussig uses Haddon's kneeling posture in another Torres Straits photo (figure 2.5) as evidence of his "sacred pose" (an unabashed "othering" of the savage).[39] But in his own book, Haddon captions this photo with ethnographic detail: "Ulai singing Malu songs into a phonograph, Gasu is beating the Malu drum."[40] I think what is most remarkable about this photo is that Haddon took this most precious piece of equipment, the phonographic recorder, to the islanders and sat it down on the ground instead of making Ulai sit on a chair at a table in the anthropological laboratory.

Finally, figure 2.6 is an informal photo of some islanders together with some expedition members.[41] Pasi is standing—*his* stance is paternalistic—with one hand each on Haddon's and Ray's shoulders. It doesn't look like these "subjects" were being regarded or that they regarded themselves as mere

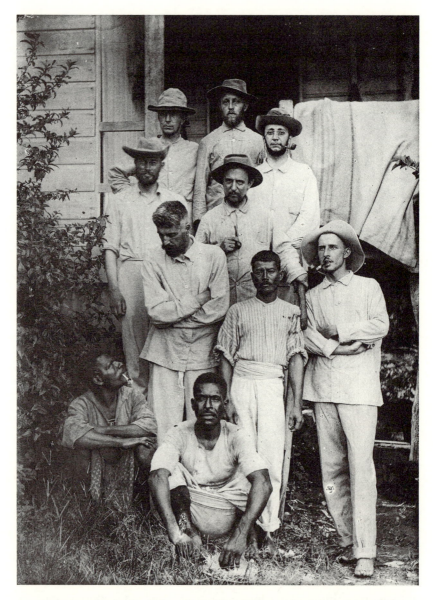

FIGURE 2.4. Cambridge Anthropological Expedition members with assistants (l-r).
Seated: Jimmy Rice, Debe Wali; First row: Alfred Haddon, Charlie Ontong, Anthony Wilkin;
Second row: William Rivers, Sidney Ray; Third row: William McDougall, Charles Myers,
Charles Seligman. Mer, 1898. Reproduced by permission of the University of Cambridge
Museum of Archaeology and Anthropology (N.22900.ACH2_003).

FIGURE 2.5. William Rivers and Tom, a Mabuiag man and one of Haddon's chief assistants, demonstrating the use of the color wheel. Reproduced by permission of the University of Cambridge Museum of Archaeology and Anthropology (N.23209.ACH2_003).

specimens. The anthropologists developed their photographs on the islands and recorded the islanders' delight at seeing themselves and the anthropologists in lantern slide shows.[42]

Music

C. S. Myers took the Cambridge Expedition approach some steps further. His studies in the Torres Straits Islands and later in the Cambridge Laboratory of Experimental Psychology focused on aural perception in music and rhythm.[43] He founded the psychological laboratory at Cambridge in 1912, taught experimental psychology, and authored a two-volume textbook on the subject. He was interested not just in recording music, measuring its intervals, and measuring reaction times in various sensory modalities, but specifically in the subjective components of sensory experience. So, for example, using a

FIGURE 2.6. Haddon and Ray having a picnic with Pasi and extended family on Dauar, Torres Strait. Reproduced by permission of the University of Cambridge Museum of Archaeology and Anthropology (N.23140.ACH2).

Wundtian apparatus in Cambridge, he could present subjects with sounds separated by various intervals.[44] The subject would try to replicate the pattern, and these patterns would be recorded on the smoked surface of a revolving drum. He stressed that, "The subject should carefully record the results of introspective analysis."[45] He also used metronomes: "The subject should observe and record the varying affective values (pleasant, wearisome, etc.) of different rhythms and the associated experiences which they may revive."[46] An "objective" accentuation could be added by enclosing the metronome in a box, which could, unbeknownst to the subject, be opened or closed. The point of the experiments was to identify the conditions under which subjects "heard or read into a sequence of beats a rhythm which was not in fact there."[47]

Throughout his career, well into the 1930s, Myers insisted that the aesthetic aspects of music and rhythm had to be understood comparatively in different cultures:

It comes about that many examples of primitive music are incomprehensible to us, just because they are not so readily assimilated as those which are more nearly related to our previous experiences. Our attention is continuously distracted, now by the strange features and changes of rhythm, now by the extraordinary colouring of strange instruments, now by the unwonted progression and character of intervals. Consequently, much familiarity is needed before we can regard such music from a standpoint that will allow of faithful description. We have first to disregard our well-trained feelings towards consonances and dissonances. We have next to banish to the margins of our field of consciousness certain aspects of music, which, were it our own music, would occupy the very focus of attention. Thus, incomprehensibility will gradually give place to meaning, and dislike to some interesting emotion.[48]

Myers often stressed the variety of emotions that music could arouse, including "joy, sorrow, tenderness, and ecstasy."[49] The crucial point is that Myers was interested in the physical world (how people perceived sound with their ears), but he held that the social and cultural world would determine how their perceptions were experienced. In his writing on music after the Cambridge Expedition, Myers may have even gone a step beyond the expedition's original extension of the Wundtian experimental method. The expedition extended Wundt's concepts of the generalized mind and of introspective training: Myers may have been moving toward a method that was not experimental at all.

Noting this moment might help us describe an ethnographic form of knowledge that is something different from scientific objectivity, and something more than mere description. Perhaps some form of intimate and emotional connection is involved, such as a form of identification.[50] We might revisit the photograph of Haddon kneeling before the phonograph and Ulai the singer. Elizabeth Edwards describes this as "subjective longing." This does not imply that Haddon actually achieved emotional intimacy with the islanders, but rather that he was open to the possibility.

My argument up to this point is that the members of the Cambridge expedition took the elements of the Wundt laboratory that centered introspection and intentional action and ran with them. They devised a remarkable way of looking at human psychology as being inextricably embedded in its context. Even the rawest, "natural" perceptual inputs from eyes, ears, nose, and skin were only graspable as products of specific human social environments.

Away from the Social

As some historians have argued, experimental psychology might seem to have principally trod a single-minded path into research models that stripped the human subject of subjectivity. Perhaps sparked by James Cattell's innovation of the lip key, there is a case to be made that there was a progressive elimination of the *experience* of subjects from psychology. Kurt Danziger has emphasized that where the effort has been made to reintroduce subjectivity the refusal has been absolutely relentless. "It became a key principle of the dominant model of psychological experimentation that the subject's experience was to be discounted. Attempts to change this state of affairs have always evolved the most determined resistance."[51] The point of my excursion into the Cambridge Expedition is to show how Wundtian experiments were carried out in the Torres Straits Islands in ways that honored the importance of the islanders' subjective experience.

I was happy to learn that the anthropologists of the Torres Straits expedition thought that they needed to go barefoot and sit on the ground in order to share the islanders' sensory environment. But back in the United States, some early psychologists were not so happy about experiments built around the idea of scientists sharing a sensory environment with subjects. A controversy exploded across the pages of young psychology journals. To understand how, in 1913, the young psychologist John Watson could demand in no uncertain terms that psychologists abandon trained introspection of the Wundtian type altogether, threaten dire consequences if they did not, and largely succeed in dominating the field for a time, I needed to see how far into introspection psychologists went in the years before 1913. In those years, subjects were assumed to bring their daily lives with them into the psychology lab where their individual life experiences played a role in experiments.

Titchener and Introspection

Edward Titchener was an American who had studied under Wundt in Leipzig. As a professor at Cornell, Titchener had an impact on American psychology in part through his college textbooks, which were widely used as practical manuals in experimental psychology courses across the country.[52] Like Wundt, Titchener was interested in "the generalized, normal, human, adult mind."[53] He thought the aim of psychology should be to understand human consciousness, which he also called "introspection" [*Selbstbeobachtung*]. And it was this capacity that required extensive training in the laboratory before anyone could produce scientific data in experiments.[54]

Meanwhile, other methods were surfacing, in concert with Cattell's experience in Wundt's lab—for some reason, Cattell was unable to produce the reaction times that the Wundt model required. Why was that? For Wundt, all consciousness was made up of sensations compounded into representations in the mind. When, by means of the will, attention was brought to bear on certain representations, they became more or less intensely present to consciousness. When the field of attention was broad, Wundt called that *perception*, which was of low intensity. When the field of attention was narrow in focus, Wundt called that *apperception*, which was of higher intensity.[55]

Experimentally, Wundt varied the instructions to subjects. As Kurt Danziger explains, in one trial the subject would be told to concentrate on his *muscular* response to the stimulus. In another the subject would be told to concentrate his *senses* on the stimulus itself. Wundt held (and some experiments showed this) that the muscular response was faster and more automatic than the sensory response.[56] He thought this was because more consciousness or introspection was involved in the sensory response than the muscular response.[57] The muscular response time for all subjects could be shortened simply by adding practice sessions; the sensory response time for all subjects could be lengthened simply by adding further steps in what the subject was to pay attention to.[58]

As we have seen, Cattell found himself unable to produce the two different response times expected by Wundt.[59] It is not hard to understand why Wundt found Cattell's experiment "incomplete." Because Cattell had removed consciousness or introspection from the experiment entirely, he could only be measuring muscular response time and not sensory response time.[60] For his part, Cattell doubted whether Wundt's sensory responses existed, or if they did, whether they could be measured.[61] In that case, the logical thing was to focus on what *could* be measured—namely, muscular movement of the lips, which, he thought, was tied directly to the brain.[62] Cattell could vary the experimental conditions even without introspection: letter stimuli could be presented slower or faster; words could be presented with other words that either did or did not form a sentence.[63]

A rash of papers appeared in the journals by dissenters such as Mark Baldwin, contesting Wundt's claim that practice made the muscular response shorter. Baldwin held that individual differences in muscular reaction times persisted even after extensive practice. Another psychologist brought in two well-known concert pianists to suggest that their different musical styles (technical vs. emotional) resulted in different reaction times. What was at stake was one's status as a "competent" subject in an experiment. According to Cattell, Wundt regarded him as "not competent." Cattell thought Wundt had accused him of being "incapable of finding" the required distinctions, ["*Cattell konnte weder . . . Unterschied finden*"], rather than that Cattell had a different psychological style.[64]

The debate turned on "competency" and "proper" results. Wundt's moral condemnation of Cattell was repeated with Lightner Witmer, a student Cattell sent to study with Wundt. As recounted by historian John O'Donnell, Witmer wrote that Wundt "excluded" him as a subject because his sensory reaction times were too short. Witmer added that Wundt advised him to "practice so as to increase my reaction time and presumably make it truly sensory." But Witmer admitted that he was "disgusted at this suggestion."[65] Denied competence as a subject by Wundt, Witmer returned to the United States and founded his own psychological clinic.[66] The debate was to be won for a time by the preponderance of evidence from American experiments conducted by J. Mark Baldwin that showed the "generalized mind" produced by practice was concealing individual differences based on prior habits: previous training about how to pay attention and previous education. Another way to put this is that the Wundt lab's training could not erase the life experience of individuals.

Baldwin—Introspection's Problems

Baldwin's entry into the debate began by stressing how important it was that the physical setting of experiments be comparable. All three of his subjects (he called them "reagents"), who were the two authors of the article and a student, were placed in the same setting at the same time of day. At the time, the Wundtian assumption was that motor reactions are always faster than sensory reactions. But Baldwin's experiment showed that there were subjects "whose sensory reactions to sound are shorter than their motor reactions." Speaking to Wundt, Baldwin argued that saying the differences are due to the competence or *Anlage*—aptitude—of the reagents is circular: the only evidence of *Anlage* is the ability to give the required results, the results that the Wundtians consider "proper." Baldwin thought the question should be: "What of these very differences of individual *Anlage*? How did they arise; what do they mean; why do they give different reaction-time results?" Baldwin was insisting that the subject's life before and outside of the laboratory would strongly influence his performance in the lab and in the experiment. The relative quickness of the "muscular" reaction found in some subjects cannot be taken to be a universal fact. He thought that we must ask where the *Anlage* of a quick muscular reaction came from in each individual's life. Otherwise we would be assuming the *Anlage* of some must be found in all, which would make our research a "handmaid to dogma." People who do not have the special *Anlage* Wundt required find it difficult to attend to the specifically muscular part of a movement.

Asking such people to focus their consciousness on the muscular component "embarrasses, confuses, and delays the execution of that movement" in people whose lives outside the laboratory give them more facility with sensory responses than with muscular ones.[67] For Baldwin, one subject's inability to produce Wundt's patterns meant that he had a different *Anlage*, worth studying, not that he failed to produce the *Anlage* Wundt required. He was neither incompetent nor improper.

Angell—Reconciliation?

The next year (1896), fellow psychologists Angell and Moore described a way to reconcile these approaches. They began by broadening Baldwin's characterization of where individual differences of mind could originate. Initially, they agreed with Baldwin's finding that different individuals have, from their practices and habits in daily life, different minds. Then they introduced two capabilities that subjects might bring with them into the experiment in different amounts: habit and attention. They were also alert to the two aptitudes that Baldwin found could differ among individuals: sensory and motor reactions. As they saw it, subjects entered the lab differently: some started out with more motor skills and others with more sensory skills, depending on their daily lives. With practice, the weaker form became more reflexive and its time became faster. As reflex increased, attention decreased and gave over to habit, which could now "cope by itself." Going beyond Wundt as well as Baldwin, they paid detailed attention to the role of habit. If a subject came into the experiment with stronger sensory skills and weaker motor skills, for example, his sensory mode would weaken after practice. "The sensory mode passes more completely under the control of habit and thus leaves the faster time to the motor form." The reason habit slowed down the weaker form is that habit, if in control, tended to be stabilized and fixed rather than adaptive and improving. Where attention rather than habit is exercised, Angell thought, there is the "opportunity for continued variation."[68]

This arcane debate laid the groundwork for a departure from the ideals of the Cambridge expedition. In search of the "generalized mind," early anthropologists expected to find it anywhere they looked, even among the faraway peoples of the Torres Straits Islands. By the end of the nineteenth century, the door had opened to reveal that people fell into different types, with different minds. Through this door, some psychologists could proceed to a form of social Darwinism. Historian John O'Donnell tells us that Cattell spent a year in England working on psychometrics in Francis Galton's laboratory, a famous nursery for social Darwinist accounts of race and eugenics.[69] Subsequently, according to historian Kerry Buckley, Cattell wrote for popular science magazines, advocating combining Galton's ideas on eugenics with psychological tests to "influence the future of the human race."[70]

In the next developments in psychology, the theoretical ideas about habit held by those psychologists who were moving beyond Wundtian introspection, such as Baldwin and Angell, became a road left untaken. However, habit, seen as a form of routine practice—an intrinsic part of the Wundtian experiment—did not at all disappear from the structure of psychological experiments, but rather was pushed so far into the background that it became taken for granted and virtually invisible.

J.B. Watson and His Ultimatum

Seeing how deeply psychology experiments were involved in measuring introspection, I often wondered how introspection had come under ill repute in psychology, which had certainly moved the field away from the emerging focus on life experience in the Cambridge Anthropological Expedition. Several of my interlocutors told me that the reign of introspection was ended in 1913. In a lecture at Columbia, John Watson, then a junior scholar in the field, claimed that experimental psychology could only join the ranks of the natural sciences by eliminating introspection from experimental protocols. His language could hardly have been stronger: "Psychology, as the behaviorist views it, is a purely objective, experimental branch of natural science which needs introspection as little as do the sciences of chemistry and physics." Once psychology eliminated reliance on human consciousness in the form of introspection, Watson argued, the path would be open to treat research on animal behavior as directly comparable to research on human behavior. In turn, the results of psychological research would be vastly more applicable in practical ways:

What gives me hope that the behaviorist's position is a defensible one is the fact that those branches of psychology which have already partially withdrawn from the parent, experimental psychology, and which are consequently less dependent upon introspection are today in a most flourishing condition. Experimental pedagogy, the psychology of drugs, the psychology of advertising, legal psychology, the psychology of tests, and psychopathology are all vigorous growths [sic]. These are sometimes wrongly called "practical" or "applied" psychology. Surely there was never a worse misnomer. In the future there may grow up vocational bureaus which really apply psychology. At present these fields are truly scientific and are in search of broad generalizations which will lead to the control of human behavior.[71]

In Watson's view, when experiments measure only behavior and not consciousness, "broad generalizations which will lead to the control of human behavior" seem within reach. Watson was serious about literal control of human behavior, and even threatened his fellow psychologists if they failed to fall in line:

Should human psychologists fail to look with favor upon our overtures and refuse to modify their position, the behaviorists will be driven to using human beings as subjects and to employ methods of investigation which are exactly comparable to those now employed in the animal work.[72]

Humans kept in cages, to control their environment? Running in mazes so their behavior is observable? And rewarded with something immediately gratifying—Money? Candy? Alcohol?

In a later version of the lecture published in 1919, Watson agreed heartily with Cattell's turn to brain-based responses. The goal of psychology was not to establish social or moral standards but to formulate "laws and principles whereby man's actions can be controlled by organized society." The behavior society required of people changed over time, and psychology had to keep pace, by "determining and developing methods of instructing" them. [73]

Watson's threatened forms of control seem impossibly extreme today. But we should keep open the question whether, using means other than mazes and cages, psychological methods may have been silently welcomed into public culture with results that make mazes and cages seem harmless. Today, when people take personality quizzes because they are fun or required for employment, they are producing behavioral data. As we have recently learned, such data, innocent as it seems, can be used by organizations to control our actions, how we vote, where we shop, and what we buy.

World War I and Watson

World War I, a perfect test case for the application of Watson's psychology, came along at the right time. Before the war began, as Kerry Buckley recounts, Watson "pointed out that an entire range of tests could be developed to select and classify military personnel. Rapid mobilization depended upon the efficient management of men and resources. Psychologists, Watson argued, had the experience and techniques to provide scientific methods of personnel selection and training."[74] Led by Robert Yerkes, famous for his animal psychology and president of the American Psychological Association when the war began, "[t]he military would also serve as a huge laboratory for the development of methods and the accumulation of data." Tests developed by psychologists primarily measured mental ability. This allowed "rapid selection of exceptional men and the elimination of those unfit for service." The military cared little about the validity of the results: it simply wanted the "ability to quickly classify personnel according to a predetermined level of skills."[75]

Nearly two million recruits were tested with Yerkes' instruments and deemed to exhibit superior, average, or inferior intelligence. Historian Daniel Kevles' meticulous research describes the result:

> Quick assignment was at a premium in the wartime army. Personnel officers, after they had assigned recruits on the basis of occupational experience, would allocate the remainder of a draft batch on the basis of intelligence scores. They distributed the men so that each company received what the Committee on Classification of Personnel called "its pro-rata share of superior men, average men, and inferior men." Many commanding officers found this method of placement so appealing that they requested draftees of a specific measure of intelligence.[76]

But when all was said and done, the military had its doubts:

> In reality, the testing ended because of the military's fundamental objections to the program. The arguments of the War Plans Division showed that the psychologists had never overcome the army's wartime antagonisms. The army had not previously "required any psychological aid in discovering

men of superior intelligence"; it did not need this now. In addition, military officers could select men for particular duties better than "civilian scientists whose knowledge of military affairs is usually meager."[77]

At that time, competition among experts blunted the opportunity that psychological testing had to operate in the military world.

Despite this wartime military resistance, in Nikolas Rose's unforgettable terms, "psychology was a 'generous' discipline; it gave itself away to all kinds of professionals from police to military commanders, on condition that they came to think and act, in some respects, like psychologists."[78] This generosity led to the "enlargement of morality." In such places as the asylum, patients were released from imprisonment and instead enmeshed in corrective moral treatment. Anyone could see the appeal of such a soft technology with therapeutic promise. Along the way, the original linkage with the culturally contextualized research of the Torres Straits anthropologists was lost. And so was appreciation of how very social the production of psychological facts is. One of the legacies of the introspective method is the imperative for experimenters to practice experimental tasks in the same social setting so that their results when they perform in experiments as subjects will be comparable. "Practice" continues today in experimental psychology alongside ideals of objectivity and leads us afresh to the realization that entirely social elements are necessarily present even in contemporary psychological experiments.

3

Experimenting Scientifically

Experiment continues to be the major occupation of psychologists; by that
route psychology became an accredited science.

—JOSEPH JASTROW, *AMERICAN SCHOLAR*, 1935

WHEN I began this project, it never occurred to me that I was already participating in experiments on human subjects when I used social media like Facebook. I didn't fully understand what a scientific experiment was—in psychology or any other discipline. Many years later, one of my key interlocutors,
Dr. S, would summarize the goal of my project as describing the "ether of
psychology." The experiments I observed in the laboratory, not to mention
those run on social media sites, would certainly turn out to be central to that
ether. Early on, even though I didn't realize their importance, experiments
were my only route into psychology labs. I signed up for anything I could that
was explicitly labeled a psychology experiment. Everywhere I traveled, I
signed up to be a volunteer subject in psychology experiments through public
bulletin boards or websites in psychology departments on the East and West
Coasts.

Some were restricted by age (but not many), all required normal vision
with glasses or contacts, and after a certain point—not until years into my
study—a few stipulated that subjects could not be taking SSRI drugs, which
are used for the treatment of depression and anxiety disorders. Despite these
constraints, I was still very busy. At one of the first experiments I attended in
a social psychology lab, I was asked to read illustrated short stories about several characters. My field notes described them briefly:

FIGURE 3.1. University bulletin board seeking subjects for psychology
experiments. Photo by author, 2013.

The first story was about a guy of indeterminate ethnicity. From his photo
he could be Middle Eastern. He got a law degree and self-published a book.
After a celebration for his book publication, he got drunk, drove his car into
a tree, and became paralyzed. A photo shows him sitting in a wheelchair.
The next story had a photo of a very thin shrunken guy, who could be
African-American. He was successful in getting an advanced degree and

then got diagnosed with schizophrenia. Since the diagnosis he has been on and off the streets.

Next, I saw a photo of a white guy and learned he was caught selling pharmaceuticals from the company he worked for because of his gambling addiction. Last, there was a photo of a white guy in a wheelchair. He had been an emergency room worker, and he was responsible for prepping a room for an fMRI. He told the incoming firemen to remove all metal because of the powerful magnet in the scanner, but one fireman forgot he had a knife in his pocket. The knife flew through the air and severed the emergency worker's spine.

My field notes continued:

> While reading, I asked myself what the experiment would be trying to understand: Prejudice? Stereotyping? Judging responsibility? Attitudes toward persons with physical or mental disabilities?
>
> When I finished reading the fictional stories, a grad student walked me to the lab room across the hall, where there was a computer monitor with a chair in front, electrodes draped everywhere and another monitor to the side. I sat in the chair in front of the monitor and the grad student cleaned the left side of my forehead, temple, and cheek. She put a hairband on me and attached electrodes carefully to my face. Readings appeared on the monitor to my left, which I could see clearly. The grad student told me that these electrodes would measure small facial movements of which I was unaware, which would indicate emotional responses to photographs presented to me on the computer screen in front of me. The photos would depict those individuals in the stories I had read. I would press keys on the keyboard to register my responses to these images. For example, I would be asked to rate each one from 1–10 on trustworthiness. A software program would tally the results. My responses would be produced, she told me, by specific parts of my brain. Later I was tested on which photographs I could remember and how accurately.

Although what the experimenter sought was data about how my brain reacted to the photographs, there were elements all over the place that puzzled me in this experimental setting. For example, although the monitor I was to attend to and make my responses to was right in front of me, just on my left was another monitor that showed the varying electrical impulses from my electrodes. I mentioned to the experimenter that I could easily see the readout of my own responses, and she said, "That's fine, it doesn't matter." But it

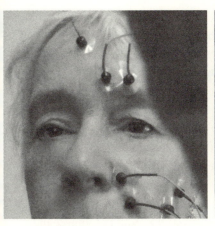

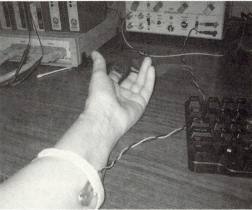

FIGURE 3.2. Author with electrodes on face to capture changes in expression. Photo by author, 2009.

FIGURE 3.3. Author's arm with attached electrodes that will deliver mild shocks in an experiment. Photo by author, 2010.

mattered to me. I couldn't help trying to catch a glance of the varying signal and wondered how this distraction might affect my responses. It seemed to me I was treated as an object that could be manipulated, controlled, by the investigator's confidence about what mattered.

In another experiment, I was shown a long series of scenes with a range of emotional valences. Some were violent and frightening, some warmhearted and appealing. It was exhausting to register how "agitated" each scene made me feel by clicking a mouse along a scale on the screen. After about twenty minutes of this, I was given a "break" during which I was to watch a video online. The video, meant to be neutral, unstimulating, or even boring, was a 1972 documentary about the making of the Boeing 747. I started making a mental list of items that "agitated" me: among other things, I saw bulldozers clear a beautiful, virgin pine forest north of Seattle to build the Boeing plant (the largest industrial plant in the world). The video showed many flights of an airplane indistinguishable to me from the ones I witnessed, living in lower Manhattan, crash into the Twin Towers on 9/11. This was my rest period! Of course, I am much older than the typical college-age subject, and most of them would not have been in New York City on 9/11/2001. This experiment took place in 2009, and 9/11 happened eight years before. So, a seventeen-year-old would have been only nine years old during 9/11. The video might well have helped most subjects to rest and be ready to undergo the next session, where their memory of the scenes and figures in the first session would be tested.

In this experiment, I was given a simple explanation of what was being measured: only my emotional responses (happening in one part of my brain) and my memory (happening in another part of my brain) were recorded. Yet the experimental setup seemed to me imbued with social meanings the researchers deemed extraneous to the experiment. The lab group doing the study was interested in social phenomena such as stereotyping, but at first glance it seemed they did not consider that the apparatuses themselves could play a social role in the experimental setting. The lab group assumed that the readout monitor and the "break" video were technologies that would not interfere with the subject's experience. Were subjects assumed to be inert objects rather than lively participants engaged in social interactions with subjects? Was the objectification of the subject so profound that both the subject and the machines seemed devoid of social life? Was there some kind of statistical averaging they could do that would justify ignoring individual outliers? I might have been the only subject to be agitated by the Boeing documentary, but how would they take account of other sorts of perturbed data? I determined to begin exploring how and in what ways the subjectivity of people participating in experiments is or is not involved in those experiments.

Since the world I was plunging into felt exceedingly alien at first, I paid close attention to what other scholars had to say about the role of human subjects in experiments. Most scholars who wrote about the experience of subjects in experiments were historians of psychology. The guiding question I gleaned from these scholars was: Are the life experiences of the participants in experiments eliminated? For example, as I already mentioned, Kurt Danziger remarked on the progressive elimination of the experience of subjects from psychology and pointed out that wherever the effort has been made to reintroduce it, the refusal has been unyielding. Later in the 1990s, Jill Morawski wrote about multiple attempts to deal with the "impoverished image of the subject" inside psychology and in the humanities.[1] Also in the later 1990s, historian Betty Bayer wrote of the phantoms that have apparently been eliminated from psychological research but actually continue to haunt it: "subjective desires, epistemological uncertainty or doubt, the encumbrance of the body, unsteady splits between subjects and objects, and deception."[2] I wondered how these phantoms remain despite determined efforts to delimit experiments in order to exclude them. From another discipline, Dr. A, a linguist, told me during my fieldwork that in psychology, "You can't theorize unless you run experiments. You have to earn the right to theorize with subjects in experiments, and that means silencing the subjects. This is done on the grounds that what subjects say would be mentalistic and subjective. So, language from subjects is driven out." I wondered exactly what of the subject's experience is driven out. Is experience driven out in all psychology experiments or only in some? Is all experience "silenced" or only some? Is the effort to ignore experience a large or small effort?

This chapter provides a first look at these questions, while describing the basic elements of a psychology experiment. I will follow the path of my research, looking at what, from my point of view, seemed like obstacles to scientific results. When I looked from the researchers' point of view, I found out that what seemed like obstacles to me vanished once I understood the criteria of a good experiment.

What Are the Ingredients of an Experiment?

I quickly saw the centrality of the experimental method. The experimental method is often described as the gold standard of scientific research across the board, including psychology.[3] Historian Andrew Winston makes it clear: "Despite widespread disagreement on fundamental issues in psychology, there is a remarkable social consensus on the definition and role of experiment. In nearly all modern texts, experiment is defined as manipulating an independent variable, holding all other events constant, and observing the effect on a dependent variable."[4] But I was puzzled by how participants (ordinary, everyday people rather than animals or molecules) could be harnessed to the requirements of this experimental method. How can we understand the concept and practice of the experiment in psychology labs where human beings both design experiments and serve as subjects in experiments?

Formal Characteristics: Dependent and Independent Variables

I learned in my psychology classes and labs that good experiments need to have a number of formal characteristics. Understanding these characteristics is hard going, but it is necessary because they lie at the heart of psychological research. Bear with me! For a start, dependent variables need to be distinguished from independent variables. I found this distinction hard to understand, and so I asked, "Dependent on what and independent of what?" Dependent variables are dependent on what the experimental subjects bring to the experiment; independent variables are independent of what the experimental subjects bring to the experiment. To use a homely example, suppose I wanted to find out whether marathon runners would run faster listening to faster music than to slower music. I would select a group of runners who ran marathons on average at the same pace. Then I would divide the group of runners in half and ask one half to run listening to slow music and the other half to run listening to fast music. The fast tempo of the music would be a variable added by me, as an experimenter, independent of the runners, and hence would be called an independent variable. Independent variables like my fast versus slow music conditions would be meant to cause a change in the dependent variable of how long it takes the runners to complete the same marathons: I would be predicting that there would be a significant difference in the runners' race times between those listening to slow music and those listening to fast music.

The setup for most psychology experiments is simple. The subject sits before a keyboard and monitor. Stimuli are flashed on the screen, and the subject presses designated keys to indicate her response according to instructions: "yes" if it is a word versus "no" if it is not a word would be a simple example. The subject's behavioral responses (the dependent variables) are measured and recorded by software residing in the computer that produces a data file listing the numerical value of the independent and dependent variables on each trial for each subject. In this case, the independent variables might involve differences in the shape, color, or sound of the stimulus in that trial. One dependent variable might be the response—that is, yes, it is a word or no, it is not a word. Another dependent variable might be the amount of time the subject took to make that response (the "reaction time"). Reaction times are often included as a dependent variable to indicate the amount of mental activity subjects require to do the tasks in the experiment. Today, longer reaction times are generally thought to be correlated to more extensive or complex brain activity.[5]

An example of a classic experiment involves measuring the so-called Stroop effect, a standard measure of specific cognitive functions. Literate, English-speaking subjects see simple color words (*red, green, blue*) displayed in various colors on a computer screen. They are instructed by the experimenter to press, as quickly as possible, the key that indicates the color in which the word is displayed. They are explicitly told to ignore the meaning of the word that is spelled out. On "consistent" trials they see the words appear in the appropriate color (for example, *red* in red letters or *blue* in blue letters), and on "inconsistent" trials they see the same words appear in an inappropriate color (for example, *red* in blue letters or *blue* in red letters). I have tried this in my anthropology classes, and my students' reaction times to name the colors in the inconsistent conditions are always longer than in the consistent conditions, implying that more cognitive activity is required to respond when the word and the color are mismatched than when they are appropriately matched.

Even within this formal structure, researchers can gather subjective reports from participants. In such cases, the protocol might include a questionnaire asking about participants' cognitive or emotional states. Participants might choose points on various self-reported scales (for example, *anxious* to *calm*, *unhappy* to *happy*, or *not confident* to *very confident*). These scales are meant to measure aspects of subjects' inner psychological states (experiences) numerically, but of course the participant is constrained in what he or she can report. That is, the participant can only match his/her subjective experience with the choices given in the self-report scales. There is not usually an opportunity to write in experiences not included in the scales, such as *irritable, resentful,* or *jovial.* The choices allowed to participants are presented as if they were unambiguous and universally understood names of stable emotional states. Nonetheless, ambivalence often surrounds these kinds of data. Sam, who works on the aesthetics of music, does not like to use scales. He said frankly that he prefers to work at the implicit level where people's conscious experiences are not influenced by being asked to make such ratings. "Their own understanding of themselves is often sort of problematic and flavored by various biases and heuristics." Dr. M told me that allowing more open-ended answers would be a problem. "There are no right or wrong answers. So how would you code them?" The standardized scales handle this problem.[6]

These are the simple elements of a behavioral experiment, but they are also the basis of experiments using more elaborate technological methods to measure dependent variables such as electrical activity on the scalp (EEG) or blood flow within the brain (fMRI). When an experiment is finished, if all goes as hoped, the experimenter will see "an effect," which is demonstrated when subjects produce statistically significant different responses and/or reaction times under different conditions defined by the independent variables. Psychologists say some colleagues are especially good at "getting effects." Others are not so lucky.

It is fair to say that nearly all publishable results from cognitive psychology labs come through the process of experimentation. Earlier textbooks in the field are unabashed in stating the fundamental nature of the experiment. The experiment is considered the idealization of the scientific method because it produces descriptions of causal relationships using fully developed methods of controlled observation. More recent scholarship has clarified that the experiment does as much to shape future questions as it does to answer current ones. An experiment is not the elemental unit in science, like the final step of a single staircase. An experiment is like a step, but one that leads to a landing from which many further staircases are now visible and from which the stairs taken previously may appear in a different light.

The way current research depends on previous research became clear to me in an experiment in which I was fitted with electrodes on my wrist that would deliver a mild electric shock. I was given a finger strap that measured my skin conductance (sweating). I was shown pairs of faces expressing anger, then asked to solve simple math problems. Along the way I was intermittently given a shock, then asked to respond to a Stroop Color and Word Test. Finally, I filled out a self-report questionnaire on my emotional state. In between tasks I saw what I thought of as a "cross"—a white plus sign on a black background on the screen. Although the "cross" had not been explained, I took it all in stride and tried my best. By this time, I was very perplexed by the world I had entered. Even after the experimenter's cogent debriefing, I asked a postdoc from the lab to chat informally with me.

I told him that I felt like a problem subject. For example, in the Stroop test, there were four keys with patches of different-colored paper taped to them. I could recognize that the paper patches were from a standard pack of pastel Post-it Notes: pink, yellow, light blue, and light green. A word appeared on the screen that I thought was colored like the light green of the pastel Post-it, so I hit the green key. After several iterations of this, a word in a deep forest green appeared on the screen, and I realized that this was actually the green stimulus! My previous choices should have been yellow. I asked the postdoc,

> From your point of view, with random subjects coming in, how do you think about these perturbations? I have felt something like this in every experiment! I feel I am not performing well or don't understand properly. There have been all kinds of different ways this has happened. Do you handle this statistically?

He told me that the processes they are studying are not consciously accessible or controllable.

> What we find across forty participants we can be more confident about. We use a large sample, and if something happens in two-thirds of participants, we consider there is a general effect. It is improbable that all forty people will go wrong the same way.

I asked about the accuracy of their measurement of emotional responses given that I was so discombobulated by the experiment. He said,

> The questionnaires that are used have been validated with a lot of work. They are chosen because it has already been shown they are meaningfully related to the phenomena. There are researchers who develop those questionnaires and that is their scholarship. We buy them, and we use them.

The questionnaires and scales came with assurances of their validity from previous studies, and researchers trust those assurances.

Who Can Participate and Why?

In the case below, at a public university, students in introductory psychology classes were given course credit for participating in experiments. The university ran a database where they could sign up.

The scene: A room with about twenty computer monitors and keyboards in cubicles with low partitions. I was there with Randall, from Dr. J's lab, to help with logistics. Because the experiment involved "forced failure," it utilized a general knowledge quiz whose difficulty the computer carefully tailored to the subject's performance, to keep each student's failure rate at 65 percent. The Institutional Review Board for the Protection of Human Subjects (IRB) worried about the negative effect this failure rate might have on students already anxious about their performance on tests. The result was an agreement to screen potential participants for depression and for suicidality in particular. Each student had to fill out a standard screening questionnaire for depression called the Beck Depression Inventory (BDI). Each had to agree or disagree on a scale. "I think I am worthless" and "I would kill myself if I had the chance" were some of the extreme responses possible. If a student scored too high on the BDI, Randall would escort him down the hall, out of earshot of others, and graciously thank him for his interest. Randall would gently explain that he was not eligible for the experiment today but that he would get course credit anyway.

On one occasion a student scored so high on the BDI that she activated the emergency plan insisted upon by the IRB. Randall had to immediately walk her to the university health service and wait to see that she was seen. Immediately! This left me, the anthropologist, in charge of the complex protocol. Luckily, the computer software functioned properly and was self-explanatory to these seasoned participants. When Randall returned, the students were still busy with the tasks in the experiment.

While Randall was away, I took the opportunity to try the protocol myself. The questions were very hard. Only occasionally did I know the answer for sure, and I often guessed, which meant I was usually wrong. Even doing this for only fifteen or so minutes I was already feeling stupid.

What is the capital of Romania?
What is the name of the river that runs through the center of London?
Who was the Vice President of Thomas Jefferson?
Whose picture is on the $10 bill?
What is the highest mountain in South America?

Upon his return, Randall came over and hunkered down next to me. I told him I felt stupid. He said, "Good! That is the point." He told me his first experience with the protocol also stressed him out in the same way. The goal of the experiment was to induce the trait he was studying, repetitive negative thoughts (RNT), in half of the subjects but not the other half. (I have changed his research topic slightly for the sake of anonymity.) He would compare the performance of the two groups in remembering what they had learned.

As the students finished, Randall debriefed them one by one. They almost all wanted to talk. They recounted how much they wondered about what the experiment was for, and how relieved they were to find out their performance was artificially adjusted by the computer so that they would fail 65 percent of the time. Randall asked each of them to verbally promise not to tell other students because it would ruin the experiment going forward. I was dumbstruck at the depth of feeling and extent of communication from the students about their experiences. I was not allowed to take notes on this material because it was not included as data in the lab's IRB application. Nor did anyone else. The feedback from the participants did not become data because it did not fall within the parameters of the experiment, nor was it quantifiable.

Some people were not able to be participants because the experiment might create a mood or emotion they could not tolerate; in other words, some participants' reactions could not be counted because they fell outside the experiment's paradigm. In terms of my guiding question about whether the experiences of subjects—the dependent variables—are eliminated from experiments, one could look at this in more than one way. I could focus mostly on the feedback from the students, which was not taken in as data. But in other ways I could see that the individual experiences of the participants counted so much that some were turned away to avoid causing them too much stress. The students were trusted with not telling others about the experiment. The protocol was imbued with empathy for the participants and belief in their reciprocal good faith. Sociologist Abraham Kaplan once remarked that "the scientist observes his data with the tireless passion and energy of an anxious mother," and this protocol was certainly constructed with attention worthy of an anxious mother.[7] The protocol achieved this by creating a tiny and ephemeral social world that carried all the social and intellectual preliminary work of the lab with it. The subjects were socialized into this small world and carefully looked after; they were trusted with keeping this small world available for future participants.

Building on Proven Methods

During his PhD progress report, Randall described an "induction" (a technique also called a "prime") that he planned to use in an experiment to study RNT. An induction or prime is a step built into an experiment's protocol intended to have a specific effect on subjects. The idea is to "prime" the subjects the way you might "prime" a water pump to enable water to flow. Randall's faculty committee asked him how he knew that his induction was increasing the trait of RNT. He explained to me, "You have to know that the measure for manipulation of RNT is sensitive, that it is actually creating the thing that you want to study." Randall tried to convince the committee by saying, "The inductions that we are using have been used in other studies, so we've got evidence to support the effectiveness of this manipulation." He told me that they said, "Okay, fair enough," and allowed him to do it. Yet again, as with the emotional scales I described earlier in this chapter, researchers explained and justified methods because they had already been used in published work, work that was deemed valid because peers had judged it worthy of scientific interest. How very different from my field of anthropology! When editors describe anthropological journals, articles, or books, they often mention the value of innovative methods. The journal *Cultural Anthropology* seeks articles that are "innovative in form and content." The abstract of an article I was asked to review highlighted its "novel methods." Things are different in experimental psychology: though researchers may seek novel findings on little-studied traits or in newly constructed conditions, they can rely on a stable foundation of proven methods. I almost feel envious of what it would be like to have highly specific, widely established methods I was expected to build on. In psychology, researchers use a trusted experimental method to find novel results: they are not necessarily expected to devise novel methods. If we accept that methods handed down from one cohort to another in a discipline are social phenomena in the same way that any teacher-student relationship is, then this aspect of experimental psychology is far more intertwined with human relationships than anthropology, where each researcher aims to invent his or her topic anew and where innovative methods are highly valued.

When she read a draft of the previous passage, Dr. J clarified her take on the matter, agreeing only in part:

> I would say that this is not entirely true, but rather that we try to limit our novelty to only one (or maybe two) dimensions. If there is too much novelty, we can't relate it back to other work in the field. Sometimes the experimental paradigm is novel, in that it hasn't been done exactly that way before. In general, the idea is to build upon and extend work. But I should say that this also limits paradigm shifts because of the pressure to integrate with the existing paradigm. The threshold to shift away from that previous way of thinking can be quite high.

So, it would be better to say both fields study novel dimensions and develop novel methods, but psychologists are more tethered to building on and extending previous work in their field than anthropologists. Psychologists are a bit like farmers who till the soil as generations before them did, but improve the quality of the soil, develop new plants and fertilizers, and gradually expand their lands. They are socially embedded in intellectual communities seeking to build a cumulative set of objective procedures. Anthropologists are also embedded in intellectual communities, but theirs are frequently devoted to questioning the very meaning of key concepts and engaging in fierce debate that rarely allows a consensus. They imagine themselves on modern-day expeditions, striking out for unknown territories and hoping to develop altogether new tools of analysis. They might cast a respectful glance over their shoulders at the paradigms used by prior anthropologists, but only in the solitary process of forging new ones.

Learning Technique

Established methods must still be learned anew by each generation, and sometimes the craft involved is both delicate and intricate. I came to Dr. J's lab for a training session in how to set up a participant for an experiment using electroencephalography (EEG), which measures electrical activity in the brain by means of sensors on the scalp. (I will describe the ins and outs of capturing and measuring brain waves a bit later.) When I came in, Ulla, the graduate student in charge, was reading an early edition of a book about EEG technique by Steve Luck. It is a practical instructional manual. I logged on to Amazon and ordered copies of the latest edition for both of us. She was taking notes in a notebook on each chapter: she noted technical terms—dipole, waves, voltage—none of which she had understood before. We were going to run an experiment with a lab volunteer to practice the technique while referring to Luck's book and lab manuals developed by Dr. J.

Our volunteer was sitting in a chair in a small room. First, her head was measured from the top of her scalp to the bridge of her nose, then around the circumference of her head to determine her cap size. The cap was black, made of a stretchy netting with many electrodes, each designed to sit next to a different area of the scalp. Front, middle, back, sides—each electrode was labeled with a sticker on the wire leading to it. Other wires trailed off the cap to be attached to the face, above and below the eyes. Gel was kept in a large jar labeled "electrode gel." I asked to smell it, and as she handed the jar to me, Ulla said it smelled like glue. I said that it smelled like kindergarten. We poured a few ounces into a plastic cup. Once the cap was on our volunteer, Ulla, another student, and I stuck an injection plunger with a blunt needle into each hole on the cap. Ulla instructed us to sweep across, up and down and side to side with the needle, thus parting the hair to make a good connection between the electrode and the scalp. If the participant complained, we should stop. Meanwhile Ulla attached the cable on the cap to a serial port on the computer, whereupon the computer monitor showed a map of the electrode positions on the cap. These were originally marked in pink. As we worked on each hole in the cap, the squares on the monitor changed color, shifting from pink to dark blue and then black. Hardly any turned black right away, but no one seemed to care. We worked from front to back, also re-gelling spots that were not yet black. Gradually, more and more became black. Meanwhile, the subject had actually fallen asleep. Ulla held her head, so it wouldn't droop forward, explaining that subjects get sleepy because the cap presses on their heads.

Kelly, the lab manager, came in and asked to do some gelling. She did it for a few moments and then Ulla, a bit impatient, took over again. There were lots of comments about how slowly we were going, about who was keeping track of time (an hour overall at this point) and about how important it was to go faster. When the experiment was run on actual subjects, they would have to be gelled and then they would still have to do all the experimental tasks! The concern over mastering the technique reflected concern over the subject's fatigue and patience. Next Ulla brought out the "pin": this was a sharp pin that she dropped into each hole that wasn't already black on the monitor. The volunteer, awake now, said it prickled unpleasantly when Ulla swept it around her scalp. Ulla said no blood was drawn. (I wondered how she knew.)

Finally, all the squares were black! Ulla shut down the computer, pulled the cap off, and gave the volunteer a towel for her hair. The training session was finished. All this craft was to measure the electrical response in a particular area of the brain at a specific time after a stimulus. But once the participant was properly outfitted, the actual experiment would run as a series of tasks, just like the behavioral protocol we have already heard about in this chapter. In other words, the basic structure of the experimental method is still at the heart of the research, even when the technology and craft of the EEG have to be learned and applied first. The learning and practicing of an established method are what enable the craft developed in previous experiments to be captured and passed on. Ulla learned from Steve Luck, via his detailed textbook; other students learned alongside Ulla. The electrode cap and the software worked with them as referees of whether the contacts with the subject's scalp were secure. They enfolded the subject in this practice in the sense that the faster they worked, the less they would cause the subject to feel fatigue.

Technique Can Be the Subject of an Experiment

I was at a conference for psychologists interested in the frontiers of neurocognitive research. The word was that here I might find more daring researchers who were willing to explore novel methods. Eve Isham, a cognitive psychologist attending the conference, gave a talk, which I quickly gathered was intended to deconstruct the apparatus and assumptions of a classic study by Benjamin Libet. In experiments done in the 1980s, Libet tracked EEG signals to show that apparently conscious decisions by a subject to act (by pushing a button) were *preceded* by an unconscious buildup of electrical activity within the brain. This finding raised questions about whether unconscious processes in the brain actually initiate what subjects experience as volitional decisions to act.[8] Some thought Libet had provided evidence that questioned the existence of free will.

Isham intended to show how Libet's assumptions and the standard apparatus he trusted led him astray. He had ignored the effect of his experiment's analog clock and its ascending numbers on the participants. This critique had more than ethnographic interest for me. Libet's research was being widely used in the humanities to claim that though people generally think that they can perform deliberate, intentional actions, this is a misconception. Instead, there is a moment of brain activation that precedes the participant's intention to act. The scientific credibility of Libet's experiments gave many humanists a feeling they stood on solid ground in questioning the classic assumption that people act on the basis of free will, that people have "agency."

Isham's playful and edgy spirit was clear from the first. She was going to "save free will from science." Despite the wide coverage of Libet's conclusions in the media, she would focus on the effect of the apparatus in Libet's experiment: an analog clock. The analog clock was used to measure the timing of the subjective decision to act (called W) and the action itself (called M). Libet claimed to have an objective measure of a brain state he called the "readiness potential," which occurred significantly before W. This meant the brain had "decided" to act before the person had. Scholars in a number of fields took this to demonstrate that "free will" is an illusion because there seemed to be brain activity *before* the subjective decision to act.

Like an ethnographer, Isham asked what exactly are W and M? Could the clock—an analog clock—influence participants to see their action in a particular way? Working with her graduate advisor, Bill Banks, Isham carefully modified the conditions in the experiments. She added an audible tone to the experiment, which presumably was simultaneous with the participants' actions. However, in actuality, the tone would sound *after* the participants acted. If Libet were right, the time of the decision should not have been affected by anything after the decision. However, this was not the case. Compared to conditions when the tone was absent, the subjects perceived the timing of their decision (W), as well as the perceived timing of their action (M), to be shifted later, in the direction of the misleading tone.

Isham went on to add a semantic component. She introduced a game in which the participant played against a competitor and was told he would get a quicker reward tone if he won the game. Actually, the competitor was a decoy, so the experimenter could manipulate the timing of the reward tone. If the participant thought he lost the game, his next action (M) would be later than if he thought he had won. Thus, a wider context affected the timing of the action.

The final nail in Libet's coffin was Isham's finding that there was perceptual bias related to the momentum of the clock. Libet's clock was an oscilloscope

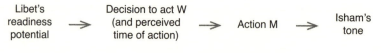

FIGURE 3.4. Timeline of Libet's experiment.

fashioned with a dot that moved rapidly around an analog clock face. If the analog clock was shown at a slower speed, M shifted backward; if Isham substituted a digital clock, W and M shifted forward. Isham had demonstrated that Libet's W and M, the moments of decision and acting, were subject to external manipulation. I was fascinated that Isham's deconstruction of Libet's findings used exactly the same experimental structure as he did—dependent and independent variables—but added different independent variables to the original experiment—the tone, the slow clock, the digital clock, and the game. Reliance on tried and true methods proved its worth and, in this case, was stretched to include questioning the conclusion of Libet's experiment. Isham's work questioned Libet's conclusions because she showed that Libet's behavioral markers for temporal consciousness (W and M) were fluid and did not correlate with neural markers for consciousness (for example, the readiness potential).

The audience at this conference, who had come to learn about pathbreaking new approaches to neurocognitive research, were delighted at Isham's creative reassessment of Libet's work. I was delighted to learn that psychologists, like anthropologists, appreciate the active role of even inanimate participants in experiments, like the analog clock.

Natural Experiments

All the experiments I have described so far were intended to discover how people who have normal cognition can process perception, memory, or learning. Other experiments I learned about studied subjects who had lost some cognitive function through an accident or a stroke, losses that had left them with deficits in perceiving, remembering, or learning. Some deficits were described as a kind of blindsight. A person might not be able to read unless the font was crossed out; a person might be able to verbally identify letters or numbers correctly under certain circumstances even though they said they could not see anything. These variations from the norm were called "natural experiments" and provided the basis for specialized lab studies. But understanding such cases is unusually dependent on the words of the subjects about what they did or did not perceive. The researchers faced a dilemma: what they called "reports" from subjects were what anthropologists might call ethnographic material. But how could anyone trust "reports," which, compared to numerical measures, might seem murky and unverifiable? In this lab, as in others, numerical precision is the goal of research. Historian Norton Wise points to the robust nature of the value of precision: "precision is everything that ambiguity, uncertainty, messiness, and unreliability are not. It is responsible, non-emotional, objective, and scientific. It shows quality."[9] In other words, reports from subjects are too imprecise to be counted as data.

Rob explained to me the rationale of studies in Dr. R's cognitive neuropsychology lab. The lab examined the capacities and the physiology of willing participants who have had cerebral accidents. Because many of their participants were about my age, I provided "normal" data—about spelling and reading—for their comparisons. I also interviewed some of their participants. Of course, experimenters working with human beings could not cause the kind of specific lesions that experimenters working with mice or rats could. Rob explained that the damage is a natural experiment that has knocked out (or impaired to various degrees) specific capacities. "What is knocked out?" I asked him. He said that both processing and the corresponding phenomenological experience are usually knocked out. He went on to describe his work with Dr. M, in another lab in the same department as Dr. R:

> This is what happens if you damage somebody's brain. For example, with Diane [a pseudonym for a subject], her ability to recognize letters was affected, and she might not be able to perceive them. It might be she can see the form of the letter without a problem, but she just can't say that form is the letter S. She can still trace the letter manually, but she can't perceive the S in the form at all—it's all jumbled. Consequentially her visual experience is just a mess.

Dr. M's lab had evidence that Diane's brain was active at the right time and place for seeing letters and processing them at a high level. I was puzzled and asked Rob how he would explain that she had this visual experience of "a mess," but nonetheless she somehow had the capacity to process the form of the letters.

> With Diane we did a classic Stroop test with normal letters, and as you know they can either be consistent or inconsistent depending on whether

the font color and the word are consistent or inconsistent. If she's processing that information you might get Stroop interference [slower reaction or incorrect identification] even though she said she can't interpret what the word is.

And not only that: she would read the words that she claimed not to be able to see! Let's say it was a green font, but the word was "red." She would say "red" and she would make that response often even though she would say, "Oh you know I have no idea what word I'm seeing." And so, you know it's being processed but her perceptual experience is not matching the information that she is getting. Her resolution is "I trust what I see in some way," but what she sees is messed up.

I then wondered aloud whether Diane knew that her response was not normal? Did she know what the Stroop test was supposed to show? Ron said, "When it was over, we explained the Stroop test and she said, 'I know, that's cool; I don't know, whatever.' I think she just thinks we're weird." Perhaps when an experiment focuses on a disability, the disabled participant might not want to know too much about the details.

It occurred to me that someone might question their data, so I asked Rob how he knew these subjects weren't faking it and whether other psychologists worried about fake reports. Rob said,

No, but at the same time people want hard evidence, which is something we haven't got. That is to say here is something that subjects don't have any control of that we can say points to this deficit precisely because it is about awareness. Awareness is something that intrinsically you know you normally have the ability to report. That has notoriously been difficult to probe scientifically or in ways that don't rely on report. You have to trust they are telling the truth in their reports.

I commented, "It's really interesting to me how you get at what their experience is, since they can't recognize letters. So, what can they do? How do you know what their experience is?" Rob explained,

With another participant, Bob, who can only recognize the numerals one and zero, you can put a triangle in one of those numerals. He says something looks different, but he can't identify where the triangle is in the numeral. He still relies on his performance, his judgments, about where things are. He gets at a loss for words when trying to describe what it looks like. He says it looks like the front of a student composition notebook.

When he tries to draw what he sees, something that is meant to represent his experience in a more dynamic manner, he imagines a flux that cannot be simply copied onto the page. And then he says the scribble he draws does not match his experience. Bob is done with us, he doesn't want to be tested anymore. We draw out these problems and bring them to the forefront. He seemed to be very uncomfortable with numbers and we would make him do number tasks a lot.

Actually, Bob did go on working with the lab, despite his frustrations.

Here, we have experiments whose parameters are, as it were, given by nature. Because the participants' perceptual apparatus is impaired, the lab has to rely on their subjective reports to figure out where the deficit in their function lies. The researchers are confronting doubt from other researchers about whether these subjective reports are scientific. The doubts could arise from the very fact that these experiments necessarily dwell on what the participants fail to perceive. This is taxing for participants, and there is a risk that a person like Bob might become unwilling to continue. But it is also taxing for experimenters, who have to rely on participants to express something for which they have no ready language.

In my interviews with the participants in this lab who were living with neural deficits, however, I only met a range of enthusiasts. Bob told me that he participates because "God saved me for a purpose." I thought he meant the purpose of contributing to scientific knowledge, and I think that is what he did mean. But when I asked him about what his particular experiments contributed he twice said, "I don't care." Diane was a long-term participant. She contributes, she told me, because it makes her feel useful, and because she gains insight about her specific brain injury. After her fMRI, when the lab showed her pictures of her brain, she felt scared but also enlightened. "A huge area of your brain is dark. But it made me say, 'Okay I understand where the problem is.' And no one knows if the brain can put that information somewhere else or find it somewhere else." Diane managed to see her participation as helpful—gaining insight, learning where her problems lie. However, as I might have guessed, sometimes the experimental tasks were troubling because they showed what she could not do well. "We were doing a little test where Dr. R may say 'good' when I got it wrong. She just means 'Good, I got what I wanted, and I finished what I planned to do.' And I don't expect her to sit there and tell me, 'You got ten wrong out of eleven.'" That would have added insult to injury.

Of all the labs I observed, this one came closest to using ethnographic methods because they asked participants to describe and to trace or draw what they saw when presented with a letter or number. The crucial factor was what the subjects reported, full stop, no matter how difficult they found it to describe or how often they felt unable to capture the experience in words at all. I can't think of many tasks harder than describing what you do not see. The members of the lab developed long-term relationships with these participants and treasured them as people who demonstrated courage and dedication and who willingly provided sources of new insights about the brain. Of course, beyond their reports, which acted like clues about where to look, research followed the standard recipe for the experimental method. Under an EEG cap or in an fMRI machine, subjects would choose answers from carefully limited and controlled options.

What It Is Like to Experience an Experiment?

Following the rules of the experimental method is clearly one of those taken-for-granted assumptions in a profession (as there would be in any profession) that anthropologists are taught to notice and ask impertinent questions about. Besides being part of the scientific method, what else, in other domains, is an experiment somewhat like? In the following, I will look at a few different aspects of the experiment. All experiments may have the same structure (independent and dependent variables, statistical measurement, comparison), but they can be seen in many different lights.

Sometimes an Experiment Is an Examination

From my first time volunteering in an experiment, I felt as anxious as any grade-conscious undergraduate student facing a final exam. Of course, I had a research project at stake, which at the time was very ill defined, enough to make anyone anxious. But though I have not been an undergraduate for decades, the fear of disappointing others and my compulsive perfectionist standards rushed back. I was determined to pay attention, follow all instructions exactly, and produce a true record of my responses.

The research assistants running experiments encouraged this. In one experiment I was told to "go as quickly and as accurately as you can." The research assistant added, "One way to give yourself a little boost is to have your hands ready on the keyboard." I got praise at times: "Beautiful! You're so fast at those." Performance anxiety afflicted me in all the dozens of experiments for which I volunteered. Somehow the overlap with a college examination flavored the experience. Sitting at a computer, listening to clear, declarative instructions, knowing there were right and wrong answers, knowing a professor had made the rules, having my responses timed: all this evoked what it was like to take an undergraduate exam. Even though I wrongly thought of the experiment as if it were an exam, my responses did not necessarily skew the experimental results. Feeling like I was being tested made sure I paid close attention and tried hard to follow all the rules. Despite helping the experimental goals in some ways, we will soon see how my compulsiveness sometimes ended up shooting myself and the researchers in the foot.

Sometimes an Experiment Is a Game

Some have said so. An historical study of post–World War II psychology manuals and handbooks revealed that some experimenters' approach to their experiments was, rather than sober and scientific, "playful 'fun and games.'"[10] Other studies of that time period have pointed out that subjects treated psychology experiments as game-like, even though psychologists intended them to be run in an authoritarian manner. It was as though, "psychology experiments [were] politics operating under the guise of science: although appearing to be science, experiments in reality constitute game-like engagements."[11] Early on I participated in a study that I was told straight off was a game. The research assistant told me that the study's purpose was to understand people's reaction to "groups defined as other. The study's benefit will be to understand and ameliorate social consequences of these feelings." I was given four sheets of paper, each with a color photo of a person at the top and a description of the person's life. Then there was a quote from a newspaper describing the person's fate, involving such afflictions as injury, illness, or addiction. The research assistant told me I would be playing a game against these four people. The otherness of the groups represented in the experiment soon became apparent as, like a good White American, I saw four different ethnicities in the four photographs—White, Black, Asian, and Middle Eastern.

I was given an electronic dollar bill and a choice to keep it or share it with one of my opponents. If the opponent shared back, I would get three dollars. Or he could decide to keep it. In either case I could punish my opponent, in dime increments. The numbers one through nine on the keyboard represented the dime increments. The Q key was for keep, and the P was for share. In each round of the game, one person's picture appeared on the monitor to show me who my opponent was. As I played, I wanted to share every time. Why would I keep the dollar? Then, when asked how much to punish, I didn't want to punish at all. But the research assistant had not told me how to not punish. So, I had to quickly improvise—and used the zero key. But I was never sure whether this response would be registered.

This experiment was literally a game, a game whose rules I would come to undermine. Being a liberally minded sort, I was determined not to discriminate against people suffering from mental illness, addiction, disabilities, workplace injuries, or racism. If we had been playing tennis, the assumption would be: follow the rules, try your best to win within the rules. If I deliberately threw the game by hitting all return serves into the net, I would be said to be violating the spirit of the game. My tactic depended on the fact that no set of game rules covers everything—the rules of tennis do not say explicitly that you must not hit balls into the net. I was told to choose a punishment from ten to ninety cents, but I was never told I could not refuse to mete out punishment. But clearly, I was refusing to play in the spirit of the game.

Seeking to understand how these experiments fit into a program of research, I emailed Tom, the postdoc in charge. Tom replied:

> Our study, in a nutshell, is aimed at discovering if social emotions affect punishment decisions. Prior research has shown that viewing a person as good or bad affects decisions to trust and modulates neural regions underlying decision-making. Our study extends this research and uses social groups that in the past elicited differing kinds of affect and differentially activated these same neural regions. Therefore, your study was a pilot study to ensure that people display differential punishment behavior, as well as to detect differences in physiological measures of disgust (the social emotion that traditionally dehumanized groups elicit).

Earlier publications from Tom's lab introduced the claim that there are neural correlates to the perception of extreme out-groups. Such perceptions emanate from the social emotion of disgust; researchers describe these perceptions as "dehumanizing." Later publications added fMRI imaging data to buttress these claims.

Even at this early stage I was impressed with how my reaction during this game deviated from the ultimate aims of the experiment. I did not want to "punish" any of the players precisely because they seemed to belong to categories of the "other," categories I did not want to discriminate against. I might even venture to say the experiment tried to dehumanize me in the sense that the option to "dehumanize" was presented as one of the rules of the game I was asked to play. So, some experiments are like games, in which subjects are supposed to play by and in the spirit of the rules. Though my results were no doubt thrown out because I pressed an incorrect key, in the hands of some researchers, my deviation could have become a "blind spot" in the experiment. As philosopher Vinciane Despret puts it in a discussion of experiments on chimpanzee tool use, "one must pay attention to the blind spots that remain in these kinds of experiments."[12] In the experiment Despret has in mind, the scientists' interpretation of their observations is that the chimps have failed to be able to use tools in a particular way. She suggests that what the chimps fail to do is to conform to human manners or cognitive habits. The "blind spot" in the experiment could lead to new questions about how the chimps interpret the experimental situation.

Obviously, participants in the othering experiment are as human as the researchers, not members of another species. But I do not think it is too far-fetched to wonder about the blind spot revealed by the assumption that participants will be willing to dehumanize other groups. And of course, the demographics of the subjects who volunteered to participate in the experiment might well have a profound impact on their responses. Most subjects probably came from the university subject pool of undergraduates. Generally, except for aiming to have both men and women among the participating subjects, demographic information is neither collected nor considered a factor in how subjects respond. Even though the students attending the universities producing the subject pools in my fieldwork probably do reflect the general demographics of the overall American population, this is not usually discussed or mentioned in publications. To leave race or ethnicity unexamined as a factor in what characterizes their subject pool risks leaving a powerful category, such as "whiteness," unseen, as "unexamined, unqualified, essential, homogeneous, seemingly self-fashioned, and apparently unmarked by history or practice."[13] In the hands of more innovative researchers, the power of these blind spots could lead to new hypotheses.

Sometimes experiments reflect a game-like notion of fairness. At a meeting in Dr. J's lab, a grad student, Randall, updated us on his ongoing research. He was studying how people learn under different conditions, such as when they are distracted by RNT and when they are not. The hypothesis was that RNT would impair learning. He was in the process of designing a protocol for the experiments, structured, as many are, with an "induction" or "prime" for the condition of interest, in this case mind wandering. Half of the participants received the induction—reading about an unhappy experience in which they did not do well in class or were not accepted by a social group. The other half would read about happy experiences in which they got a good grade or were welcomed into a group. Both groups would be tested with the set of general knowledge questions I described earlier, which the computer would automatically adjust to make everyone fail 65 percent of the time. At the end of Randall's presentation, Dr. J interrupted with an objection that I found eye-opening. She explained that the happy examples described an event whose outcome generally represented success for the participant. But the learning task was designed to make them fail—the computer automatically adjusted the participant's score to fail 65 percent of the time. So, the two experiences didn't go together. The participant who had read about happy experiences would want to win but be unable to—because the failure rate was set at more than half. Randall's experiment broke the rules—like an unfair game that no one could win. Randall immediately took the criticism to heart and reworked the protocol to avoid such a catch-22. In this case, the initial protocol was faulted for demanding something of participants that would put them in a difficult quandary. Instead, Randall changed the protocol to reveal the difference between recalling a *neutral* experience and an *unhappy* one. The same way of structuring an inquiry—the experimental method—can be used to create a closed system governed by the experimenter's own cognitive habits (as in Tom's punishment experiment), or an open one that takes seriously what participants experience (as in Randall's RNT experiment).

Sometimes an Experiment Is an Ordeal

In another experiment, I looked at photographs of people and animals superimposed into various settings. There were torture victims, a person being shot while a large knife was held at his throat, horribly mutilated, deformed, emaciated, diseased cats, a dog killed brutally, a tiger with a huge chunk of bloody meat in his mouth, a fawn in a grove of trees, a snake coiled with its tongue out, a Doberman with a huge, open, toothy mouth, a puppy with fluffy fur, a butterfly, a person pointing a gun at me, a flower, a bloody corpse, two rabbits smelling a flower, a woman holding a dead man, happy babies, a Black man holding a gun on another Black man, an Indian child, a Black man holding a knife on a White woman, a dead fish, an attacking dog, an old woman, a woman nursing her baby, a disfigured man, a drunk homeless man, kids play-ing, a wounded dog. The settings into which these figures were superimposed included an ocean beach, mountain meadows, waterfalls, deserts, dusty plains, domestic interiors (a Middle Eastern living room, a man cave, a kitchen), an empty parking garage, offices with people and without, urban streets with traf-fic, deserted streets, Las Vegas casinos, a tropical forest, a corporate meeting room, a lighthouse on the coast.

For each pair I was to say where my reaction fit in a range of excitement—from numb, to middling, normal, or excited. Two drawings of Lego-like figures appeared on the monitor—on one end, the figure had a small dot on his middle, and on the other end, he had a large, sparking star. I was to pick a number from one to nine running along a continuum under the figures. Obviously, I had absolutely no context for understanding the extremely alarming photographs or the strange Lego figures. Once again, I felt cornered, like a student taking an exam on unfamiliar material. I hunkered down and tried to follow the instructions.

After a break, I was again shown photos of people, animals, and settings. Now I was instructed to say whether I could recall these photos from the earlier ses-sion. I could choose from a range of possible degrees of certainty: "I am certain I saw it; I guess I saw it but am not sure; I am certain I did not see it." I found this very difficult and felt little confidence that any choice I made was correct.

Later I came to understand the Lego figure (it is called SAM—Self-Assessment Manikin) and the source of the photos (they came from IAPS, the International Affective Picture System). The SAM represents a standard scale for participants in experiments to register where they are in terms of affect, arousal, and dominance.

IAPS was not hard to track down through an internet search. It is a set of hundreds of photos of people or animals in different settings. The system was devised at the University of Florida and, according to its technical manual, it was "normatively rated" there. This means that emotional responses to figures in different settings were recorded for hundreds of undergraduate students, and their scores were averaged.

Regardless of the demographic composition of the undergraduates, each of them is treated as an everyman representing the universal human subject. Any researcher can request a set of these photos for use in experimental stud-ies. (I did.) Since the "normative" response to the photos has been determined already, experimenters can compare the scores of their participants under the specific conditions they devise to the normatively rated scores.[14] Perhaps a

FIGURE 3.5. Crocodile, an image of the sort used in IAPS studies.
Image by William Warby, CC BY 2.0.

FIGURE 3.6. Sleeping baby, an image of the sort used in IAPS studies.
Image by William Warby, CC BY 2.0.

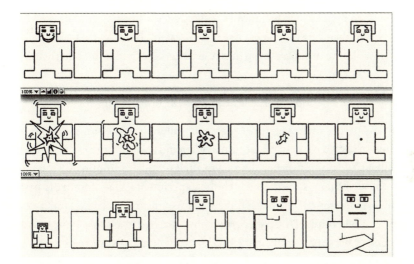

FIGURE 3.7. Self-Assessment Manikin (SAM). Copyright © 1994 by Peter J. Lang.
Published in Sidowski et al. (1980) and Bradley & Lang (1994).

TABLE 3.1. International affective picture system (mean values of a sample of pictures)

Description	Valence mean	Arousal mean	Dominance 1 mean	Dominance 2 mean
Snake	4.09	5.61		4.43
Crocodile	5.35	5.67	4.66	
Baby	6.49	3.80	5.81	
Wounded dog	2.47	5.75	3.86.	

Source: Lang, P.J., Bradley, M.M., & Cuthbert, B.N. (2008).

few undergraduate psychology majors had heard about SAM and IAPS in their courses and understood where they came from. In my naive state, I experienced this experiment as an ordeal. The recording I made of myself doing the experimental task was filled with dismayed comments: "Oh my god"; "What on earth is that image?"; various expletives. The researchers certainly did not intend to make me undergo an ordeal. While the consent form I signed said I might experience mild discomfort, the researchers could not have predicted how upset I would be. The dismay of a participant like me, someone who was not knowledgeable, speaks to the depth to which researchers and students are embedded in their own techniques and practices. The instruments, SAM and IAPS, have been, as they say, "normatively rated," but they have also become "normal" in the ordinary sense that researchers are accustomed to them.

Sometimes an Experiment Is a Drama

As a key part of their structure, many experiments include an "induction" designed to elicit a particular emotional or cognitive state. Others present material like IAPS photos that are known to elicit particular emotions. So, it seems fair to ask if there is a way in which the experiment is like a dramatic performance. In the terms of Russian director Konstantin Stanislavski's method acting, we could think of the participant being coached to assume a role based on his or her personal emotional experience evoked by words or images. The emotions evoked might reasonably be understood as coming from the social context depicted. In IAPS images, people pointing guns are racially marked by skin color, and settings are geographically marked by architectural design. The emotions evoked must be imbued with associations subjects have previously made within particular cultures.

Even in studies that give no credence to the social or cultural context of the subject's experience, coaching of actors can be involved in the preparation of the experiment's stimuli. In some classic studies of emotion, such as those by Paul Ekman, the experimenters actually used actors who were coached while observing themselves in a mirror.[15] They were instructed to display facial expressions that designated a limited number of basic emotions selected by the experimenters. Ekman's studies worked under the assumption that humans could infer emotional states from facial expressions, and that such inferences are universal.[16]

If experiments have a performative aspect, this does not necessarily diminish their scientific validity. But acknowledging this would make it clear that participants have a deliberate, active role, albeit one that usually conforms to social and cultural expectations. Perhaps we could say that subjects are called onto the experimental stage, expected to perform an impromptu skit informed by their own cultural assumptions.

Interpretations

My point is that even in a scientific laboratory, structured practices governed by rules and held robustly in place by tradition and proven efficacy have a lively and varied existence as they are instantiated in social life. The psychological experiment, like all human examinations, games, ordeals, or dramas, is open to multiple interpretations. Diane tolerated having her deficit made plain in return for greater insight about her condition, while the lab saw her as a unique window into how the brain functions. After seeing the various ways in which experiments can be experienced (as an examination, a game, an ordeal, or a drama) we can realize that the same experimental structure can play out in different ways, depending on the sensibilities of the subject, the object of the experimental study, and the mechanics of the experimental apparatus. Seeing a structured practice taking on different meanings in different contexts is not unique to scientific labs. The same thing occurs for other structured practices in ordinary life. Cooking a meal, knitting a sweater, or fixing a clogged pipe could be experienced as routine and boring habits to honor a customary division of labor, as fearful and desperate efforts to stave off an emergency, or as warm-hearted generosity to celebrate an occasion.

In his book *Actual Minds, Possible Worlds*, social psychologist Jerome Bruner describes how determined people are to make human stories out of their experience at every opportunity. In experiments done by Fritz Heider and Marianne Simmel in 1944, people even interpreted geometric shapes like triangles and squares as human figures and imagined them interacting intentionally. I had trouble understanding how this finding could have come out of an experimental setup, but it did. This happened in a different subfield of psychology, social psychology, where subjects were asked to watch a video of a sequence of moving geometric figures. Invariably, people interpreted them as lovers in a chase or bullies bent on destruction. The difference between this study and the model of the experimental method I witnessed in fieldwork cannot be overstated. The subject's response was open-ended, not restricted to a set of choices. The researchers wanted the subject to talk back rather than to conform to a limited set of conditions. The "experiment" Bruner describes could be a part of an ethnographic study in an urban neighborhood or village and could no doubt reveal different ways of constructing stories. Of course, as an ethnographer, Bruner's case feels familiar and right to me.

But I have come to see that the experimental method has strengths that are different from, but not necessarily less powerful than, the kind of open-ended ethnographic inquiry where anthropologists spend most of their time listening to what people say. If the researcher sets the conditions into which the subject is invited and then is expected to conform, like a mannerly dinner guest, data can be generated that is quantifiable and hence comparable. Along the way, the sensibilities of subjects are not at all ignored. At the very least, their potential fatigue, boredom, or stress affect the length and content of experiments. In this sense, there is no question that psychologists do care about the experience of subjects. I heard many lab discussions about how long an experiment could last before subjects would become tired or bored. The dependency is mutual: a tired, bored, or hurting subject would not produce good data. These psychology researchers demonstrate all the characteristics of good ethnographers: they are empathic with their subjects, and they try with foresight to minimize the effect of their intrusion on peoples' everyday lives. Participants would not be asked to play a game that cannot be won. In some cases, their unique personal reports of experience are necessary as a hint about where in the brain their missing abilities lie. Experiments can even shine a light on a previous experimental protocol and show the effect the protocol itself had on the data gathered. To be sure, although researchers do pay attention to the needs of individual subjects, the experimental method requires them to transform the responses of subjects into numerical measures. They must also erase many specific differences among subjects in the service of identifying the norm. I emphasize that the requirement for much of the lived experience of subjects to be stripped away in order to produce an experimental result may be the most fundamental implication of this chapter. But I would also note that the stripping away is required of researchers even though they are empathetic and kind to subjects every chance they get.

To return to my questions at the beginning of this chapter, we can now see that the experimental method allows another step to be added to the staircase, building on previous studies whose conditions were specified and whose results were quantified. In published accounts of research findings, we ordinarily only hear about the last step in the staircase, but we do not learn about the work that precedes its installation. We do not hear about the subjects who were not included because of their depression. We do not hear about the arduous process of learning the techniques required by the experiment. We do not hear about how the needs of subjects are considered. Anthropologist Don Brenneis wrote, "Teaching and learning, intertwined practices rich in particular cases, accounts, and examples, are central in the shaping of scientific imagination." But despite their importance, this "nexus rarely figures in either public or practitioners' understandings of science, effaced in favor of broader, overarching, patently theoretical frameworks."[17] In bringing an ethnographic approach to psychology, I have had to extend my observations to include both long before and long after any experiment. In a longer time frame, the ethnographic method of close up, open-ended observation can show us that the experimental method has a hidden, open-ended side where subjects live, interpret the experimental method in various ways, and influence the design of the experiment itself. The tracks I followed from the beginning of an experiment to its completion included many forms of sociality: learning, interpreting, listening, responding empathically. None of this ever gets into published papers. You could say I was covering their tracks like a reporter; you could also say the psychologists were "covering their tracks" to seem more scientific.

4

Normalizing Data

Further, just as in physics and astronomy, so can we also in psychic measurement neglect at first the irregularities and small departures from the law in order to discover and examine the principle [*sic*] relations with which the science has to do. The existence of these exceptions must not, however, be forgotten, inasmuch as the finer development and further progress of the science depends upon the determination and calculation of them as soon as the possibility of doing so is given.

—GUSTAV THEODOR FECHNER,
ELEMENTS OF PSYCHOPHYSICS, 1860

NOW THAT I have laid out all this detail about the experience of being a participant in psychological experiments, readers might be left wondering how, with such an obstreperous subject as me, researchers ever get telling results. One answer is that my responses might well have been erratic enough to warrant being thrown out. They would not be discarded for no reason, but because they were far enough off the average range to be questioned, for good reason. Being able to disregard erratic responses depends on having enough subjects. The more subjects you have, the easier it is to designate some responses as unusable and still have enough subjects left to make an adequate sample. In the labs, subjects have to be recruited with some kind of reward: they might get credit for a course assignment, or they might be paid a token amount. The expense of this and the hassle of organizing the schedule for when subjects participate, a place where they can sit, and a computer they can use make getting large numbers of subjects impractical. Generally, in my fieldwork labs, the number of subjects were in the range of forty or fifty at most.

No matter how many subjects are in an experiment, there is still the question of why most subjects fall within the average responses and do not have to be rejected. How is it that subjects are, so to speak, domesticated so that they act like mannerly dinner guests? That question has an answer, but it relies on something I totally failed to notice at this stage, even though it happened to me in every experiment. The answer lies in the tacit "practice" that subjects are asked to do before every experiment, which I will turn to in chapter 8.

Before getting to how subjects are "domesticated," I need to explore how data are domesticated. The data an experiment produces has to pass muster before it can be analyzed. Between the experiment itself and published findings lies the process of "cleaning" the data. Psychologists are extremely careful about ensuring that the databases they use in experiments represent an appropriate range of people. This is essential if a researcher wants to study how the responses of a group of experimental subjects compares to the responses captured in a larger database of subjects. But this would be pointless if the larger group were biased in its composition. The larger database should include old people as well as young, men as well as women, and so on. When the responses in the database are "normalized" (we will see shortly what that means), they are made to represent a demographically representative section of people and not a limited one.

The technique of normalizing data does not belong to experimental psychology alone but is widely used in statistical operations in many fields: health, finance, the military, law enforcement, education, and so on.[1] In all cases, obtaining a set of data from an appropriate range of people involves using categories that are conventionally understood and in common use. Experimenters define categories such as age, gender, race, or socioeconomic status based on conceptions of these categories that are commonly accepted both within their discipline and more broadly. Of course, the assumption that any such categories are unambiguous and universally understood would run into particular trouble when faced, say, with "intersectional theory" in the social sciences, which sees race, gender, and class as inextricably intertwined; or "gender fluidity" in contemporary social experience, which blurs the boundaries between male and female.[2] Generally speaking, in my fieldwork, experimenters assumed that potential subjects would understand the kind of categories that commonly appear on a health questionnaire or a census form and be willing to use them in identifying themselves. Recruiting an equal number of subjects who self-identify as male or female, for example, makes the study representative of the general population, as far as gender goes. Since, in cognitive psychology, the presumption is that cognitive processes such as remembering, paying attention, or perceiving shapes are universal human capacities, the emphasis is placed on seeing how these cognitive processes vary under specific experimental conditions. The conventional categories used to diversify a subject pool are taken for granted as researchers pursue the overriding goal of studying cognitive capacities shared by all.

Selection

Before going further, I need to address the basic question of who decides which participants' responses become part of a data set. Historian Georges Canguilhem used a passage in the Bible to think about who is authorized to select a sample from a large group of people. Who "selects the selector"?

> When Gideon takes command as the head of the Israelites and escorts the Midianites beyond the Jordan (The Bible: Judges, Book VII), he uses a test of two degrees that permits him to keep only ten thousand out of thirty-two thousand men, and then three hundred out of ten thousand. But this test owes to the Eternal the finalization of its use and the process of selection used. To select a selector, it is normally necessary to transcend the blueprint of technical selection procedures.[3]

Clearly, God devised the test of two degrees and selected Gideon as the man to choose which of his army would fight the Midianites. Canguilhem suggests that psychologists designate themselves as the selectors of who takes part in experiments. Perceptively, he notes that the selection of the selector should "transcend the blueprint of technical selection." His point is that the rules of selection determine who will be chosen but not who will choose them. Accordingly, tennis players should not serve as their own referees. So how is the selection of participants done in psychology?

In recent decades, psychologists have relied on participants who come mainly from large introductory psychology classes. Sometimes the students are required to participate in research as part of learning how experiments are conducted in psychology. Recently some institutional review boards (IRBs) have become concerned that such a requirement might be coercive. As we saw earlier, some labs have responded to this difficulty by returning to a nineteenth-century practice and using their own lab members as participants. Most have continued to use university students as participants in experiments in return for pay or course credit. Many have also added websites where interested people not at the university can sign up. The top of the selection funnel is wide, but being chosen as a participant depends on the researcher's need to have comparable numbers of male and female participants or the like. Generally, it is assumed that students at the same university will all make good subjects and will certainly produce comparable data that can reveal cognitive characteristics that hopefully will be found in other populations. This assumption has been questioned, since American college students might well not be representative of the gender, age, or ethnic makeup of the general population.[4]

Despite the homogeneity of American college students, who are relatively privileged in many ways, it did surprise me that the students' diverse experiences, knowledge, and life circumstances were apparently considered comparable. Somehow, students who work a full-time job, who are clinically depressed, who learned English as teenagers, who are physically disabled, who grew up in another country, and so on, are all granted equality as experimental subjects. Their responses will be timed in the same way and counted as mutually comparable. Experimenters presume that any differences of this kind are minor and will "wash out" when the data are compiled statistically. Psychologists depend on the structure of the experimental design to precisely identify an element of cognitive or emotional behavior and to elicit that element in the same way from everyone, usually by measuring the time each subject takes to manifest the behavior—their reaction time.

Because experimenters are measuring time, results take numerical form, and as we will see shortly, they are then processed statistically. "Normalizing" refers to the work of understanding the results of this process of quantification and numerical averaging across many subjects and can be graphed in a "normal distribution" curve as shown in figure 4.1. Normal distribution provides a standard that enables experimenters to identify outliers and remove them, in order to find the most common, hopefully generalizable, human response to the given variables. Historically, in other spheres, "norms" have been calculated for many attributes: intelligence, sanity, and criminality, not to mention fitness, height, weight, blood pressure, bone density, and so on. In all my classes on the anthropology of science I have asked students to volunteer their height. In the aggregate, the group has never failed to produce a "normal" curve, with a few at the extremes of tall or short and most in the middle. The middle is what catches our attention, and we are right to wonder why. But it behooves us to discover what normalized findings depend upon, because it is these normalized findings that permeate the news. Media versions of experiments in psychology labs inform us daily about the "normal" human psychology of adaptability, intimacy, kindness, loneliness, memory, and vulnerability.

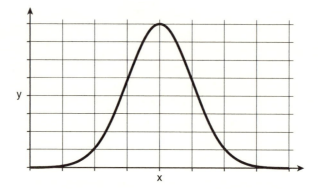

FIGURE 4.1. A normal curve. Drawing by Kara Healey.

Here again is the common assumption embedded deep in the field that human psychology, like human anatomy, is universal. Structures in the brain, activity in the brain, processing of emotion or risk, cognitive processing of language—all can be studied in ways that are thought to reveal attributes of human minds that could, given appropriate evidence, be generalized to people outside the study group. Most of us would go along with this notion at an abstract level: strong negative emotions like fear or anxiety would probably produce activity in only certain areas of the brain, which could be measured with fMRI. But from an anthropological perspective, problems arise with the move from the abstract to the particular. In an experiment early on in my project, I was asked to look at faces of White men. The faces all looked fierce and angry to me. Along the way I was given shocks. The experiment was a pilot project to determine whether seeing an angry face together with a shock would affect the subject's conditioned learning more than seeing an angry face with no shock. Afterward, I talked with Jon, a postdoctoral fellow, about the faces: Who were they? Did it matter that they were all White? Jon told me that behind the experiment lies an evolutionary concept about the human species: many people have spider phobias, but hardly any have car phobias, even though we are more likely to die in a car crash than from a spider bite. He pointed to negative emotional reactions that were established early in human evolution and were therefore common to everyone. At that point, I tried to be more direct.

I asked if there was a reason he only presented White male faces in the experiment. Jon explained that they were all Swedish, and they all expressed anger. Shifting ground slightly, he pointed out that all cognitive psychology relates back to animal research. He went on to say that in animal experiments, researchers have identified the neurological fear circuit in rats, so experiments with human subjects have to be simple and obvious, in order to mimic the rat scenario. He suggested I should read articles by Paul Ekman, who took photographs of European faces to New Guinea and found that New Guineans recognized the same emotions that we do.

Jon was giving me a whole series of reasons why the specifics of the faces—their ethnicity or gender—could be ignored in favor of universal reactions based on developments in early human evolution, or on traits we share with other animals. He was citing Paul Ekman's classic studies on cross-cultural constants in emotion, which, I noted to myself, have been roundly criticized in the humanities and social sciences. I could see his point, but I was somewhat astounded at the level of abstraction Jon was interested in. I kept thinking that when I (a woman) saw angry men, it would be different than it would be for a man. If I were a Black woman or man, how different would it be to look at angry White men? There is no question that Jon's lab understood the importance of race and gender in culture generally. Other experiments in his lab looked directly at the effects of implicit bias about race or gender. What struck me was his ability to adjust the focus of his gaze from a close-up level, where such differences mattered, to a faraway and abstract level, where universal features of the human mind could be discovered. Changing focus in this way, increasing the scale of what is being studied so dramatically, depends on a crucial underlying assumption that at least some psychologists share: there are universal features of the human mind that are not affected by specific cultural characteristics. Nor do the experimenters' specific cultural characteristics matter. Historian Jill Morawski has shown that psychologists seldom focus on the race of the experimenter in charge of participants, most of whom are White. As a field, they shy "away from examining whiteness."[5] As we will see, experimenters do take account of cultural variation in their subjects, and they consider the selection of subjects to be a crucial concern. But they pay less attention to whether the homogeneity of the *experimenters*, in terms of race, gender, or socioeconomic standing, might affect how research questions are selected or explored. As Canguilhem pointed out, psychologists seem to have selected themselves as the selectors of participants in their experiments.

Amazon Mechanical Turk

While marveling at the presumed ability of psychology experiments to infer universal properties from a diverse university population, I was intrigued to hear that experiments might now also include a broader, thoroughly international population. This became possible through a technology called "Amazon Mechanical Turk." One of my psychology colleagues mentioned Amazon Mechanical Turk in passing and enthused about it. "I could do a whole study in a weekend! The subject pool takes forever, and you often run into problems like subjects not showing up."[6] What is Amazon Mechanical Turk?[7] You access it through a website run by Amazon. With the help of guides and templates provided on the site, anyone can design a project, which might be an experiment or a questionnaire, and offer it to crowdsourced "workers." Anyone can apply to join as a worker, but beginners are only given access to a limited number of jobs. As you complete jobs and perform more complex jobs, more opportunities open up. I searched on "cognitive psychology" and joined a few simple projects as a worker. The work is divided into Human Intelligence Tasks, which at the time paid about thirty cents each. Estimates are hard to come by, but one curious worker reported that after three hundred hours, his average pay per hour was about three dollars, far below minimum wage in the United States, although not necessarily in other countries. More recently, after a hiatus, I requested more work. I was told, "We regret to inform you that you will not be permitted to work on Mechanical Turk." The word on the internet is that Amazon has started limiting the number of workers to prevent having too many workers for too few jobs. No one outside Amazon will ever know because their "review criteria" are proprietary and will not be disclosed. An algorithm is probably determining whether or not to select applicants.

The impetus behind most Mechanical Turk projects seems to be marketing. How will consumers respond to a variety of fashion styles or products: which jeans or shoes do you like better and why? But since the format presents a visual stimulus (a photo, for example) and a range of responses that can be timed, there is every reason to use it to conduct psychological experiments. Amazon gives experimenters good reasons to participate: the technology is scalable, meaning you can hire only as many workers as your project requires at a given time; the "sentiment ratings" are easy to collect and understand; the cost is low.

The name of the technology and the vision of the workforce it implies may be in accord. The first "Mechanical Turk" was an eighteenth-century traveling fair curiosity.[8] The Turk was a male figure with dusky skin, a head turban, flowing embroidered clothes, and a fur-lined vest who sat at a table with a chessboard. Aided by a whirring set of cogs and wheels, he would play chess with his customers. Referring back to this antique mystery of the "Orient" makes so much sense. The Turk knew what moves to make; Amazon's Turk will tell

FIGURE 4.2. The original mechanical Turk. A "chess machine" built by Wolfgang von Kempelen in Bratislava, displayed between 1770 and 1810. Image by Sueddeutsche Zeitung Photo / Alamy Stock Photo.

you what moves to make as a marketer of goods or a student of psychology. The original Turk concealed a human worker under the chessboard; today's Turk conceals an artificial intelligence algorithm behind its operation. The otherness of the "Oriental" Turk points to the incorporation of a far larger population of workers than a university could provide. The Turk also pushes low-skilled laborers farther away, out of sight and out of mind for the marketers, programmers, business innovators, or entrepreneurs who are running projects on the site, and whose highly valued creative work is kept clean and unsullied by the tedious labor on which it depends.[9]

Having been foiled as a worker, I went to the site and registered as a "requester." (You can too.) I designed a simple project with questions and a range of sentiment ratings about the field of anthropology. I refrained from posting my project, but I could have. To accept the kind of data my project would have generated as comparable to data from a university's subject pool, I would have to accept not knowing whether the participants speak English, whether they are sitting at a desk or on a beach with a laptop, whether they are cooking dinner or watching TV, whether they are in a noisy space or a quiet one—all these factors are invisible. For marketers, perhaps this anonymity reflects the online purchase of products—anytime, anyplace—perfectly well. For psychologists, the willingness to tolerate the invisibility of the participants' environment speaks to the power of the experimental method to isolate and hone particular cognitive or emotional responses. Anyone anywhere can record their "sentiment ratings" and generate numerical measures that will then be taken to represent *universal* human psychological reactions.

Normalizing Data

Whether a data set comes from Amazon's Turk or a psychology lab, it must still be normalized. I will return to techniques we have already encountered—IAPS (International Affective Picture System), EEG, and fMRI—to see exactly how the data they produce is normalized, that is, how data is compared to find the characteristic result for a given group. The "normal distribution" refers to the characteristics of a particular group of subjects. Many of my anthropology students were about five feet, seven inches tall, which would be represented by the peak of a normal distribution curve. The students who were much taller or shorter were represented by the two trailing sides of the curve. The normal distribution accurately represents the height of this particular group of students. We could compare this distribution to the distribution of student heights from other universities, or from other countries or cultures. Thus, the normal distribution of heights represents the most frequently occurring heights, not the average distribution of heights.

Normalizing IAPS Results

When the University of Florida sent me the set of IAPS photographs, the instructions explained,

> The IAPS was conceived as a catalog of pictures that represents the entire range of emotional reactions potentially obtainable in this medium. Therefore, users are advised that it contains some images of violence, as well as some images that are judged to be erotic, fear evoking, disgusting, and/or repellent by some viewers.

Crucially, each image has been shown to hundreds of experimental subjects, who were asked to register their emotional reactions. According to the instructions,

> it is the inclusion of the normative ratings that we have collected, obtained from hundreds of participants, which allows researchers to select pictures with known hedonic valence [a measure of whether participants see the pictures as pleasurable or painful] and arousal properties [whether participants feel stimulated or unmoved by the pictures].

Over the years, hundreds of University of Florida students have evaluated their response to the IAPS photos using the Self-Assessment Manikin (SAM) ratings of valence, arousal, and dominance—the Lego-like figure I described in chapter 3.[10]

If you were to use the IAPS photos in an experiment, you would be able to know in advance what the normalized values were for each picture, at least for the student participants in Florida. Depending on your purposes, you could choose pictures with high or low values on any of the SAM dimensions, so you could be certain that your participants were being stimulated in the appropriate way. You might have to ignore the fact that some of the descriptions of pictures in the database seem rather culturally specific: "attractive female," "grieving female," "angry face," "terrorist," "drug addict," and so on. Some of the animals might not be familiar to everyone: Mickey Mouse, the jaguar, or the crocodile, for example. Nonetheless, the assumption is that IAPS can be used for any subject population.

In this project, I have been surprised again and again by how much my primary interlocutors had already anticipated the problems I spotted, like the culturally specific nature of some items in the IAPS. This was illustrated yet again when Dr. J mentioned in a lab meeting that she had "renormalized" the IAPS photographs. She previously taught at a prestigious private university before moving to an urban branch of a public state university system. By paying close attention to what the public university students were doing, she realized that compared to private university students, they were markedly more efficient with their time. "Dithering to pick the right choice" was replaced by "if you can't get it, move on." To make sure her results were comparable, she added a step that forced the state university students to wait between tasks. She also told us that the IAPS photos included a crocodile. University of Florida students would have some context for this creature, but northeastern urban students at a public university might not. Presumably, her private university students might have had broader experience in a wider cultural world and might have heard of the University of Florida Gators football team. The Florida scale had a relatively high valence score for "crocodiles," about the same as for "musicians." Dr. J thought such a high valence would be more likely in southern Florida and probably would not be the norm for urban northeastern public university students. Whatever the reason for the high Florida valence, Dr. J went to the considerable trouble of renormalizing the pictures she wanted to use. She had to set aside time and money to enroll her public university students in sessions where they would record their valence scores on her subset of IAPS photos. I cautioned myself never to assume how technology will be used based on its written instructions. Dr. J took the rules seriously, to heart, and in renormalizing, acknowledged how the differences in students' lives imbued the IAPS photos with local rather than universal context. The extra care Dr. J used may not be acknowledged often enough. Historian Jill Morawski lamented that "conventional histories overlook the routine interactions that transpire in [psychology] experiments and, in keeping with the science's ethos, take the hundreds of thousands of individuals who have served as subjects to be stable and interchangeable entities whose dispositions are irrelevant to understanding the science."[11] Dr. J showed me what lies behind the science's ethos when normalization is used to take problems of selection that reflect the characteristics of different populations into account. However, from the point of view of an anthropologist, even Dr. J's extra effort felt rather limited: in the end, we still did not know how to characterize her urban student body. Were their valence scores for IAPS images different from the private university students and the Florida students' scores because of their socioeconomic status, their higher average age, their affinity for a vibrant and diverse urban culture, or something else? Those questions could be ignored once the normalized scores were in hand.

Averaging Signals from ERP

In Dr. J's lab, Ulla was learning how to set up a participant for an EEG study. The study would focus on a particular feature of the electrical activity in subjects' brains, called the Event-Related Potential, or ERP. As I mentioned earlier, I read the textbook she was consulting, *An Introduction to the ERP Technique* by Steve Luck. My goal was to write up a short, nontechnical description of the technique that I could present to my class in the anthropology of science, so students could understand the fieldwork I was doing. Here is what I came up with:

The participant wears a net cap with scalp electrodes that send electrical signals from the participant's brain activity over time to the computer. The signals are transformed into a wavelike path (a waveform) on the computer as time goes by. This process is called the EEG, short for electroencephalography. Then the Event-Related Potential (ERP) is extracted from a particular part of the EEG waveform. The ERP is a specific response—as the name indicates, the ERP is an electrical "potential" that is related to a specific event. The event (usually a stimulus in an experimental task) is time stamped on the waveform, so you can see clearly how many milliseconds after the stimulus the ERP occurs.

The history of the ERP sheds light on why it is useful. In an experiment in 1964, subjects were fitted with electrodes on their scalps, which were connected to devices that could record electrical responses. In the first trial, the subjects were presented with a warning sound followed by a visual target. There was no task. In spite of that, the EEG recorded a signal. This was surprising because subjects were not doing anything except waiting. But their brains were doing something! In their second trial, subjects heard a warning sound, and then they were asked to press a button when they saw the visual target. In the second trial, a large voltage change was observed at certain electrode sites during the period between the warning sound and the appearance of the target. This could not have been simply a sensory reaction to the warning signal, because it depended on the subject's *preparation* for responding to the coming visual target.

In 1965, the P300 component was discovered. The "P" stands for "positive" and the "300" for the average number of milliseconds the signal occurs after the initial stimulus. The P300 is a large positive signal that looks like a spike. Subjects were told to expect a visual or auditory stimulus. When subjects *could not* predict whether the stimulus was going to be auditory or visual, the stimulus elicited a large peak at a point on the EEG waveform at P300. The peak was much smaller when the subject *could* predict the kind of stimulus. There was great excitement at being able to record human brain activity related to cognition. ERP provides high resolution information about the exact time the brain responds to uncertainty. The ERP allowed a measurement of the timing of voltage difference in brain responses while anticipating unpredictable versus predictable stimuli.

To get a P300 result, software has to filter the raw data to remove noise from the participant's eye and bodily movements and other extraneous sources and [to] amplify the signal. Then the waveforms of each participant on all their trials are averaged. As complicated as this process is, Luck's informal style summarizes the process well. Quoting his PhD advisor about how to interpret the waveform, "Upward-going deflections are called *uppies,* and downward-going deflections are called *downies.* Because of noise, some trials will have an uppie at a given time point and others will have a downie, and these uppies and downies cancel out when many trials are averaged together. Given a finite number of trials, the uppies and downies will not be perfectly equal and will not cancel out perfectly, so some noise will remain in the averaged ERP waveform. However, the uppies and downies that remain in the averaged waveform tend to become smaller and smaller as more and more trials are averaged together."[12] As the P300 response becomes clearer through averaging, the experimenter can say whether or not there is cognitive activity at P300 produced by one task (say one that caused uncertainty) but not by another (say one that did not pose uncertainty).

My anthropology students were puzzled by how psychologists justify the averaging of signals. Coming from a field where individual responses are not numbers but words and gestures, they had trouble picturing how anthropologists could average anything. But of course, even without having numbers, anthropologists do average responses in a way: we use the words "typical," or "usual," or "often heard." So, the difference is a matter of degree. In ERP data, individual responses do vary, just as they do to the IAPS. Precisely because individual variations are not the same, producing uppies and downies of different sizes, averaging the signals is necessary. The average represents what is common to all the subjects amid the inevitable individual variations. Whether we are concerned with normalized results from IAPS or averaged results from ERP, the numerical logic of this is indisputable. The unease I felt as an anthropologist came from the lack of any way to explore why people produce such different perturbations with their brain activity. What would happen if individual signatures were calculated from each person's waveform and participants could be interviewed about their experiences during the experiment? Of course, the positive or negative charges do not indicate moods, but what if the uppie participants were experiencing pessimism and anxiety and the downie participants were experiencing optimism and composure? Might such a difference affect their response at P300? I suppose the answer would be that the optimism or pessimism of individual participants was not the object of the experiment. It is the fact that there is a statistically significant response at P300, even after the variations have been averaged out, that matters.

Averaging Signals from fMRI

To see another version of how subjects are compared, I volunteered in Dr. R's lab to have a brain scan in an fMRI machine that would provide "control" data for another participant in my age group. I provided, so to speak, a "normal" brain, whose data could be compared to the other participant, whose brain had undergone a stroke, providing a "natural experiment." One practical difficulty in using a fMRI scanner is that no metal can be present inside the machine. This presents a serious problem for headphones, which ordinarily depend on metal components. Highly specialized headphones for fMRI use can be purchased for a price, but I had already heard from frustrated students that they do not work very well. During my session, I wore the special headphones and had at hand a soft bulb I was to squeeze if I had an urgent problem. I was told not to squeeze it for a trivial question like "how much longer will I be in here?" but only for emergencies like a panic attack or an important physical need. My field notes detailed the experience:

> I was rolled into the machine on its moveable bed, and the machine started up. It made a whirring, grinding, banging noise but it was not as loud as I had imagined. The technician started the first run, but I could hear nothing at all in the earphones! The sound was totally murky. I felt dismay trying to decide what to do—stop the run or go on guessing randomly. In doubt, I pushed the emergency bulb. The technician turned off the machine and rushed in. She checked the earphones and found that only one was working. So, she got another kind of earphones with blue plastic nubbins that stuck in each ear. The machine started again. Again, I could hear nothing, and pushed the emergency bulb. This time the technician came in and shoved in some pillows to push the phones closer to my ear. The machine started up again. I decided that there was no point in further alarms, so I just went ahead, thinking to myself that I was actually able to make out only about one out of three words. Obviously, this didn't matter for the visual tasks, where I only had to say "upper case" or "lower case." But it really mattered for the spelling task. I heard a word I was supposed to spell. Was it "pan" or "can" or "pant" or "tan"? I was sweating and upset because obviously I couldn't be sure I had heard right. It did occur to me that the real test might be to see how I reacted to this stress or how long I would go before squeezing the bulb. The series of words alternated with pictures of faces and houses, first focused photos and then pixelated photos. Then

there was a series of words alternating with consonant clusters. A graduate student had told me earlier, "Do not read the words! Let your brain do the work. Do not say the words to yourself. Do not name the people or the house styles. Let your brain do the work." I felt this was really impossible: how do you see the word "book" and not read it? I tried but felt like I was unable to follow the instructions. Even hearing that I shouldn't name the faces tempted me to do so. Yet again I felt like a bad subject.

After my session, I met with Dr. R and Karen, one of her graduate students, to discuss the experience. I started with questions about my ability to hear.

"As you know the earphones weren't working so well," I began. "And I was terribly worried about not being able to hear and trying so hard to hear. So, there was a lot of emotion. You just sort of can't help it. I really wanted to do this right, and kept asking myself 'should I squeeze the ball?'"

"You were worrying about showing the emotion?" Dr. R asked.

"Yeah," I agreed, "and should I squeeze the bulb? Because maybe I should just go with it and try to do the very best I can."

"When there's a really clear event causing a problem, we will very often not use the data from that period of time," Dr. R explained. "We'll look at the data run by run, and if that one looks unusual we'll just discard that one—if there's some big event like that. Sometimes we just can't use any of the data because of something that happened throughout the session. There's just too much going on."

I had not realized that it was acceptable to discard data as long as you had a good justification. My fMRI was the worst-case scenario, when the data might be altogether outside the norm and had to be thrown out. However, Dr. R continued, it is always true that "people are doing all kinds of things other than the tasks we ask them to do. I mean you're thinking about stuff. The experiment doesn't fully occupy your time. And there's also time between the trials. And so your brain is doing more things than just the tasks that you're asked to do."

"The logic of it," Dr. R continued, "is that usually what we're doing is actually comparing activation of your brain in two tasks or in two kinds of stimulus conditions. In part of your session you were looking at words. And in another period of time you might be just looking at checkerboards. So before, in this particular experiment, we were interested in trying to identify what parts of the brain are active for reading. What we would do is compare the activity at every point in your brain. During one period, you were looking at words; during a second period, you were looking at checkerboards. And the basic reasoning is that words are going to recruit areas that involve reading more than checkerboards."

When I was doing reading tasks, she explained, "areas that are really reading areas would be more active."

I persisted: "Even though there is all that extraneous worrying and thinking?"

"Yes," she replied. "The other thing is that we also assume that this kind of background stuff is more varied and more random than the actual task that we're looking at. And so, every time you see a word, the reading area is active. This other stuff that's going on—like one moment you're thinking about lunch, the next moment you're thinking, 'Oh my God. Am I doing this right?' All these things more likely than not accumulate in sort of the same area. So, they're going to be smaller signals and might cancel each other out. It's kind of part of the noise."

"So what do you call this process of combining signals?" I asked.

"It is called averaging. The other averaging that goes on in a lot of these studies is that we combine data across individuals. So again, one person happens to, for whatever reason, be thinking about food the whole time, let's say, and their food area's active, but nobody else's is. When you combine the data across everybody, that food area is just not going to end up being consistently active. Only the things that are consistent across everybody will end up being strong enough to be statistically significant."

I knew that "statistically significant" meant that a relationship between variables was caused by something other than chance. I felt better able to understand the assumptions here. It is as if subjects were the many cars driving across a suspension bridge. Some drive fast, some slow, some placidly, some erratically. But all of them are able to successfully drive across the bridge because of how the bridge was structurally engineered. It is as if the cognitive structures being sought are like the principles of physics that hold the bridge up.

I was struck by how similar this argument was to the averaging in the ERP.

"That's a pretty persuasive argument for the fMRI imaging being meaningful—that you can do this," I conceded. "Because it could be that the emotional experience of somebody like me who is test anxious would wipe out everything. But it's very persuasive if that's actually how it works."

"There's an area of the brain that's particularly involved in emotion," Dr. R reassured me once more. "And it could be that area would be particularly active for you because you're more anxious than somebody else. But unless everybody is, or most of the majority of subjects are, it's not going to end up being a significant result."

In the midst of all my worrying, Karen had loaded up the scans from my fMRI on the computer. Dr. R asked, "Do you want to see your fMRI images? If you want to, only if you want to." Of course, I eagerly wanted to see them, and we went to Karen's computer monitor.

Spontaneously, I said, "Oh my God. It's beautiful."

"She is modest," Dr. R joked.

But it was no joke: I was dumbfounded to see the inside of my brain. Karen guided me to my scans for the part of the study where I was looking at pictures of houses and then faces.

"These yellow and orange clusters are the areas of your brain responding to the faces," she explained. "And the blue and green are the areas responding to the houses."

I was astonished.

"Good grief. I wouldn't have believed it," I said.

"What we normally see is that these two blue areas in the Para hippocampal gyrus are active for seeing houses. So that's pretty normal," Karen said. "And these little yellow ones right here are the fusiform gyrus that activates for faces. So, you display pretty much normal activity."

Taken aback, I asked, "Normal? Why would the brain activate different areas for houses and faces?"

"Well they both share features," Karen said. "So, you see a house, and it's got the doors and the windows. And they're generally usually in the same arrangement as the parts of faces. Yet people's faces are more familiar. You see lots of faces every day, but it's a little more meaningful than the houses are, per se. So that could be why they develop in different areas."

Still incredulous, I blurted, "Amazing—but you were hoping for it to be just normal, right?"

"Yep. You can see there're a lot of other activated areas as we move towards the frontal cortex. So, this activated area right here on the right side of the brain is for face recognition as well. However, on your left side we find an area for words, for reading and spelling. So, it was nice that you showed that consistent result."

"Consistent? Yeah, right," I said, by which I meant, "Unbelievable."

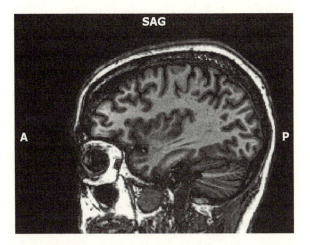

FIGURE 4.3. Author's fMRI scan. Photo by Dr. R's lab, 2010.

"And then I can show you an activated area on your right side for reading," Karen continued. "So, Emily, you have bilateral activation, which is nice. We usually tend to see it more localized in the left."

Completely wrapped up in the way averaging had allowed my scans to show clear results as predicted, I wondered, "How much of the process of getting rid of the noise gets written about in a published paper? Would it be in a footnote or something?"

"No, it's in a paragraph. It's about the fMRI software for preprocessing or that sort of thing. But a little paragraph, and it's actually stated what the steps were. It does not really go into depth in describing what the software does. But we do three motion corrections. So, we correct for motion because nobody can lie perfectly still in the scanner."

What a comeuppance. I thought that I had uncovered a flaw in the whole method because my emotions and anxiety seemed to flood my experience of the experiment. Nothing could have impressed me more that averaging signals reveals common patterns and eliminates noise than being told my brain scans were normal and consistent with previous data for this task.

I was left wondering about the "little paragraph" in a published paper that describes methods for getting rid of noise. Such brevity is understandable given that filters for motion corrections on fMRI data are standard practice, well known to researchers. Motion corrections are conventionally accepted in the field and need no justification.

Reaction Time

Another convention runs through all of the examples of normalized or averaged data. That convention is the use of numerically measured reaction times. In my fMRI session, the data that were averaged were numerical measures of neuronal activity. Researchers detected a significantly larger amount of neuronal activity (blood flow in a specific location in the brain) when I saw an image of a face or a house compared to when I saw no image. This neuronal activity could also be mapped to different areas of the brain. So, in fMRI studies, both the quantity and location of neuronal activity are what matter. ERP studies measure only the spike in neural response that occurs at a predictable interval after a task is initiated. Some tasks lead to a spike and some do not. The *location* of the brain activity is only generally known from the location of the electrode on the head, but the *time* of the activity is known precisely.

The most venerable and most common numerical measurement in behavioral experiments like those discussed in chapter 3 is "reaction time." Experiments in psychology based on reaction time began with the nineteenth-century work of Dutch ophthalmologist Franciscus Donders. He devised experiments that involved different tasks. In one, subjects would simply recognize that a light had turned on. In a more complicated experiment, subjects would choose which light had gone on. Subjects took less time to perform the simpler task than the more complicated one, and Donders concluded that he had discovered a measure of the duration of different mental processes. Reaction time, precisely measured, was a potentially crucial feature of mental activity. Joseph Jastrow was an early American psychologist who, following Donders, laid out the premise of reaction time:

> It follows, as a very natural consequence of the modern view of the relation between body and mind, that mental processes, however simple, should occupy time. It being established that so comparatively simple a process as sensation involves the passage of an impulse along nerve-fibres, it is plain that the rate of travelling of this impulse sets a limit to the time of the entire process, as well as of all more complicated mental operations in which sensations are involved.[13]

Apart from his scientific research, Jastrow was in charge of the psychology exhibits at the Chicago World's Fair in 1893, where experiments based on reaction time were set up to educate the public: "as Jastrow put it, 'to render visible to the public' the nature of the problems that psychologists were considering."[14]

The exhibit [. . .] included a working laboratory set up, not to conduct research—although photographs of numerous university research laboratories were displayed on the walls—but as a testing room where, for a small fee, fairgoers could have their sense capacities and mental powers tested.[15]

The exhibit occupied two rooms, and in the second room there were eight tables displaying various devices to test sensation and reaction time.[16] The tests were given to everyone who visited, to "convince Americans that the answers to psychological questions resided within the laboratories of the universities, and not in the hands of mesmerists, spiritualists, or phrenologists."[17]

> Visitors would be given a clipboard and laboratory score sheet. There they could move among a number of experimental stations to measure their accuracy of movement, reaction time, color vision, sensitivity to pain, judgment of weights, memory, and so forth, recording their measurements on their scoresheets.[18]

As the first attempt to introduce psychological tests to the American public, the testing room demonstrated the methods experimental psychologists were then using to test the range, accuracy, and nature of what they called "some elementary mental powers" and also to collect data for a larger study of the ways in which such factors as age, education, gender, race, environment, social status, and physical development could affect those powers. An army of graduate student volunteers brought to Chicago for the occasion tested thousands of the fair's visitors.[19]

By the time of the World's Fair, reaction time was established as a core value, a key tool, and an unquestioned metric for experimental psychology, one whose utility for averaging individual responses and describing norms had been disseminated in public media. The focus on reaction time and the accompanying restriction of the subject's experience to a timed reaction amounts to an instance of what Kurt Danziger classically called "the isolation of laboratory products from the personal and cultural reality that produced them."[20]

The isolation did not, however, take place once and for all in the past. The isolation of "laboratory products from the personal and cultural reality that produced them" must be done over and over. To see this isolation in process, I turn to a current study in Dr. J's lab. The study fell under the heading of "social decision-making" with a focus on "trust." A lab meeting was scheduled to introduce the project, and the meeting included—besides me as the lab's

Where Men's Senses Are Tested.

FIGURE 4.4. "Where Men's senses are tested," from an article about a psychology exhibit at the Chicago World's Fair, *Chicago Daily Tribune*, 1893.

FIGURE 4.5. "Testing the accuracy of aim," from an article about a psychology exhibit at the Chicago World's Fair, *Chicago Daily Tribune*, 1893. Graphic prepared by Ralph Guggenheim.

anthropologist—grad students, undergrads, Dr. J, and a visiting professor from another university who planned to collaborate in the study.

Dr. J began with a definition of "trust":

> We assume there are two kinds of people interacting and call them "trustor" and "trustee" for short. The trustor may or may not trust the trustee depending on the circumstances. The preconditions for trust are:
> —Trustor has dependence on trustee: the trustor has low confidence in his or her own knowledge, which motivates active information seeking, and motivates acceptance of information provided by trustee.
> —Trustor does not have confidence in his or her own decision-making.
> —Trustor has vulnerability: the decision outcome carries value, and a poor decision risks loss.
> —Trustor has uncertainty. The trustor cannot predict 100% how the trustee will behave.

This model assumes (as did the ensuing lab discussion and the publications that lab members referred to in the discussion) that people only trust in certain circumstances, as specified above. I found this somewhat startling. As an anthropologist, I had been trained that human life is social through and through, always involving something like trust relationships (or else distrust), generosity (or else selfishness), openness (or else secrecy). I was startled because although the psychological model recognized that trust could be present or absent, there seemed to no place for what lay in between these alternatives. In my training, I would always expect many subtle social and cultural variations to lie between the opposites.

Dr. J explained that the project about trust aimed to model experimentally a specific context in which the subjects would decide an issue involving trust or mistrust. The subjects would be shown one or another human face that communicated either "trustworthiness" or "untrustworthiness." Then the experiment would measure how exposure to these faces affected the subject's performance in a decision-making task.

While these faces were being projected on the slide screen, a lively discussion of the experimental design took place. But I was distracted. Finally, I raised my hand and asked, "Which of these faces is supposed to be trustworthy and which untrustworthy?" Every head in the room swiveled around to look at me and several people said, disbelievingly, "the left one is trustworthy!" Dr. J defended what was obvious to everyone else: "We normed all these faces and included features for attractiveness and intelligence. We threw away the middle [where there might have been disagreement] and used the extremes where virtually 100 percent of people were in consensus on which face is trustworthy and which is untrustworthy."

The visiting professor turned to me and asked, "How about for you? Which is trustworthy?"

"I would have a really hard time deciding," I said. Confronted with skeptical looks, I elaborated: "I am thinking, hmm, this guy could be feeling poorly today but be especially empathic and trustworthy, that guy might look friendly but actually be a snake: you know you can make up this long story . . ."

The visiting professor interrupted, "Oh you really trained yourself! This is your anthropological training, right? We should study you! This would actually be a good study because you have been trained to be very open to everybody, right?"

I had, just like that, been isolated from the general population because of my anthropological training and deemed to belong to a special population. Dr. J then picked up another aspect of my intervention.

"This is a very good point," she said. "The 'trustworthy' judgment happens very quickly in the experiment. You have an initial impression that happens within 200 milliseconds. In that circumstance, you would probably have responded to the left one as untrustworthy. But if we have more time to sit around and think, 'I know somebody who was smiling all the time, but he was really fake, and this other guy looks like he could be an interesting person.' It's different if you aren't given time to make up a story about the person."

We have just been taken back to Jastrow on reaction times: the coin of the realm is the speed of neural reaction in milliseconds. This is what isolates the reaction and enables it to be meaningful. A signal from a specific part of the brain is relevant, but made-up stories about trust are not. What interests me, however, is the way a broader kind of "trust" sneaks back in, despite the experimenters' efforts to confine and isolate it. What sneaks back in is "trust" in the historically established assumptions of the field, like the importance of reaction time as a direct link to neural processing. It is as if the specified domain of "trust-mistrust" floats, even for psychologists, on a broader kind of trust in a larger field of commonly accepted tenets, what Wittgenstein called the "scaffolding of their thoughts." Their defining distinction between preconditions for trust and no preconditions for trust is "held fast by what lies around it"—namely, things that stand "unshakably fast" in a "system of what is believed."[21] The "system of what is believed" is that reaction time indicates the duration of neural activity and that the experimental design can isolate and

define something like "trust" in specific ways. While my psychologist interlocutors would clearly accept that an anthropologist could have other interests
in stories about "trust," they were confident that the reactions they measure
occur too quickly, that the reaction time is too fast and too short to possibly
be influenced by something like cultural conceptions about trust.

The psychologists isolated me (as an anthropologist) from the norms of
experimental psychology, and they have isolated "trust" and "social decision-
making" into specific contexts. But like members of any academic discipline
they cannot isolate themselves from a broader kind of trust in the scaffolding
built by their common history. Canguilhem wrote that the selection of the
selector should "transcend the blueprint of technical selection." In a way, disciplines like psychology and anthropology do not "transcend the blueprint of
technical selection." As an anthropologist, I was not acting outside the blueprint of my field in telling stories about trust any more than experimental
psychologists were acting outside their field's blueprint when choosing participants, measuring their reaction times, and averaging them. Inevitably, academic disciplines rely on their own criteria for selecting who can participate
or what approach is important. Since each discipline shares trust in its own
conventions, anthropology and psychology are distinct. But in each honoring
our own conventions, we share common ground.

The establishment of reaction time as a metric allowed for the numeric
measurement of brain activity and the calculation of averages and norms. In
this respect, the experience of subjects—their subjectivity—could be largely
silenced, especially by focusing on fast reaction times. But though subjects are
counted one by one as individuals, experiments are not conducted in an asocial environment. The discipline of psychology brings powerful social conventions to bear at every point. All of this will be omitted in published papers and
media coverage, which then cannot help but carry an ethos of the isolated
individual into the wider culture. But observing the journeys traveled by psychological experiments up to publication makes the social context they depend on clear. It is ironic that making the social context of the experiment
invisible eliminates the many contextual referents that would make the experiment more intelligible.[22]

To establish "clean" data sets that are representative of general human cognitive capacities, psychologists depend on numerical measures. The valence
of IAPS (International Affective Picture System) images, the spike of an ERP
response, the amount of neural activity in an fMRI, and reaction time in a
behavioral study are all numerical measures. Only data in the form of numbers

can be normalized, or averaged and precisely compared. These are powerful tools! Even a skeptical anthropologist like me felt astonishment at the way averaging fMRI data revealed the predicted pattern of activity in my brain. Of course, extracting only numerical measures from an experimental setup has to ignore a lot, such as the definition of what counts as trust, the individual anxiety of participants, the racial history of the Amazon Mechanical "Turk," or the White faces in a study of anger. The power of focusing on numerical measures is that one can calculate statistical significance, average a range of responses, or decide to count different individual responses (from students or Amazon Mechanical Turk respondents) as comparable. This power comes at the cost of flattening the complexity of participants' experience and risks reproducing racial and gender disparities.

5

Delimiting Technologies

Many crucial choices about the forms and limits of our regimes of
instrumentality must be enforced at the founding, at the genesis of each
new technology. It is here that our best purposes must be heard.

—LANGDON WINNER, *THE WHALE AND THE REACTOR: A SEARCH
FOR LIMITS IN AN AGE OF HIGH TECHNOLOGY*, 1986

IN THE intimate space of the experimental psychology lab, the task of delimiting the strengths and weaknesses of technologies was taken very seriously. Most of the lab training about what technologies can and cannot do well focused on tools to scan and image the brain, tools that emerged after the "cognitive revolution." I heard many explanations of why the cognitive revolution made understanding the brain a primary concern. As Dr. R put it, the cognitive revolution was fought against behaviorism. "It assumes that cognitive processes, although invisible, are 'real' and can be measured—just like subatomic particles are invisible but their presence can be inferred and measured." This revolution took to task John Watson's portentous words of 1913: "The time seems to have come when psychology must discard all reference to consciousness; when it need no longer delude itself into thinking that it is making mental states the object of observation."[1] Watson ushered in the era of behaviorism, arguing that only behavior—and not consciousness—could be seen, measured, and analyzed scientifically. Watson's insistence on the primacy of measuring behavior has not disappeared from psychological experiments. Most students in the labs I followed began their graduate research with behavioral studies. Building on Watson's exclusive reliance on behavior as opposed to consciousness, they assumed that their contemporary studies could shed light on cognitive processes like learning because reaction time to a stimulus was taken as a measure of brain activity. But they could well hope that interesting results from their behavioral experiments would eventually allow them to use EEG or fMRI to detect the timing or locations of the psychological traits they observed behaviorally. Behavior was the *starting point*, the hypothesis-generating point, but no longer the end point. Dr. G, an experienced elder in one psychology department where I did fieldwork, told me that this was because, not long after Watson, H. O. Hebb, an important forebear of Dr. G's, turned the tide. Hebb argued against the conclusion that observing behavior was the only relevant source of data for psychology. In *The Organization of Behavior: A Neuropsychological Theory*, published in 1949, Hebb proposed that the material basis of mental concepts lay in neural structures called "cell assemblies." Hebb's ideas were spread worldwide by his students, who established laboratories to study how behavior was based in neural structures. Basically, human mental processes such as remembering, forgetting, fearing, hating, paying attention, not paying attention, and perceptual processes such as reading, spelling, or identifying became treated as processes in the brain that people themselves could not be aware of. The result of these brain processes could be described in nonspecialist psychological terms ("I remember," "I forget," etc.), but that level of phenomena was relegated to the unscientific, left to the artist, the writer, or the anthropologist. What psychologists had called "introspection," Dr. G explained, was abandoned as "too murky," a "blunt instrument." What came to matter was identifying the parts of the brain involved in "remembering," etc., and how they interact. Later, Dr. S summarized the situation: "Historically, they thought by introspection you could get access to the *processes* behind perception. We don't think this anymore." Of course, he would agree that ordinary introspection (self-examination) still goes on, but that it cannot reveal the steps in cognitive processes.

Understanding the Limits of Tools

In the last chapter, I explored how researchers average together individual results from the current technologies used to detect brain activity. The next step is to understand more about how researchers work with technology to delimit their experimental design and capture specific data. Luckily, creative work in anthropology helps us to understand "things," such as tools, instruments, or devices in new ways. In classical Western epistemology, thought and concepts are distinguished from material things. The current anthropological insight is that this classical epistemology may mislead us when studying other cultures. Mental concepts might not be distinguished from material things in the same way, or in any way. What Western eyes see as inert objects, members of other cultures might see as animate and person-like. Recent ethnographers have taken great care not to impose classical Western categories where they are unwarranted. Anthropologists are still struggling with the problem of how to describe worlds where matter and mind are conceived differently, given that Western language and practices are imbued with their own classical epistemological assumptions. A fundamental source for this work is Marcel Mauss' monograph, *The Gift*. Mauss delved into the history of how material things came to be defined as different from persons in Latin and Greek texts. He showed how the separation of material things and property from persons happened because material things became subject to market forces. In contrast, his report of ethnography from Melanesia and Polynesia showed that certain kinds of "things" were part and parcel of persons. The "gift" of what Westerners would call a "thing" to another person conveyed powerful aspects—the *hau*—of the giver along with it; for example, the *hau* might have the power to demand that it be returned to the original giver. It is hard to find a language to convey such ways of understanding the world. The task of describing how "things" operate in contemporary Western science is no less difficult.

Researchers have considered how users often give their computers person-like attributes. In my fieldwork, the technologies in frequent use were not anthropomorphized in any obvious way. But they were frequently the subject of lectures, discussions, and complaints. Perhaps too fancifully, I often imagined them as only partially domesticated beasts. I imagined the EEG as a many-armed sea creature whose tentacles gently felt the scalp and reported electrical activity, the fMRI as a roaring, wide-mouthed creature who swallowed and digested subjects inside a magnetic field. To be sure, researchers frequently talked about these tools as recalcitrant: prone to randomly detaching from the subject or stopping for no reason. The technologies also were commonly seen as "speaking" to researchers in a sense. They gave signals, which had to be interpreted, "cleaned," or "read." One common way researchers interacted with these technologies was to delimit their capacities as tools: to say what EEG, fMRI, and behavioral tasks can tell us about cognitive processes, and what they can't.

EEG

As I mentioned, I had hands-on experience attaching electroencephalograph electrodes to subjects' heads. This required placing the weblike cap on the subject's head and then using a pin to puncture the outer scalp while applying gel to each electrode, usually about sixty-four of them. Grad students checked the contact between each electrode and the computer software frequently, reapplied gel, rechecked the software recording, and so on. After all this, the experiment proper began, with subjects carrying out a series of tasks to test, for example, how they learn and remember under specific conditions.

The goal, in brief, was to measure electrical signals from all the electrodes attached to different parts of the scalp. The computer software detected and stored all the waveforms recorded by each electrode—called a channel— measuring fluctuations in electrical voltage emanating from neural activity in some region of the brain. As I described in the previous chapter, one particular aspect of the waveform, the event-related potential (ERP), is considered especially useful. Since the EEG is very sensitive and accurate about the time at which the fluctuation of a waveform occurs, the polarity—positive ("uppies") or negative ("downies")—and amplitude of the ERP at a particular time can be detected with a certain amount of assurance. So as subjects perform tasks, the time of the ERP is recorded by the computer together with the voltage measurement—this is called an event code. Subjects' recorded waveforms can be recorded before, during, or after the task and then examined in detail. As I explained earlier, certain spots in the timeline have proved to consistently produce significant results at certain locations on the scalp. The one called P300, for example, is a positive increase in voltage that occurs at 300 milliseconds after a stimulus and is detected at the electrode placed in the left upper parietal area—the region across the top of the head but behind the frontal lobe.

In any one subject, responses 300 milliseconds after a stimulus are averaged together by the computer. Then that average is compared to averages from the other subjects in the experiment. What does it mean if the data show a consistent, statistically significant ERP for a particular task? Lab members told me it shows which perceptual processes are involved in specific tasks. As my ERP manual taught, "ERPs can be used to isolate specific cognitive processes [...] The main advantage of the ERP component is its ability to track the time course of processing, not to measure the operation of specific neural systems." In other words, we can learn when certain types of cognitive processes are happening in what order, and roughly where they are occurring. However, the

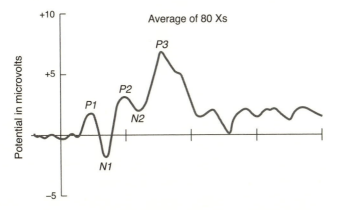

FIGURE 5.1. P300 spike in the ERP waveform. Graphic prepared by
Ralph Guggenheim.

manual continues, "it is difficult to determine the exact location of the neural
generator source"—that is, where in the brain the signal originated. Nonetheless, "ERPs provide high-resolution temporal information about the mind and
brain that cannot be obtained any other way."[2] As we will see shortly, EEG
recordings are composed of signals of interest from cognitive processes in the
brain, but also contain signals from "noise"—due to head or face movements,
blinking, or twitching. To heighten the signals of interest, experimenters use
various filters in their software to reduce this noise.

The above paragraph is inspired by Steve Luck's confident textbook about
running an ERP experiment. What professors teach students in lab meetings
can significantly differ from the upbeat tone of a textbook. In lectures I heard
during lab meetings, the focus was on the mechanics of the technology and
the brain, but also insistently on the limitations of the technology. These lab
lectures were part of how students learned both what the technology of EEG/
ERP *could* do and, just as importantly, what it *could not* do. The lab lectures are
therefore worth quoting at length.

At one lab meeting, Dr. J began,

Ultimately EEG is measuring what happens when a lot of these neurons are
firing in synchrony. They are firing at the same time in roughly the same
place, and when that happens you generate a field potential. That potential,
while too small to shock your neighbor, is enough that if we amplify it
properly with our sophisticated $50,000 worth of equipment, you are able
to see it on a computer screen. That is what EEG is measuring. That thing

over there on the left, that is a neuron, a schematic of a neuron, and it looks like some sort of alien.

Dr. J was drawing on the whiteboard, and I copied her drawing into my notebook.

Again, EEG is good at some stuff and not at others. One thing EEG is very good at measuring is [the activity of] neurons in the cingulate cortex. You probably don't even know what the cingulate cortex is, but the cingulate cortex is slightly older, not quite as new as the neocortex but not as old as the hippocampus. It is a five-layer piece of cortex that kind of goes right above the *corpus callosum*. Does anyone know what the *corpus callosum* is?

The group drew a blank.

It's this big, fat, thick cluster of axons that link the two hemispheres together (the right hemisphere and the left hemisphere) and there is a big, thick band of axons that link them, that allow for inter-hemispheric communication. Right above that is this thing called the cingulate cortex, and the neurons there are kind of oriented very nicely, perpendicular to the top of the head for most part. There is a really nice orientation, a lot of pyramidal cells and because they are pyramidal cells they have an open electrical field and they are pointing straight at your electrode. So, when we look at the P3a [a component of P300], this is coming from the cingulate cortex and that is why the signal pops out.

Dr. J continued with a discussion of what EEG can measure:

The basic thing about neurons and pretty much the entire brain is essentially there is input, there is integration and decision-making, and there is output. Our behavior is often similar too. We have decision-making processes to decide what you want to do with the input, and then we have output. In the neuron we have a place for input, which are our dendrites. So other neurons coming in here can talk to this neuron, whisper in its ear, and say, "I think you should fire now." Basically, we sum together all the different inputs, the many inputs on one neuron, sum them up and if they reach a certain threshold at this point right where the axon hits the cell body, the neuron fires what is known as an action potential. That results in essentially this change in polarity across the cell membrane that shoots down the axon and ultimately to the next cell which could be right here or could be in a completely different part of the brain. Inputs come in here,

Pyramidal Neuron

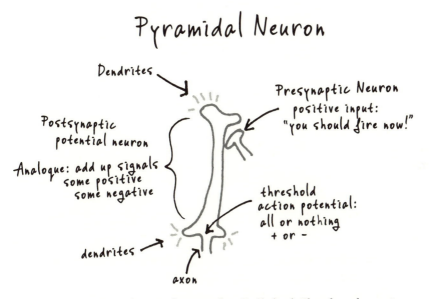

Dendrites

Postsynaptic potential neuron

Analogue: add up signals
some positive
some negative

Presynaptic Neuron
positive input:
"you should fire now!"

threshold
action potential:
all or nothing
+ or -

dendrites

axon

FIGURE 5.2. Author's drawing of a neuron from Dr. J's sketch. Photo by author, 2018. Redrawn by Kara Healey.

decision-making is right here, a decision is made (if it reaches threshold) to fire and it goes down the axon as the action potential. You can also miss threshold, maybe there wasn't enough [excitatory] input to hit threshold, in which case no action potential is generated. Action potentials are all or none. They either happen or they don't. You need to reach threshold. If you go above threshold you don't generate a bigger action potential. You either hit the threshold or just barely hit the threshold and that is good enough."

I was struck by the way Dr. J brought these physically interacting parts of the brain to life. First, the neuron is an "alien," then we humans make decisions on the basis of input and output just like neurons, then the neurons "talk to each other" and "whisper in each other's ears." An action potential reports a "decision." More elaboration was yet to come.

However, before we get to the action potential, there are what they call graded or analog—not digital on and off but analog—signals that are building up and adding together, summing together for this thing on the side, whether it hits threshold or not. We call these post-synaptic potentials because they are happening here on this neuron. This neuron in this model is called the postsynaptic neuron because it is receiving inputs from other neurons. This is the synapse, the little gap here. This is the presynaptic neuron, sending information. This is the postsynaptic neuron receiving the information. Sometimes the information can be things that excite the neuron, basically make the neuron more excited, more likely to fire the action potential. Other things are going to inhibit the neuron from firing an action potential. It's kind of an algebraic sum of all the excitation and all the inhibitions that reach this point and if the excitations exceed inhibitions and reach the threshold, then you fire [an action potential].

Now Dr. S was describing the neuron that fires as "you" firing: you and the neuron are excited on the basis of information you receive or inhibited on the basis of other information. But charming as this scenario is, Dr. J quickly set limits on what the EEG can measure. She continued,

What we measure with EEG is not an action potential because action potentials are very fast. They dissipate quickly from the neuron. Typically, what we are measuring are the slower graded excitatory and inhibitory postsynaptic potentials. We are kind of looking at the input side of things. When we measure EEG, we are looking at how things are input to different areas of the brain rather than the decision to fire or not. That is the nature of what we can see on the scalp, those are the kinds of potentials that can be detected in that area on the cortical surface, with our method.

I thought this might count as a major disappointment. Dr. S was saying that with this method we can't measure action potentials! In a culture where we all want to know where the action is, where we want to be party to decisions, where firing is the subject of movies about rockets and employment performance, the EEG can only measure inputs. Disappointing as that might be, at least we can get a fix on the signals that can lead to action potentials, the combination of excitatory and inhibitory inputs, right?

Wrong.

Dr. J broke the news:

Guess what? You cannot tell if you are seeing excitation or inhibition simply based on the direction of the waveforms, unless you have x-ray vision and you can go in and know exactly what layer the inputs are coming from and the orientation of the neuron. I have tried but I just gave up. We just don't have access to it. We have to be kind of agnostic about if we are seeing excitation or inhibition. We just know we are seeing neurons that are acting similarly. There are enough neurons that are acting in this way that they are summing up to make a recognizable deflection; we just don't know if it is excitatory or inhibitory.

It's sort of disappointing, you know? It would be nice to know if it was inhibition or excitation.

She added that in an fMRI,

You might think "I am seeing increased blood flow so there must be excitation," but the fact that a brain area is active does not—even in fMRI— reveal whether its effect on other neurons is to excite or inhibit them. It is always tricky.

It is also tricky to separate signal from noise. The technology creates a world that researchers inhabit. Dr. J put it like this:

EEG is all about signal and noise. Your whole life is about signal and noise. All about cost and benefits and signal and noise. Every imaginable aspect of the apparatus is considered along these lines: What metal should the electrode be made of? Tin or silver? Where should the ground electrode be placed? On the nose, between the eyes, on the earlobe, chest, or mastoid? Should you keep the electrode site moist with a gel or a sponge? All of these choices are considered to avoid muscle movements. We say, "Muscles swamp the brain!" or "Eye movement is among the worst curses of EEG." We try to be as precise as possible when monitoring eye activity because it is something we need to remove. The better we are recording it the better we can remove it. "Eye movements are the enemy." They dominate the EEG.

Each eye is like an electric battery, and when it rotates it alters the signal in numerous electrodes.

It is clear Dr. J was speaking to neophytes in neuroscience whom she expected would be setting up participants and running them in ERP experiments. Still, she bent over backwards to explain the limits of this technology. She summarized her qualifications in an emphatic way: "Not only can EEG not measure action potentials, it cannot tell whether the postsynaptic potentials are excitatory or inhibitory." Disappointing indeed, but better forewarned than under an illusion. EEG has enemies: the body and eye movements of the participant, including scratching, fidgeting, smiling, frowning, or blinking. Much statistical calculation by software and manual coding by lab members must happen before a signal emerges victoriously.

Experimenters and Subjective Judgments

We have already had a taste of the large amount of work it takes to segregate the experience of subjects from data, and I was soon to learn that psychologists must also devote considerable effort to segregate their own subjective experience from experimental data. Ulla was teaching me how to "clean" data from an EEG session. We were looking at a computer screen displaying a software program that can organize the data from the electrodes on a subject's scalp. Each electrode traces a separate line on the screen, with obvious variations in amplitude. But we sometimes faced signals that Ulla described as "messy" or "noisy" or "crazy." So, we began to remove these by selecting them with the mouse and deleting them. I wondered what we were looking for? "Anything that could cause perturbation of the brain activity," Ulla said. "Extraneous eye movements, like a blink, scratching the eye or face, touching the face, moving the eyeglasses, emotional expressions at the temple, dozing off." Ulla's job was to identify all these perturbations consistently and remove them. Subjects cannot always be disciplined enough to provide quietly attentive, calmly relaxed responses to tasks. Hence Ulla had to remove the traces of unruly bodies so the data would be "pretty," "clean," and "smooth."

I sat beside Ulla as she worked her way through one trial of one subject.

"The eye is connected to brain activity. It's best to take out the eye movement, and hope the effect is still strong enough," she said as she selected a swath of data and deleted it.

"They blink! This is a blink. If you select this one and I select that one, we are going to get different results. So, it's very subjective."

"What's subjective?" I asked.

"Eye activity. And these are sweat potentials—sometimes if they are sweating you see this effect. If there are a lot of them I just leave them in, but if there are just one or two I take them out."

"I'm amazed at how much is judgment! I was assuming all this would be automatic, that you'd push a button," I said.

"Even if you find a good example of an eye blink and tell the software to take out anything similar, it may not correct for other ones properly. This is like a scratch of an eye."

"Oh my god," I said.

"It should be taken out. Anyway, I'll take it out. Here's a better blink—I'd keep this in because it's not too noisy but again I think it's like subjective."

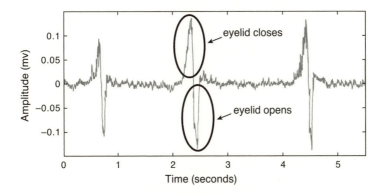

FIGURE 5.3. Subject's eye blink in the waveform from an EEG.
Drawing by Kara Healey.

Ulla was fully aware of the subjectivity involved in choosing which parts of the signal should be taken out. She assured me that studies had shown years ago that having different researchers clean EEG data "did not differentially impact results."

I jumped to a speculation. "If you showed the participants like you are showing me, that would be amazing."

Ulla was unsure, but as she thought about it, she said, "I think it would be great to show them this and then if they get tense they can kind of self-monitor."

More errors piled up as we watched the EEG signal run by: "Wow, that person had something in their eye. This is line noise because the electrode was not attached well. This is from neck muscles. Anger is the trigger for that. These are alpha waves, probably because her eyes are closed. The signals are coming from the back of the brain. Maybe she is asleep or just inactive or using imagery."

In response to my continuous gasping, Ulla summarized, "This is life inside psychology."

"Do you ever compare how you would clean a file compared to others in the lab?" I asked.

"In my group Dr. J was more conservative, others were less conservative. I was in the middle. But I go over all the trials in my study so there is consistency from trial to trial," she replied.

Finally, when the data are cleaned, and consistency is checked, the findings might make clear a large number of cognitive processes: Does uncertainty induced in the subject lead to a large P300 response? Do males and females differ in their responses to uncertainty at P300?

Randall, also a graduate student in Dr. J's lab, expanded on my experience cleaning data with Ulla. He showed how he cleans up an Excel spreadsheet containing data from a behavioral study.

> You may need to eliminate someone because their engagement or perception of the task is outside of the norm. There are many things you need to analyze up front to make sure that your dataset is good. You look at the normal range and then if you see someone who, say, puts a 1 for everything, then you eliminate them. You can do almost anything as long as you declare what you are doing and as long as it's systematic and ethical. That is a given. You cannot eliminate a subject unless you have a quantitative measure for why this person doesn't meet your expectation for the group. Qualitative observations also count. If you are there and see a person moving through the tasks quickly and not paying attention, that's a valid reason.

Randall explained further,

> You don't want to eliminate unnecessarily. In some cases, even though you have this outlier, you can run the analysis with and without that person, and if there is no effect then you can leave it in. We have to clean our data, process our data. And the period of processing takes forever. We meticulously look for errors—it is not good enough to say "here's my data, let's use it." We have to keep a system, keep an eye on things.

To produce "clean" data, students have to work long and hard. They consult guides, including manuals that give detailed instructions and records of data cleaning that can be used to compare lab members' different subjective judgments. The process is lively: the number of active neurons increases or decreases; subjects blink or move; lab members interact with noisy, messy data that has to be painstakingly and consistently smoothed and cleaned.

fMRI

The EEG, within its limits, can identify brain waves called ERPs and place them accurately in time. Currently, what some call the "Holy Grail" is the fMRI scanner—that large magnet inside which subjects do experimental tasks and produce data about the three-dimensional *locations* where brain activity is taking place. The fMRI seems like the Holy Grail in part because it is expensive. Universities with medical schools rent their fMRI machine to psychologists, but there are no in-house discounts. If you are a graduate student, you have to depend on your lab's PI having enough grant money to support an fMRI experiment. The ability to track brain activity in space was still regarded as somewhat miraculous in the 2000s. Dr. R said,

> fMRI is an amazing technology because it depends on blood flow. Whoever would have thought that you could measure this! If someone told me you could take a magnet, and then use it to detect the energy of protons, which means there is more hemoglobin and more signal, I would have thought they were crazy.

EEG is a stable, classic technology, whereas fMRI is the new kid on the block. Just like the EEG, the limits of fMRI are now well known. Textbooks are frank about its limitations and tradeoffs. On the web there is even a satirical mockup of a conference poster about avoiding false positive signals in the fMRI machine. Tongue in cheek, the authors explain that "One mature Atlantic Salmon (*Salmo salar*) participated in the fMRI study. The salmon was approximately 18 inches long, weighed 3.8 lbs., and was not alive at the time of scanning."[3] Even though the participant was one dead fish, some (false positive) signals were recorded by the fMRI. Joking and skepticism aside, the fMRI basically increases spatial resolution at the cost of diminishing temporal resolution and sensitivity.

Today, fMRI technology is seeking new frontiers. At her university's medical school, Dr. R told me, they were "testing an even stronger magnet" that may provide even finer spatial resolution. The safety of this project is still being assessed.

"Someday soon, will everyone upgrade?" I asked.

"Someday," said Dr. R. "We have done some safety stuff, but what's tricky is although there is a stronger potential signal, the amount of noise is also stronger. So, we still have the problem of separating signal from noise, and that problem might even be bigger."

Dr. R remarked on the surprising connection between "more hemoglobin and more signal." The fMRI detects changes in blood flow in the capillaries that pervade every part of the brain. Increased blood flow in particular parts of the brain is taken to indicate increased neuronal activity there. Subjects inside fMRI machines are given tasks that carefully pinpoint different cognitive functions like memory or attention. As the subject performs these tasks, the fMRI machine scans the brain and produces functional images (the "f" and "I" in fMRI) of how much blood is flowing in different regions of the brain. When I first began taking classes in neuroscience, I was intrigued to find that the latest technology relied on that anthropologically rich bodily substance, blood, to detect the ethereal activity of neurons. Although the fMRI depends on blood flow in the brain, at that time, in 2010, I looked in vain to find popular graphic illustrations of the role of blood in the fMRI. Cognitive neuroscience texts showed many fMRI images of neural tissue but often lacked pictorial representations of the blood vessels that permeate the brain. More often than not, illustrations only showed the brain itself, and not the rest of the body. Popular media accounts typically glossed over the function of the blood in favor of the detection of neural activity. This is a narrative from an educational video, in which the blood's function was described in words and images at first:

> When a particular area of my brain is working hard, extra blood flows there [we see images of blood flowing into capillaries in neural tissue] through my arteries to provide energy for the active nerve cells. The scanner can detect these changes in blood flow, giving us a completely new window into the fascinating world of the mind. Using this technique, we can actually watch the brain work.

The video then showed the surface of the brain's gray matter turning on its axis, isolated from any body part, with different parts highlighted in color, while the narrator said, "this part of the brain is where we process all sounds, and this is where we appreciate music. Amazingly, there are even separate bits for melody, for rhythm and for pitch." What we were shown were images based on measurements of increased blood flow, but mention of the blood had been left behind, and neural processing—for which the blood is a sign—had taken its place.[4] Pure neural processing, not the messy, blood-filled body, is surely the Holy Grail of what the scanner can detect.

Over the years since then, accessible accounts of fMRI in journals and textbooks and on the web have fully included the role of blood flow and elaborated on the way blood operates in an fMRI. Most notably, reference sources now actually illustrate the link between blood flow in the body and the signal the fMRI can detect. A teaching video from Oxford Sparks shows the entire body of a person moving his hand, the flow of the oxygenated blood needed by a particular part of his brain to orchestrate that movement, and the spinning effect on the hemoglobin in the blood in the brain that makes it detectable by a magnet.[5] The blood and the body are back for sure, as the technology becomes less opaque. fMRI is also increasingly open to scrutiny for validity. An article in *Frontiers in Neuroscience* claimed in 2012 that there are 6,912 strategies for analyzing fMRI data, resulting in a possible 34,560 different maps of the brain.[6] As a technology matures, its limitations become more evident.

The Person in the fMRI Scanner

Subjects also have to contend with the limits of technologies. I often heard reports of subjects who spoke of the output of technologies as a part of their bodies, reminiscent of Mauss' anthropological insights about the *hau* associated with a gift.

I asked Dr. R, "Do you ever ask people what is like when they see their brain?"

"Most people want to see their brains," she replied. "One subject gave the picture to her mom for Mother's Day." But there was also one subject "who would not give scans to us to publish. He did not want them published. He felt it was too personal, like getting undressed in public. So, of course we did not use them."

"If the person has a deficit, can they see the problem?" I asked.

"Not really, but it can be a delicate situation," she said. "It can be scary. If there is a pretty awful big hole, then you can really tell."

I recalled that when I saw my own fMRI scan, I worried about what looked to me like dark cavities, even though I knew that they were called ventricles and that everyone's brain has them. Perhaps my ventricles were too large? Dr. R asked if I knew why the ventricles are there. I drew a blank. She then explained that they are spaces in the brain that produce, hold, and transport cerebral spinal fluid that have no blood vessels within them. Reassuring me, she said that ventricles look like blank spaces in an fMRI, but they are crucial to what a normal brain needs in order to function. Embarrassment at having holes in my brain faded away.

Sometimes people resist having their brains exposed. Other times subjects compulsively do whatever they are told not to do, in a form of oppositional perversity, even in an fMRI machine. In one fMRI experiment, my instructions were to *not read* the words that would be shown on the screen, but just to *look at* them. This was a puzzle for me since my everyday life was spent reading all day long. But I set my mind to do it. Then I noticed letters and words on the machine itself. Later I thought about an experience kayaking on the Rogue River in Oregon. The guide would patiently draw a map in the sand on the shore showing each rapid's obstacles before we began. "Go to the far left of this rock by the rock wall, do not stay in the middle of the stream whatever you do. People have died in this rapid if they go down the middle." Something always took hold of me despite my best efforts. Whenever they told me *not* to do something, I *would* do it. I went straight down the middle of the rapid and somehow survived. In the scanner, just the same, I found myself visually gripped by the embossed manufacturer's words and kept reading them over and over again. "Toshiba Vantage Galan Toshiba Vantage Galan." I worried about this failure.

I took my concern to Dr. R. I told her and her colleague Karen that I found myself wondering afterward about two things in the instructions. One was, "When you see the words, just look at them; let your brain do the work. And don't read the words."

Karen explained, "Well, I didn't want you to look at them and be like 'cow,' 'dog.'"

"Yes, you said don't say words to yourself or out loud or in your mind," I said. "But then when it came to the test in the machine I thought that I didn't know how to not read a word."

"No, you should read the word," Dr. R explained. "I think Karen was just trying to say, 'Don't move your mouth when you read.' Maybe that's what we need to say more specifically."

"That would clarify it better," Karen echoed.

"Well, I just found myself unable to—" I said.

"—Of course," Dr. R interrupted. "Reading is absolutely automatic. And that's what it should be."

"Okay, so I didn't miss the boat on that one?"

"Not at all," Dr. R confirmed.

Karen agreed. "Yeah, you just passively do it. It was just we didn't want you to be like . . ."

". . . moving your mouth," Dr R. filled in. "Or with the consonant strings, attempting to make them into words. And then the faces—don't make up stories."

"Some people try to give them names for familiarity purposes or something," Karen explained.

"I don't know that you need to improve the instructions, but I just have to say that some people like me are incredibly perverse. When I am told not to do something, like 'Don't name them,' I can't help saying to myself, 'Don't call him Bob. Don't call him Bill.' But then I have already given them names."

"That's really funny," Dr. R said. "Did the instructions make it a little unclear?"

"No, I wouldn't say they were unclear at all. They were very clear, but I'm reporting to you the complexity of being a subject in this situation and trying to follow directions."

"Well, it becomes a salient, like a magnet. On the experimenter side you're not able to see whether the person maybe seems confused about something and then say, 'Well, what we really meant was blah, blah, blah.' And the person may not feel like it's a situation where they could ask, 'Well, do you mean blah, blah, blah?' because it's so formal."

In agreement, I would say that the huge, rumbling machine is intimidating. Anyone could figure out that time in the fMRI must be expensive and that its time should not be wasted. There is something frightening about its noise and the caution against having any metal. Many people ask whether their tooth fillings will fly out. This is not a situation where a student or volunteer would feel comfortable insisting on having the instructions clarified.

Behavioral Technologies

Although it has no metal, no chips, and no electricity, the experimental method should surely be considered a technology. In chapter 3 I described how the method is put into practice and held to its purpose despite obstacles created by obstreperous subjects. I now look at how the characteristics of machines can create further difficulties for harnessing subjects and getting them to produce what an experimental psychologist would consider usable data.

I had signed up to participate in an experiment that I was warned would include mild shocks. Two electrodes were attached to my fingers to measure how much I was sweating, an indication of stress. Another electric wire was attached to my forearm to deliver shocks. The experimenter took care to adjust the current, so I would clearly feel the shock but would judge it just uncomfortable, not painful. My task was to choose more or less risky bets, to win or lose actual money, starting with the thirty dollars in cash I was given at the start. The aim of the experiment, as I discovered when it was over, was to study whether the anxiety caused by random shocks would affect my willingness to risk losing a bet. Would I become averse to loss and hedge my bets? After each set of trials, I had to pick a point on a scale to register the range of my feelings: calm, tired, drowsy, hungry, anxious, fearful, happy, angry.

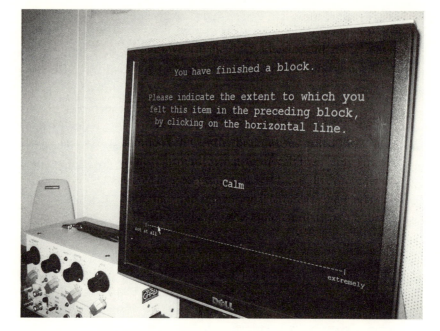

FIGURE 5.4. Slider to indicate the subject's level of calm during an experiment.
Photo by author, 2010.

The typical small, windowless room was warm. Too warm. After I was hooked up to the electrodes, instructed, and given a practice session, the experimenter left the room. No phone or alarm button was within reach. Nothing was unfriendly about this. But harnessed as I was to the electrodes and anxious as usual to be a good subject, as the room heated up, I began to sweat, and the greater conductivity from this moisture made the shock feel stronger and stronger and the pain worse and worse. The tape I recorded during the session is full of my dismayed cries!

As a subject I found this experience unforgettable. Not least because in the end I had won seventy-two dollars. When my tasks were finished, of course I told the student what had happened. He apologized but assured me that any unusual variation caused by my discomfort would not affect the experiment. At the time, I didn't know enough to ask how that could be. In retrospect, I imagine that the perturbation in my behavior would easily be handled by discarding my data if it was too far from the norm. Certainly no one meant to subject me to painful shocks. I am sure, however, that I continuously logged my feelings as "angry" because I felt trapped and in pain. In this case, the experimenters had clearly delimited the signals coming to me and going out from me to the software. Numerical measures of my skin conductance went out from me, as did my log of feelings. Numerically measured shocks and carefully calculated options for how much to risk came to me. But external, environmental conditions that no one anticipated combined with the settings of the machine to perturb the validity of the experiment, at least in my view. Ultimately, they would certainly be able to justify discarding my data and to use other subjects' data to decipher how anxiety (caused by random shocks) would affect subjects' willingness to risk loss. The recalcitrant elements in the experiment, which could not easily be anticipated, were the heat of the room, the sweating of the subject, and the conductivity of moisture. All these are mundane physical aspects of the environment that nonetheless delimited what data could be used.

I discussed a similar dilemma in a conversation with Dr. B early in my study:

"I was a subject in this test of reading ability. There was a huge battery of tests. But one of them had words that were quickly appearing on the periphery of my vision. Just really brief exposures on the left, the right, randomly, and I was supposed to read the word. And I couldn't do it well at all."

Guessing where I was headed, he replied, "And then you moved your eyes or your attention?"

"I was supposed to be looking at the fixation point in the middle of the screen. I knew I wasn't doing well, and I had been told that it would be really hard. So, I knew it was okay that I wasn't doing well. But I couldn't help myself. I started trying to guess where the next word would appear. I was looking left, right, left, right, left, right, trying to guess. Oh, there were just three lefts, so there's going to be a right. Afterward I told the experimenter about this and she just said, 'Hmm.' I mean, I would think that would be disturbing, it might have disturbed the data."

Dr. B agreed. "I would be concerned. If subjects reported they were doing something like that, I'd be concerned."

"So, it would matter."

"It would matter."

"That's reassuring. So, it's interesting that the experiment sets a sort of normative standard within which you can assume the subject will fit. But there's no feedback from the subjects about what's actually going on."

Later, I told Randall about this experience and he was reassuring.

"I'm sure you were not the only one in that study that had difficulty staying in the center. The brain biases our visual attention and where our attention goes; I mean for safety our brains are tuned by evolution from the highest order of species all the way down to see something in the periphery. And you have a reaction to go to that thing if it's moving or flashing."

"It flashed."

Randall said, "Yeah, you want to go there. Now not only are you supposed to not go there, you're supposed to understand what's there. So, it makes perfect sense for you to deploy your attention where you get the most vivid and rich contextualization of what the thing is. So that would be very anxiety inducing."

"It was very hard. It was almost enough to induce a panic attack," I said.

In this case, an ancient evolutionary adaptation showed up to interfere with the production of usable data.

On another occasion, I was a volunteer in an experiment about "attention and impulsivity" in which my performance would be compared to other subjects. I was told to look at the white dot in the middle of the screen. Then I would see striped rectangles appearing to the right or left of the dot and they would blink. I was told to press the R or L key to say on which side the stimulus, the striped rectangle, appeared. This sounded easy, but there were also empty rectangle shapes popping in and out, which confused me. I was given a practice run and did not do well. But on the first block of tasks I got 97 percent right, and the research assistant said anything over 90 percent is no problem. As the experiment went on, the empty rectangles appeared randomly, sometimes over the striped rectangle and sometimes not. Finally, during a short break, I asked if I was supposed to look at the striped boxes? No, I was told, look at the white dot but "focus on the striped stimuli." Now doubly confused, I translated: "You mean focus on the striped stimuli with my peripheral vision?"

"Yes."

The stimuli only appeared for a second, if that. The speed threw me at first, and I was surprised that I had to react so fast. To do well, I had to constantly tell myself to pay attention and slow down. I had to concentrate and actually think before reacting and to deliberately separate the task into steps: see, think, press. If I managed to do this, I would get most of them right. A few times I got 100 percent, and the grad student gave me a thumbs-up. There was definitely positive reinforcement for good performance going on! I was left wondering whether it mattered to the data whether the subject divided the task up as I did. I used a kind of mental discipline to improve my performance, which was my way of deliberately paying attention. Attention was the topic of the experiment, but despite their efforts to delimit what influenced my attention, the main thing affecting it was my desire to get a good score. That in turn impelled me to devise a mental crutch I would ordinarily never use to score well. Only the time it took me to respond correctly or incorrectly got into the data. My mental crutch was invisible. But it was powerfully present anyway, an active participant in the experiment that might have perturbed the results.

Conversation as a Technology

Because EEG and fMRI devices are made of metal, wire, and chips, run on electricity, are integrated with software on powerful computers, and produce quantitative information, no one would hesitate to call them technologies. In my own field, I had been trained to consider the spoken word, together with gestures and expressions, as a kind of technology with which to detect different peoples' understandings of the world. In particular, I learned to value conversation, where more than one person is interacting, prodding, confounding, debating, agreeing, or joking. Did my psychology interlocutors find conversation useful at all? The one time a PI in my fieldwork pointed directly to psychological research as a "conversation," he was not talking about experiments but about the presentation of experimental results in a poster at a conference. Dr. S explained that a poster is very much a conversation in which collaboration is born, questions are asked, praise is given, doubt expressed, or interest articulated. As I myself observed at conferences, poster presenters hone a short talk to explain the carefully chosen and formatted charts, graphs, and text on their poster. Freewheeling conferees gather around the speaker, coming and going as they please. If they arrive in the middle of the talk, they simply wait until some listeners leave and the poster presenter starts all over again. I often saw researchers from different countries exchange contact information with the speaker or each other, sign up to receive an electronic copy of the poster, or propose comparative collaborative research projects.

But on other occasions I thought opportunities for conversation were being disallowed. Wade was doing his first experiments with participants, who either did or did not have knowledge of a second language written with a non-European alphabet. The experiment was to take place in two sessions a few days apart. In a lab meeting after the first session, Wade mentioned that participants had commented about "capital letters" after the first session of his experiment. Since there are no capitals in non-European alphabets, he was trying to understand why subjects were seeing them. But the lab members were not pleased. Wade recounted to me the negative remarks people made in the lab meeting: "Lab members said, 'What do you mean? What are subjects saying? What are you asking?'" His answer: "Well, you know, I was asking them how it seemed because I'm just curious. I like to know what they think they were doing." The response from the lab members was, he said, "Don't ask."

> They were like "no!" I guess I was trying to see—one, just to be sociable in hopes they will return for the second session, and then, two, to kind of inform myself. I was wondering what the subjects think may be going on. The lab's caution to not do this might have been coming from the idea that subjects' intuitions can be very wrong and things like that. So, I think they were saying there's no point in asking, like just don't bother, kind of.

Wade thought the message was that he shouldn't talk to participants at all, and in fact I think this was the intended message. He thought the lab was concerned about keeping the conditions of each experimental session exactly the same for the sake of consistency.[7] Given that the experiment was still ongoing—continuing into a second session—every subject should hear the same thing in order to make different trials comparable.

Later I tried reframing the issue with Dr. R. I asked her whether it would be right to say that in Wade's initial experiments, some of the subjects' reactions were interesting to him, like the naive subjects thinking there were capitals when there couldn't be.

"Would it be right to say those responses could lead to further, more refined experiments even though they were not the point of the experiment?" I asked.

"Absolutely. Insights, information, whatever, come from wherever they come from," Dr. R explained. "We just take them when they come to us. Could be you could just have a dream, see it in your tea leaves, wherever it is, whatever happens. Of course, it's not like I can read tea leaves, but these sorts of things, they are potentially data. They are not maybe very well organized at that point. It is possible that one could have come to that conclusion by actually looking at the data we are collecting. But we haven't set out to look at that, so we could have missed it entirely. These are sorts of things we hadn't planned on, but they maybe were revealed in this sort of bottom-up way. There is a lot of stuff going on, and so you get your ideas wherever they come from, and paying attention to what your subjects tell you can sometimes set you off on some path."

"They will give you a clue?" I asked.

"They give you clues—that's why I love testing people myself, because there are clues and then you can pursue them and evaluate them in a more systematic way, and sometimes they turn into nothing but sometimes they turn into things. So, the answer to that is yes."

Given Dr. R's lab's focus on the neural locations of language, the clues she referred to would ideally have been ones that pointed indirectly to neural processes that subjects could not be conscious of.

Clues that subjects might provide about their unconscious processes are one thing, and clues about conscious processes are another. Anthropology is deeply indebted to conversations with people about their consciousness of the world around them. Wade was trying to include such conversations in his experiment in the face of a lot of doubt about their value. In spite of the general lack of conversational interactions with subjects in psychology labs today, a few psychologists in the 1960s were willing to investigate the conscious experience of subjects. For example, Saul Sternberg raised unconventional questions about the experimenter's relationship to the subject. Dr. B had suggested I read Sternberg's work. In one of Sternberg's experiments, subjects were asked to remember a short string of letters, such as "a, n, l, c, d." Then they were shown a single target letter and asked to quickly say "yes" or "no" to indicate whether the single letter was in the string of letters they had memorized. The results showed that the longer the string of letters, the longer the subjects' reaction times. Their reaction time increases were the same whether the target letter was present in the string or not. Sternberg concluded that this must mean subjects were doing a "serial-exhaustive" search, meaning they mentally scanned the string letter by letter all the way to the end before saying "yes" or "no." They were not performing a "serial self-terminating" search in which they would stop searching when they reached the target letter. Sternberg went further by asking his subjects how they had performed the search. Surprisingly, he found that not all subjects thought they had engaged in "serial-exhaustive" searches. "Perhaps because of its high speed, the scanning process seems not to have any obvious correlate in conscious experience. Subjects generally say either that they engage in a [serial] self-terminating search, or that they know immediately, with no search."[8] Sternberg's conclusions have been controversial and have inspired a wealth of literature both pro and con, including a recent paper he wrote as a "defense."[9] Insistently, Sternberg says that subjects' consciousness can be affected by the experimental design: whether they get feedback about their reaction times and their accuracy; whether they are given material rewards. He summarizes, "It is not clear how much to trust the data from studies that do not provide feedback and performance-based incentives, such as studies in which students are forced by a course requirement to serve as subjects."[10] For Sternberg, my conscious experience of using a "mental crutch" could be a factor to investigate, compare, and control, as part of the experimental design. I found it remarkable that Sternberg asked subjects explicitly whether the reported reaction times that he was measuring had a correlate in conscious experience.

I asked Dr. B, "what happened to that interest in conscious experience? I really want to know that."

"You've just been in some experiments that maybe take a little strategy, and the experimenter might ask you what you thought you did?"

"Something like that."

"Sometimes it's done," Dr. B explained, "but mostly it's not. It's data! Why isn't it considered data? It's not data because people are thinking somehow it's not data. But I don't know what happened to that. I think it may come back. I mean, now there's supposedly this push to understand the scientific basis of consciousness. But nonetheless it's almost disregarded. In the last experiment I did with the assistance of a grad student, we didn't ask anybody what they were doing. But the last experiment where I ran all the subjects myself because I didn't have an undergraduate assistant, I had great conversations with the subjects afterwards about what was going on. However, I don't think I included any of that reported data in the write up."

"I've seen that, too, during that little debriefing afterwards," I agreed. "Stuff pours out from subjects about what the experience was like, doing the experiment. And in one lab, I asked Wade, a grad student, if I could treat what subjects said after an experiment as my data, and he said, 'I cannot authorize you to notice anything they're saying, even though it is like a flood of stuff.'"

"I've designed an experiment and run subjects, but the experiment didn't go the way I wanted," Dr. B said. "And I would just ask subjects and they would say, 'Oh, yeah, this is what I'm doing.' And it would be different from what I intended. But you don't do that too much, and it doesn't get reported as data very much."

"That's what's so fascinating. Is it correct that if you designed the experiment well, it doesn't really matter what they think is going on?" I asked.

"It depends on how much you're interested in that, doesn't it?"

"Would you be interested in that? Say, a hypothetical situation where somebody is running a bunch of experiments, an experiment with a lot of subjects, and I was able to interview them, officially, about their experience, would that be interesting?"

"Going back to Sternberg, I don't know how to put Sternberg's original model into what people's subjective experience is, right? It could be that his model of serial-exhaustive search is wrong and it's really something more like what the subjects tell you, except for some other reason it showed this exact pattern of reaction times according to the model of serial-exhaustive search. Right? And it could be that the subjects are right, or it could be just there's not a lot of access to some mental operations."

Pursuing this thought, Dr. B added, "There are a lot of things you don't have conscious access to, for example, color constancy. When the light illuminating an environment is really red, this shirt, for example, will still look blue. In different light, then it might look pink or purple. There's plenty of processes that we know you don't have access to, but that doesn't mean that it isn't an interesting question. We were trained *not* to be phenomenologists. But that's stupid."

"Well, you have a lot of wisdom along these lines," I said.

"If I was learning about crab endocrine systems, my intuitions wouldn't help me very much," Dr. B continued. "But my intuitions would help me understand my human subjects. And my intuitions may be totally wrong; in fact, they usually are wrong. But there's nothing wrong with keeping track of them as data."

Dr. B was the most adventuresome of my interlocutors, ranging widely and willingly beyond the standard boundaries of the discipline. Calling his discipline stupid for ignoring phenomenology is about as gutsy a response as I could have imagined. Dr. R was younger and more dedicated to the norms of the discipline, despite the originality of her research topics. I spoke with Dr. R and Karen after my own experimental run in the fMRI.

"So at any point in any study anywhere along the line does anybody ask the participant what it was like for them going through the machine?"

"We don't," Dr. R said firmly.

Karen chimed in. "Informally, I guess. Every now and then at the end we'll be like, 'Well, how was that?' And the common response is, 'I'm pretty tired now' or 'It was boring.'"

"Some people do what's called a debriefing where they very systematically explain to you a lot about the research," Dr. R said. "And they have a series of questions that they ask you because they want to know certain things. They might be worried about certain biases you might have. It's not unusual to do that."

"Yeah, but what would the *goal* of that be?" I asked. "I mean why would someone else do that debriefing thing?"

"Well, sometimes people might have some kind of deception or manipulation they did that you didn't know about—I mean, not an immoral deception or anything. But maybe you were looking at words, and that was fine, but what they were manipulating, let's say, was your response to food words. There's nothing about the instructions that had anything to do with food or food words. But unbeknownst to you—at least not specifically told to you—every so often there were food words. And maybe the order in which the food words appeared was relevant for some hypothesis they were testing. Or maybe food words always appeared right before an emotion word—'angry'—or something like that. They could have some kind of thing they're trying to do."

"Some little subterfuge of some sort?" I guessed.

"That's right. And that's really what the experiment is about. And maybe it's important for them that you were not aware of it. And so then in the debriefing you might ask the subject, 'Did you notice anything about the words that were presented?' 'Did you notice anything about words that tended to be presented together?' And then the participant might say, 'Oh yeah, I saw that every once in a while, there was a food word. And I realized after a while that before a food word there was always like an angry word or something.' And so, then the researchers might say, 'Well, let's not look at your data' or 'We'll treat your data separately.' So that would be a reason to debrief."

The main reason consciousness is irrelevant in experiments is, as Dr. B said, "there are a lot of things you don't have conscious access to." But he also acknowledged that he was interested in the question. "Suppose it comes out that people don't have access to actually how they remember things," he said. "Well, that's interesting."

Whenever I heard comments from other subjects, either muttered while in an experiment or expressed during a post-experiment debriefing, I felt this might be important material. But I was ethically not allowed to take note of any of it. This material was not included in the IRB agreement of any of my labs, so I could listen but not treat these things as data. The words went into the ether (unless a lab person like Wade told me about them during an interview) even though they could have been important to improving the data from the experiment or the comfort of the subjects.

Publication as a Technology

So far I have focused on the difficulties of harnessing technologies for specific purposes: not knowing whether a signal is exciting or inhibiting, having to help the signal emerge from noise, contending with perturbations from subjects' movements, or making do with increased blood flow as a sign of neural processing. Given all this, one might wonder what actual contributions these techniques are able to make to our knowledge of how the brain or mind

works. If we remember that most cognitive processes of interest in experimental psychology are not accessible to conscious awareness, then all information
about the location or timing of cognitive processing in the brain is a significant
new contribution to knowledge. Through a great deal of experimental effort,
psychologists have determined from the EEG that as the milliseconds pass by,
certain times (100 milliseconds, 300 milliseconds, 400 milliseconds) are associated with particular kinds of cognitive activity. At 100 milliseconds, the
brain is processing low-level data like seeing or hearing; at 300 milliseconds,
it is processing higher level functions like decision making; at 400 milliseconds, it is processing unexpected novel information. So, experimenters can
design experimental tasks or stimuli that sort out when a response is detected
and therefore what kind of cognitive processing is going on. A classic EEG/
ERP (event-related potential) study in 1980 by Marta Kutas and Steven Hillyard, for example, showed that a novel semantic stimulus ("he took a book out
of the dog") produced a large response at 400 milliseconds, while an ordinary
semantic stimulus ("he took a book out of the library") did not. Hence the
experiment could show that the response at 400 milliseconds involved higher-
level semantic processing.[11] This was important because it demonstrated that
a longer delay was evidence of more complex cognitive processing.

In fMRI research about where cognitive activity is located, a 2001 study by
Paul Downing and colleagues showed that *specific areas* of the brain activate
more strongly in response to images of body parts than to any other objects.[12]
Perhaps this showed that the brain is modular, with specialized locations for
specialized stimuli. Further research by James Haxby and colleagues (also in
2001) showed that the *pattern of activation* in certain broad regions of the brain
correlated with images of different kinds of objects (faces, houses, cats).[13]
Thus research could progress from the idea that the brain is modular (specific
brain locations process specific stimuli) to the idea that cognitive processing
is overlapping and distributed.

Randall tried to give me a sense of what it means to get from the moment
when the subjects walk out of room to being able to use their data.

The gap is huge, and we have to devote a lot of time to this. When you read
any published paper, *none* of this stuff is ever written about. Of course, there
is a huge section on method, and it will detail a little bit about how your
physiological response or brain data was processed. Because we are interested in these waveforms, we tell you which waveforms enter in, how we
got them, and how we created our averages. But those steps between getting

data from output to readable format no one ever describes. And there are lots of ways to do it, so shedding light on this needs to be done. Wouldn't this be insightful for you and your audience!

In describing the "huge section on method," Randall is alluding to the strict rules for publishing papers in psychology journals included in the frequently updated *Publication Manual of the American Psychological Association*. The rules dictate precisely and in great detail the form and content of the thirteen expected sections of a published paper, from title to appendixes. Information about participants is required, but only at the level of demographic variables: gender, age, race, education, and so on. The elaborate recipe for publication runs to 272 pages in the Sixth Edition.

I felt strange when I realized that my interest focused on a part of psychology experiments that is not included in the final published articles. If what I saw as an ethnographer does not count as knowledge for the science of psychology, what use is it? Perhaps the obstacles to a published result, including what Randall called "the gap," could be seen as handrails on the steps of knowledge. You can climb the stairs without holding on, but you would be missing important parts of understanding how scientific knowledge is produced. Psychology as a discipline may have contributed in some ways to the dominant view of human beings as individuals acting to pursue their interests without reference to their social worlds. As I described in chapter 1, I have found that the life of experimental psychology up to the point when an article appears in print is, ironically, filled with complex relations between subjects and researchers, between researchers and their technology, and among researchers. Omitting all these relationships from publications leaves us with the impression that individual responses from subjects demonstrate the universality of human cognitive features. However, putting social relationships back in the picture of how knowledge is produced helps restore the complexity of the contexts in which human cognition is studied.

Precisely because the psychology lab is so full of social relationships, the ethical concern for teaching students how to reckon with what their tools can do well and what they cannot do well has been built into the ordinary course of training in classes, seminars, and lab meetings. In the labs, many research agendas coexist, but they all share the goal of illuminating universal aspects of how the human brain functions, how it understands, remembers, appreciates, or learns. Such delimited theoretical goals are no doubt put under pressure by the imperative to obtain grant funding in order to carry out research and support students. Researchers might be forced by practical necessity to accept funding from the military or from corporations like Google, even though such funders might demand concessions driven by the desire to make a profit or acquire new customers. But the shared value placed on basic research questions about universal features of human cognition makes it incumbent on labs to insist that students learn both what their technologies can do and what they cannot do. The scrupulous attention of experimental psychologists to the capacities and limitations of the EEG, the fMRI, and behavioral studies could serve as a model of such an ongoing inquiry about the capacities and limitations of new and emerging technologies. In particular, their attention to the limitations of technologies could be a model for describing the limits of the algorithms active in digital media, which we will encounter in chapter 11, and in which our lives are now embedded.

6

Stabilizing Subjects

The experimenter "controls the conditions." He does not let things happen at random; in the ideal experiment he has all the factors under his control that have any influence on the process to be observed.

—ROBERT WOODWORTH, *PSYCHOLOGY*, 1921

LOOKED AT from the vantage point of the last three chapters, experiments in psychology bring together a bundle of loosely coordinated elements. Participants, neurons, and devices need to be domesticated, as it were, to be tamed by being delimited in their ability to emit data toward a common goal. But there is one part of the picture missing from this vantage point. That is the overarching emphasis on "control." Ideally, as many independent variables as possible should be carefully "controlled." Physicists study the interaction of quarks within atoms; chemists study the interaction of atoms within molecules; biologists study the interaction of molecules within cells. The striking thing about experimental psychology is that humans are the object of observation. While it is easy to imagine that atoms, molecules, or cells could be observed under controlled conditions in the labs of physicists, chemists, or biologists, it is not so easy to imagine how human beings could be observed under controlled conditions. What people bring into a psychological experiment is immensely variable: Where did you grow up? What languages do you speak? What kind of schooling did you have? How is your health? Who is in your family? What are your life goals? How do you feel? Just for a start.

Yet, to be valid, the experimental setting must provide a context in which people do occupy identical physical spaces and carry out carefully controlled identical tasks. In my fieldwork, I was on the lookout for what objects and practices might be enabling the researchers to compare all those different people who become subjects, presumably bringing with them a great variety of cognitive and emotional states ranging from obsession to complacency, curiosity to boredom, anxiety to calm. I imagined that comparisons across individuals would depend on stabilizing and controlling (at the very least) space, time, and motion. I was hard put to envision how psychologists accomplished all this.

Stabilizing the Subject in Space

For experimental psychology, the development of the means of stabilizing subjects in space began in the early history of psychophysics. Historically, a simple method of holding the subject's head still in space was the bite board, which was used by Helmholtz in his nineteenth-century biophysical experiments on vision and was reiterated in twentieth-century American college psychology labs. I first noticed a drawing of a "bite board" in Edward Titchener's widely used early twentieth-century American textbook for college psychology. This drawing was an exact replica of Helmholtz's illustration, published in 1868. Helmholtz needed to have exact control of the subject's head and used the bite board for this purpose. The board was coated with a sticky substance that would take an impression of the individual subject's teeth. The subject would bite the board and hold steady until the impression was set. (Helmholtz specifies only *Schellack* for the sticky substance, which seems improbably permanent. He might have meant sealing wax, which contained shellac as an ingredient at the time.) Ewald Hering followed Helmholtz's technique a year later in 1868 and explicitly added the goal of stabilizing the subject in space:

> The lacquer is softened with warm water and then the little board is grasped with the teeth so that both rows of teeth from above and below make an impression in the lacquer. Every time one again bites the board with the teeth, the latter come exactly into the old impressions and the small board will always have exactly the same position with respect to the head.[1]

Helmholtz designed the bite board to investigate something about the anatomy of the eye: When the subject looked diagonally to the side and down, could the eye cyclorotate? That is, could the eye rotate clockwise and counterclockwise while not looking straight ahead?

In Helmholtz's experiment, the subject was supposed to focus on a black strip of paper on a gray background. When the subject looked away, he would

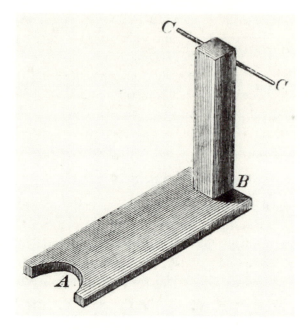

FIGURE 6.1. Helmholtz's bite board. From Helmholtz (1867), p. 517.

continue to see an afterimage of the black strip. As he focused his eyes to the left or right, up or down, the afterimage stayed horizontal. But if he turned his eyes (not his head) obliquely to the upper right or left, or lower right or left, the afterimage *rotated*: thus, proving that cyclorotation of the eye does occur. This is why Helmholtz had to hold the subject's head steady: when the subject kept his head still, Helmholtz could be sure that the rotation of the afterimage was caused by the eye cyclorotating rather than by the head moving.

For Helmholtz, the eye was a measuring device, which, as he showed, followed the rules of existing optical devices of the time.[2] In his experiments he used a simple "cross" (a plus sign) as a reference point from which to measure how the eye moved.

It was where the subject focused his vision in response to the experimenter's instruction that determined where Helmholtz would place the cross as a reference point for the subject's visual experience. For Helmholtz, the subject himself determined the fixation point depending on where his eyes naturally came into focus on something. Later, similar crosses would come to be used as the subject's "fixation point," but its meaning changed entirely. In current

FIGURE 6.2. A fixation point. Drawing by Kara Healey.

experiments, the experimenter, not the subject, determines the location of the fixation point. It is now set where the experimenter wants the subject's eye to focus.

Almost all experiments I witnessed or participated in used a fixation point. In illustrations of the method used in published papers and in PowerPoint presentations, the fixation point is shown just as it would be to the subject: in between tasks or blocks there is a slide or a portion of a slide with a cross, like a plus sign. Usually the fixation point is white on a black screen.

One day I was serving as a control subject for my age group in Dr. R's lab. Her lab assistant, Liz, sat me down and instructed: "Please focus on the fixation point. We are interested in your reaction time, so be as fast as you can without sacrificing accuracy." This was unusual. Usually nobody mentioned the fixation point. Indeed, no one but me thought it was interesting! When I asked about it, people said, "Oh, it is just to prevent subjects from looking around all over the place." Later, Dr. S told me he found this answer to be pretty offhand. He said,

> In visual perception research, it really is used to make sure the subject is looking precisely at the point where the two arms of the plus sign intersect. This defines the visual frame of reference for the presentation of other items, much like a Cartesian coordinate system is used to define locations of points in geometrical space. In some experiments it's really important to know the precise location of the stimulus (like in a study of color perception in peripheral vision).

What in one lab is casually taken for granted as something subjects will generally look at, in another is a means to a precisely aimed gaze.

In one of Dr. R's lab meetings, Wade, the first-year graduate student, was explicit about the use of fixation points, telling the group that between each pair of stimulus letters there was a fixation point. Later I told him how interested I was in the history of this device and asked him what he thought it was for. He said, "It's so that everybody would be looking at the same spot and the subjects are able to be compared." In the many experiments in which I have been a subject, very few experimenters explicitly say to subjects: look at the fixation point when it appears. One time, in an ongoing experiment I was observing, I asked Rob, the graduate student in charge, what the fixation point was for. Only then did he tell the subject to look at the fixation point. Rob explained, "I should have said something but for most people if you have a dot or a cross then that's what they are going to look at, but if you have nothing then they will look all over the place." Dr. S later confirmed that in attentional research the cross is considered a "pull cue" that "summons" attention to the center of the cross automatically.

Just how important the spatial stabilization of the subject was became clear to me in another of Rob's experiments. I was riding the bus with him to conduct an fMRI experiment at the university medical school. I wondered how he would stabilize the subject's head in the fMRI.

"They put something in between your head and the machine; one machine has a half dome that your head goes into, and it's pretty snug, but they might add some foam. We can look," he said.

I interjected, "My textbook shows various ways to stabilize the subject, including an individually crafted mold."

"I wouldn't mind that," he said, "it sounds confining. But if I *could* move my head, then I would have to think too hard about not moving my head. It's claustrophobic, or worse."

"Does this matter to your data?" I asked.

"You want to minimize movement, like to not have movement at all, but you don't want to make the subject uncomfortable. But we are already making them uncomfortable and bored! So maybe if they were more uncomfortable they wouldn't fall asleep! They will fall asleep when they have no task, when we want them to just keep their eyes open and pay attention. It's really hard. I have all this data, and I assume everyone is the same, but when I look back at my notes I see, this person was sleepy."

"You tell from the way they behave in the scanner?"

"We usually don't look. Usually we tell from some behavior like blinking a lot, or if they are slightly disoriented afterwards when you talk to them."

Soon I was with Rob in the control booth facing the fMRI machine, which was on the other side of a glass wall. I felt it was a rather surreal scene because the monitor we were watching showed the person in the scanner on one half and live TV on the other. There was a CNN crawl with the current news flashes: the White House's email had been hacked, the stock market plunged and recovered. On the monitor we could see the subject, who introduced himself as Malik, lying down in the scanner with his head held by foam pads and his feet facing us. We could see any movement he made and how he was handling the buttons. It was strangely intimate and objectified at the same time. There lay the subject stabilized in a tube with his gaze focused on one point in space while we observers saw him from the point of view of the soles of his feet. Inside the fMRI scanner, Malik was immobilized and encased in one location in space. Outside, in the control room, observers could switch between viewing his fixed location and viewing events all over the world. This difference in the extent of what we could see seemed to make Malik's confinement even more striking.

This was a study that depended on locating different visual regions for each subject. Therefore, each subject had to begin with a "reference scan," which would map where the visual portion of his or her brain activated under controlled stimuli. If the subject moved during the rest of the experiment, another reference scan would be required. When Malik's reference scan was finished, Rob told him, "Next you will see faces, scenes, and objects, also scrambled objects. Just try to stay awake and pay attention."

"Ok," Malik said.

But a moment later, Rob cried, "Oh no! We have to do another reference scan! He picked his head totally up when he said ok!"

A few moments later, Rob said, "I think he's got an itch; he just lifted his head again." Rob asked the technician to "talk to him and see if he is ok."

"Do you have an itch or anything?" the technician asked Malik. "Just try to keep your head still for the next twenty minutes."

"So do another reference scan," Rob said resignedly.

Keeping the subject still enough for an fMRI reference scan requires not only the help of the foam pads in the machine, but the determined concentration of a willing subject. Every delay costs time and money and risks breaching the limits of the subject's ability to cooperate.

FIGURE 6.3. View of a subject in the fMRI scanner while onlookers see his brain,
his prone body, and a current show on CNN. Photo by author, 2013.

Keeping a subject still in space comes at a premium because every subject has to be kept immobile in the same place so the data from all subjects can be compared. Human subjects cannot be drugged or harnessed as animals can. They cannot be "fixed" as cells and bacteria can. Their position is not solely determined by the laws of physics as the stars are. They make things difficult by having itches, being tired and sleepy, or by being bored and not following instructions. Lying very still for twenty minutes, hard as that is to do, is a challenge that subjects are called upon to meet.

Seeing how hard it was for Rob to keep his subject still, I wondered if there were any contemporary equivalent to Helmholtz's and Titchener's "bite board" with its sticky wax, which came close to a physical harness. I talked with a psychologist, Dr. M, who told me he still uses a contemporary version of the bite board, namely a chin rest, in some of his experiments.

Surprised, I asked, "But am I right that, today, in most experiments, the subject just sits in front of the monitor, and you just assume that they're going to look at the fixation point?"

"It depends on how important it is to know exactly where the person's eyes are," Dr. M replied. "So, if it's not that important, and you just want people to be paying attention to the screen, you might put a fixation dot or cross up there, just to make reasonably sure that they're looking where you want them to look. If it's really important exactly where in the visual field the stimulus is going, you may do something to fix the head, at least use a chin rest or maybe even use a bite board," he elaborated. "And you may use an eye-tracker to monitor their position. It just depends on how important it is for what you're doing. Sometimes it really doesn't really matter that much. Other times it does.

"So, you know, one of the patients we're testing has different perceptual issues in different parts of his visual field. So, we use a chin rest with him and a fixation point and, you know, occasionally, we monitor with an eye-tracker. And the other thing we do is present stimuli briefly enough that he doesn't have time to move his eyes away from the fixation point while the stimulus is still on."

Dr. M thought a chin rest would be needed "if you presented things displaced to one side or the other of fixation. In studies of split-brained individuals you need to control which hemisphere visual information was going to. You would typically have them fixate centrally and then flash something briefly in the left or right visual field, so you could be pretty confident that the stimulus was going just to one hemisphere." I recalled my own behavior in an experiment where stimuli appeared in my peripheral vision. I had felt like a disgrace of a subject at the time because I failed to keep looking at the fixation point. Now I had a glimmer of understanding about why stabilizing my gaze would matter.

The striking historical change from Helmholtz's time is that today the subject is given a fixation point which is by definition the point he or she is supposed to deliberately focus on. "Making reasonably sure" the subject is looking at the fixation point depends on subjects who have learned to play the subject role by doing what seems obviously desired by the experimenter. My experiences made it clear that control over subjects has exceedingly fuzzy lines around it. Even a subject with the strongest will in the world and no obsessive oppositional tendencies in play can cause expensive additional reference scans and emit useless data because they are inattentive or asleep. As researchers well realize, asking a subject, usually an undergraduate student who is overworked and under time pressure, to lie down and not move in the dark on a bed, while performing tasks that have no known purpose—without falling asleep—is a challenging request.

Stabilizing the Subject in Time

Fixation points and head cushions aim to control the subject in space, but experimental psychology also depends on control of and precise measurement of time. Stabilizing the subject in space is only the start; the instruments that record the time when data is produced must be exceptionally accurate. Rob suggested that I ask Dr. M about the days before computers, when researchers used the tachistoscope to achieve accuracy in the timing of events in an experiment. I learned that the tachistoscope was devised in the mid-nineteenth century to provide an accurately timed exposure of a visual stimulus.[3] The name is from the Greek words *tachisto* and *scope*, meaning "speedy viewing." Originally, a weight pulled by gravity lowered a strip of paper on which a visual stimulus (a word, say) would appear briefly between two metal plates. In between the metal plates there would be a fixation point, where the subject was asked to focus his eyes. Asking the subject to focus on a fixation point means the researcher is controlling the parameters of the experiment because she is interested in visual perception. As I mentioned, this was a change from Helmholtz's time, when subjects were supposed to control the position of their eyes because the researcher was interested in the physics and physiology of eye movement. This was a shift of major proportions. Historians Ruth Benschop and Douwe Draaisma astutely point out that after the mid-nineteenth century, "psychology presented itself not as being about the visual, but as using the visual to do something else." They are referring to James Cattell, an American student of Wilhelm Wundt, who explained the shift exactly: "You know that what I want to do is to find out how fast we think." Benschop and Draaisma say that psychologists of the time thought vision was only one route to understanding mental processes: "The eye is but one of the senses that may be stimulated for the investigation of the duration of mental processes." Accordingly, Cattell described the aim of his experiments as "looking to determine the relation between the intensity of the stimulus and the length of the reaction time," thus bringing mental processes studied by any means into the forefront.[4]

Until the advent of the computer, innumerable versions of the tachistoscope were invented and used. Devices to regulate the temporal interval between different stimuli used everything from rollers to bicycle wheels. They seem ingenious and transparent: unlike today's electronic devices, you can immediately see the operation of the weights, pulleys, and wheels.

In the past, Dr. M had used an advanced version of the tachistoscope that had a light to illuminate the stimulus for a certain time. He told me,

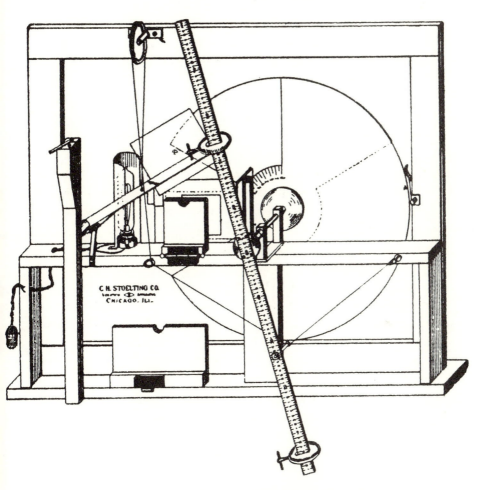

FIGURE 6.4. A tachistoscope, 1921. From Whipple (1921), p. 284.

The tachistoscopes, which we used before computers, were good in that you could pretty precisely time the presentation, the stimulus. You know, they had these light tubes that you could turn on and off with very good control. If you wanted a 10-millisecond exposure, you could get a 10-millisecond exposure. When we started using computers, then we got into the refresh rates of the monitors.

Since Dr. M could tell from my expression that I had no idea what he was talking about, he explained,

Monitors draw the stimulus from the top to the bottom of the monitor. And they only refresh the screen, say, every 16 milliseconds. So, you're basically dealing with increments of that. You had to be careful that if your stimulus was put up while the monitor was, you know, drawing down, and your stimulus was up high, then the monitor would draw all the way down and then come back up before it would get to your stimulus. That could introduce some error into when your stimulus was actually presented. You can get quite accurate timing with the computer, although there are issues you have to deal with, too. If you're having somebody press the keyboard, the computer may check every certain number of milliseconds to see if the key has been pressed, rather than the key producing an instantaneous response in the computer. So that would add some error to those measurements. If you need it [to be] more precise, you'd have to get it some other way than with the keyboard.

"So, was the tachistoscope more accurate than computers?" I asked.

"With the computer you get the data automatically recorded," he replied. "When I was first doing experiments, we had a little timer. And there were thousands of milliseconds and hundreds of milliseconds and tens of milliseconds and individual milliseconds. It wasn't even a digital display. It was a little circle, you know, like a clock position. There were little neon lights. It would light up at various positions, and you had to read it off there."

Dr. M's point was that with earlier technology, the psychologist had to literally record the subject's response time by hand. The experimenter had to note the reaction time on the timer and then record it accurately. Compared to using a standard computer and its monitor, the tachistoscope provided more accurate timing of events but less reliable recording of data. And it took far longer to collect the required data using the tachistoscope. Dr. M told me, "The main thing with using a computer though is you can do things so much more quickly. I was giving people pairs of words or simple sentences. I had to type them all out on a long strip of paper that was fed through the tachistoscope and it would take a couple of weeks to set up something that today I could set up in half an hour." A big gain in speed of research projects and reliability of recording data, at the cost of some loss of accuracy.

In today's experiments you cannot go far without learning about another temporal measurement of the subject that we have already encountered: reaction time. Wade, as a beginning grad student in Dr. R's lab, was trying to find his feet in the plethora of ways to measure his subjects' reactions in time. He let me in on the problem:

I've been going in circles, and I can't even tell you how many iterations I did of these things because you can look at the reaction times and the inverse reaction times and the raw reaction types or the adjusted ones. And then when you're doing this, starting to analyze it, you can either add in a constant so that it's a true equating metric or not, and then you can center the data or not. You can scale it to variance or not, and any combination of those. And I've done them all. So, I've got about 64 different sets of this data now. I just kept looking at all of them. I want it to be the best and I don't really know what's best, so I'm looking at everything that I can.

Not understanding any of the options he was considering, I managed to ask, "How do you pick the right one?"

The one that's most interpretable, and that's something I came to learn in this process. I think I had this idea that I'm really learning how to do science now and this is math, and so there's a right way. And then—at the end of the day it's still about interpretation. It's about building a story around what you get out of these measurements. And there's all kinds of methods for doing this. I'm asking people, well, what method is best? They tell me, 'Oh, just try some.' I guess if you assume that there's [a] kind of order in the universe, I think the idea is the structure is there in the data.

I felt the hair on the back of my neck stand up when Wade told me his research was about interpretation, about building a story. I thought interpretation and storytelling were the property of the humanities, and of anthropologists in particular! I had confused the content of research with the form of writing used to communicate how and why it is important, an elementary mistake. I now saw that data about the structure of cognition could be arranged in narrative form with a strong story line, much as an ethnography can be.

Regardless of which story Wade will eventually tell, reaction time is likely to be central. Wade told me that each subject gets a standard reaction time test, so researchers can have an idea of how quickly the person reacts to a visual stimulus and compare that as a baseline to the experimental data. In his study of a non-European script, Wade said,

If the subject is familiar with the language, certain things about the orthography will slow their reaction time down. For example, if it is a letter whose position determines its form, that should take longer than otherwise. Or a subject familiar with the language will slow down over letters that have similar forms in other parts of the alphabet. Comparable phenomena in English might be how the letter "a" becomes "A" at the beginning of a sentence; or how in handwriting the letter "u" could be confused with the letter "w."

Wade ran himself as a subject and found that his reaction time was slowed down both when he read different shapes of a letter whose shape was determined by its position and when he read letters with confusingly similar shapes.

Reaction time is a numerical measurement of the difference between the moment the researcher presents a stimulus and the moment the subject makes a behavioral response to the stimulus. We wouldn't necessarily know from our experience which of our reactions were similar and which were not. So valid findings often depend on precise measurement of reaction time. To me reaction time seemed a very elementary kind of measure, partly because it has such a long history. Reaction time was the coin of the realm in the Wundt laboratory more than a century ago. How could reaction time have remained so salient more than a hundred years later? I went in search of an answer, and Dr. M provided one, which I have hinted at before:

> We're using time as some index of operations that are going on in your brain; the assumption is that the more time you take, the more computation is going on in your head, or the more complex the computation is that's going on in your head. In that sense, time is important to us as something we can measure, that we think sheds light on how the brain works.

Although the use of reaction time goes back to Wundt's lab and has remained a standard of measuring brain activity from the 1960s until today, it is not without skeptics. At a lab meeting where Wade presented his first project, he commented that the data were "all based on reaction time." It cannot be accidental that he made this comment after a conversation with me about the history of reaction time in psychology experiments. Then, an even newer member of the lab asked, "If the reaction time is longer in one task does that mean something different is going on there? And if the reaction time is not different, does that mean the same thing is going on?" Wade looked a bit unsure what to say. Finally, he said, "measurement of this component is quite subjective, we need a study of *it*!" The moment passed, but I made a note of it. Time and again my interlocutors joined my ethnographic inquiry in ways I found open and adventuresome. I doubt I could measure up to their open mindedness if an ethnographer questioned the basic methods of my field.

How Measuring Time Changed

Wade's open-minded approach led me to an additional question. I was fascinated with the large number of versions of the tachistoscope, which could rely on gravity or motors, pulleys, discs, or bicycle wheels, and were often named after their inventors: Whipple, Wirth, Gerbrands, and so on. Rob sent me his folder of significant scientific papers on the confusability of letters from the late 1800s to the 2000s. Evidently, psychologists have long wondered why some letters in the English alphabet are more easily confused than others, a question that is relevant for teaching students to read and making print media legible. Indulging my obsession with these devices to measure time, I paid close attention to how researchers described them in published accounts. From the beginning of such accounts to the present, the length of descriptions gets shorter and shorter.

In 1888, E. C. Sanford explained that his apparatus was so satisfactory that he would venture a "rather full description" of it. The letters subjects were to identify were set in a "dark box," and the description runs for many pages. This short section gives the flavor of the detail he provided, all for the purpose of assuring that the device could accurately reveal the time subjects took to recognize each letter:

> The dark box was of simple construction, about fifteen inches square and nine deep, and was set obliquely before the machine. The letters were pasted as before on a cardboard disk and were immediately behind a centimeter square opening in a black cardboard screen at the back of the box. The disk could be turned from behind through a hole in the box. The place of the letter was indicated by pinholes pricked near it; at first by four, later by three. The illuminating flash entered the box by a cardboard tube and fell on the letters at an angle of about 40°, while the subject looked perpendicularly upon them at a distance of sixteen inches. A certain quantity of extraneous light entered the box in various ways, sufficient often to make the white square about the letter dimly visible to eyes thoroughly accustomed to the dark, but never, of course, sufficient to disclose the letter.[5]

As if this painstaking level of detail were still not enough, the article included a photograph, a diagram, and pages of charts of stimuli and results.

By 1927, the tachistoscope had become more standardized, although it could still be designed in different ways, and H. Banister simply mentioned that he used one. However, he felt it necessary to detail the exact type of material the stimuli were printed on:

> The first experiment was carried out on two groups of adults. The letters were drawn with Indian ink on white mill board. Each letter, with one exception, lay within a rectangle measuring 25mm high and 20mm broad, and the lines forming the letters were 5mm wide. The exception, "I," measured 25mm by 5mm.
>
> The letters were exposed tachistoscopically in random order for about 0.019 second, by means of a slit 37mm wide in a falling shutter. A white fixation point on the shutter indicated where the exposure would occur.[6]

A year later, Miles A. Tinker piled on the detail in descriptions of his tachistoscope and its speed, the location of stimuli, and the posture of subjects in relation to the apparatus and the stimuli. A short excerpt:

> A Wirth disc tachistoscope was used for exposing the symbols. The disc was turned at the rate of 1 revolution in .45 second by an electric motor. The constancy of the speed was tested at different intervals throughout the experiment and was found to be very satisfactory. The length of the exposure was varied by opening or closing a window in the disc. The stimuli were viewed through a small window in a gray screen located in front of the disc. This screen was extended so that no part of the revolving disc could be seen in peripheral vision by the observer. In front of the screen was a small table carrying a headrest. By this provision the subject's eyes were about 15.5 inches from the stimulus material. The subject's elbows and the paper for writing down the exposed material rested on the table. Short lines were drawn at exactly the middle of the four edges of the window in the screen through which the stimuli were viewed. The point where these lines would meet if extended across the window gave the region of pre-exposure fixation. The stimuli appeared in exactly the center of the window.[7]

Looking back in time, we see that the researchers provide stunning detail in the descriptions of their experimental equipment: what kind of paper and ink they used, what the apparatus is made of, even where the subject sits and where he writes his reactions down. As noted above, as the decades go by, the length of these descriptions gets shorter and shorter. By 1969, Dennis F. Fisher and colleagues condensed relevant aspects of their apparatus into a few terse lines. Clearly more of the elements had been standardized:

- Black Chart-Pak "deca dry" upper case letters, Futura medium font 36 point
- Gerbrands two-channel tachistoscope
- White fixation cross composed of bisecting 5/8-inch lines, 1/16 inch thick[8]

Once computers took over from tachistoscopes, the amount of detail devoted to the apparatus continued to shrink. There might be information about one or another standard font and its size, and then, as Arthur M. Jacobs describes it in 1989:

Stimuli appeared on a VELEC VS display terminal using a fast P4 phosphor. Lighting conditions were photopic [bright] and were kept identical across subjects, as were screen brightness and contrast. The display background luminance was about 0.7 cd/m^2, and the stimulus luminance was about 70 cd/m^2. Stimulus presentation and data collection were controlled by an Acorn-BBC microcomputer. The subject's eye movements were recorded using a photoelectrical scleral reflection technique and analyzed in real time by the computer, which sampled eye position at a 100-Hz rate.[9]

Once the tools become standardized by manufacturers who could be trusted to ensure the consistency and reliability of their computer and monitor brands, the apparatus could become more of a black box. By 2001, it was just about enough to say, as Liu and Arditi do, "The letter strings were generated on a Silicon Graphics IRIS computer and were presented on a 15-inch Mitsubishi Diamond Scan color monitor at the highest contrast the monitor could deliver."[10]

Occasionally, specific details about the apparatus were added: subjects used a chin rest; a mask shielded all but the center of the screen. But computers quickly became so ubiquitous and so similar that it was no longer necessary to detail such matters as the glass on the display, the chair in which the subject was seated, or the keyboard used to register the subjects' responses. Informal conventions developed, as Dr. S told me: "Researchers eventually decided (by some sort of collective wisdom) that certain variables (like the size of the letters and time of exposure) do matter and that other variables (like the kind of chair subjects sat on) do not." Even details that could vary, such as the refresh rate of the monitor or the resolution of the display, did not need to be mentioned. The machine was now doing more of the work, as Dr. M explained.

But although many elements of the experimental setting were no longer explicitly described, they continued to function in important ways, as we will see shortly.

How Aesthetics Can Be Measured

Even as psychology labs tackled complex topics like people's aesthetic responses to different pieces of music, the accurate measurement of reaction time remained central. For example, Jim, a first-year graduate student in Dr. S's West Coast lab, told me about his senior thesis (completed at a different university under a different advisor), which he did in a lab focused on music cognition. He said that all the existing studies of the aesthetics of music "were focusing on the stimulus characteristics that might influence listening time." Following that tradition, the lab was "looking at variables like how long does someone listen to music, and what sort of factors influence the sensation of *groove*." Being a Baby Boomer academic from the East Coast, I looked puzzled, so Jim went on, "Groove basically is this feeling in music that makes you want to move your body. That's called groove, and my study is sort of the operationalization of groove."

Astounded at the reach of the experimental model, I exclaimed, "You can study groove experimentally?"

Trying to calm my astonishment, Jim added that the experiment "can be fairly systematic, it's not as sort of subjective as it seems. We're doing a lot of different groove projects, and my particular piece was looking at listening time. So, strangely enough, the amount of time someone listens to music isn't necessarily very well determined by how much they enjoy it. This is sort of strange, and it's something I think we've taken for granted. So right now, there is sort of a hunt in the lab for what the predictors of listening time will be, and how complex the interactions will be, but the news isn't in just yet on that."

"Is the experiment set up so that the subject determines their listening time and tells you?" I asked.

"Yes, basically they can just click a key when they want to stop listening," Jim replied. "So, there are potentially a lot of distractor variables. After every piece, we asked them if they were distracted and filtered out those who reported being distracted, but there is only so much we can filter out. And we're hoping to sort of refine that, so we have the least noise possible. But right now, we're just looking for something to stick out. We found a number of factors that have a very small influence, but they all seem to be mediated by enjoyment. So, everything contributes to enjoyment, and then enjoyment finally directly impacts listening time. But then again enjoyment only explains less than 20 percent of the variance in listening time. There is a lot left to find, and it might just be a lot of [statistical] noise, and it might be there is something very interesting there."

"Are you allowed to ask them?"

"Yeah, we ask them questions like 'why did you continue to listen?'" Jim explained. "Their replies are very specific. They'll say something like it reminded me of a time in the past, or a movie I saw, or they'll say the melody just seemed very nice. It's very high-level language, and it's very specific. And even if you tally them up they're all very different. Familiarity is mentioned a lot, and we can actually filter that out. Because we're interested in the stimulus characteristics rather than memories that might be tied to them."

Jim articulated the main tenets of the field: a focus on systematic, measurable, and hence comparable reactions, with the hope of finding something about the music itself that correlates with listening time. But introducing "groove" as the object of study required that the experimenter admit a great variety of experiences that were all "very different." In this case it is as if there is a large opening in an experiential box into which subjects pour their memories of the past, their associations with movies, and their experience of enjoyment. But so far, nothing stands out in the box. Using this material, an anthropologist could probably write an essay about what American college students mean by groove, but, as a psychologist, Jim has to find some formal properties of the music—its rhythm, loudness, pitch, or timbre—that could "operationalize" the feeling of groove, abstracted from the multitude of experiences participants reported, and that could account for the length of time they listened.

Stabilizing the Subject with Tables

As we have seen, it is clear from the history of technology in psychology that fixation points came to be taken for granted in the experimental setup, so much so that experimenters rarely call participants' attention to them. Perhaps one reason subjects don't need to be told about the fixation point is that there is another way in which subjects are held steady in space so that comparable data can be extracted from them. This modest stabilizing technology is the table.

Like the fixation point, a table is a technology that usually goes unnoticed in psychology experiments. The table has a crucial role—to stabilize people

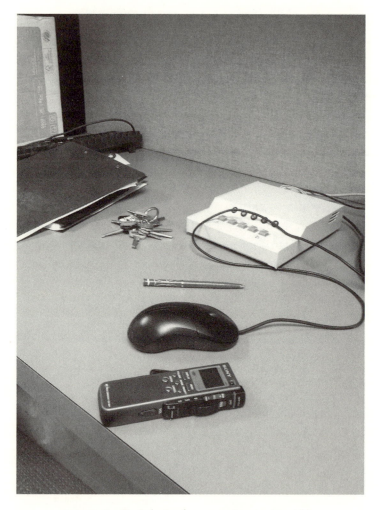

FIGURE 6.5. Typical setup for an experiment using a table.
Photo by author, 2013.

and things in space for a time. The table, with its chair, enforces a posture of attention to what is on it. It permits display and use of other tools and enables precise recording. It also allows the display of disparate materials on the same plane in space. Bruno Latour explained this, as he watched botanists in the field arranging soil and plant samples on tables: "Specimens from different locations and times become contemporaries of one another on the flat table, all visible under the same unifying gaze."[11] The flat plane provided by the table enables the abstraction of dissimilar specimens into categories.

Open and inviting as a table might seem, once you are sitting at it, for dinner or for producing data, certain forms of courtesy serve to hold you there. Alfred Gell famously described a hunting trap as a device that embodies ideas and conveys meanings because it is a "transformed representation of its maker, the hunter, and the prey animal, its victim, and of their mutual relationship, which [. . .] is a complex, quintessentially social one [. . .] Traps communicate the idea of a nexus of intentionalities between hunters and prey animals via material forms and mechanisms."[12] If the table can be thought of as a kind of trap to capture and contain a subject, it is a disarming one—it looks so placid and innocent, for something that has the potential to be a powerful constraint. The table is so embedded in the experimental context that it escapes notice, even though without it the stability of the subject in space and over time would be difficult if not impossible to achieve. Once it becomes evident that the table is an active artifact in the production of knowledge, new possibilities for opening up the nature of the experimental space in psychology abound. After our discussion of the table's role in experiments, Dr. B began puzzling about what it would take to conduct an experiment to study, say, memory outside the psychology laboratory. Could you do it in in a crowded coffee shop instead? This was disconcerting to him because leaving the laboratory would mean leaving a world of standard Steelcase tables, with its surfaces that are similarly flat, stable, and in one plane. The tables in a coffee shop might well be a hodgepodge of heights, shapes, and levels.

In my fieldwork, tables are ubiquitous. Tables, with their chairs, keep one's body in place. In all the experiments I participated in, the experimenter gave frequent and repeated instructions concerning tables: sit here at the table, pull your chair closer to the table, put your hand on the table, rest your hand flat on the table, arrange the keyboard conveniently on the table, etc. And of course, tables hold computers, monitors, keyboards, and recording equipment steady.

In the contemporary lab, the place of the psychological subject in relation to the equipment is not open for debate. The subject sits at a table and yields data to the machines. You might say that the fixation point is ancillary to the table. Early anthropological experiments also depended on tables to hold their equipment steady, at eye level, and off the ground. Photographs from the Cambridge Anthropological Expedition to the Torres Straits in 1898 make it clear that tables played an important role in the psychological experiments conducted by these early anthropologists.

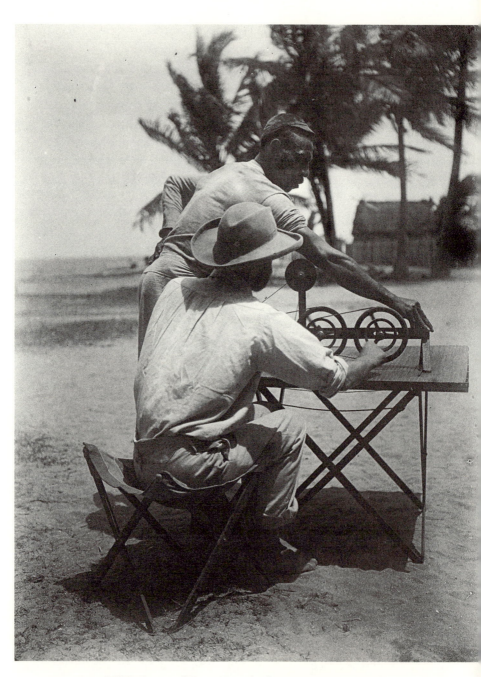

FIGURE 6.6. W.H.R. Rivers and Torres Strait islander Tom preparing to use the color wheel. Reproduced by permission of University of Cambridge Museum of Archaeology & Anthropology (N.23036.ACH2).

FIGURE 6.7. Claude Levi-Strauss in Amazonia in Brazil, 1936.
Image by Apic/Hulton Archive/Getty.

More recent anthropological work has also depended on tables, which were even used to create an island of French culinary civilization in the Brazilian rain forest. The photograph chosen to represent the ethnographic work of French anthropologist Claude Levi-Strauss in his obituary showed him in a Brazilian rain forest standing by a table made of sticks lashed together.[13] Anthropologist Laura Bohannan says that among the limited bits of advice given to her about how to do fieldwork in Africa was this: "You'll need more tables than you think," a remark she attributed to Evans-Pritchard, a founder of the field.[14]

Tables have also been used to corral thought, to guide the reader's mind along a certain course, as in the classic and often-quoted examples from Plato and Marx: everyday objects that illustrate the concept of a form for Plato or the concept of a commodity for Marx.[15] As usual, such objects do not determine their own use. "Table" is also a verb, as in the phrase "table it," in which the "table" holds items of business steady and unchanged in time. There are myriad practices in meetings involving tables of all kinds, which exert a certain force in governing how matters proceed. Think of referring to "what is on the table," "setting an agenda," "laying a question on the table," "taking a motion from the table," and so on.

By now you might be wondering why the graphic display of data enclosed in columns and rows is also called a "table"! It might have something to do with early scientific collections, arranged in flat boxes divided up into little square compartments. Or perhaps the table as a graphic form derives from the medieval practices of counting money on tables marked with squares. The table—as a piece of furniture with a flat surface and legs—and the table—as a display of facts in columns and rows—might both trace their genealogies to the Latin *tabula rasa*, literally "scraped tablet." The tablet was wax, and it could be heated and smoothed (scraped) to yield the literal origin of the epistemological "blank slate." Whatever the historical link between the two kinds of tables, they both remain intriguing forms of everyday technology, guiding and adjusting our posture and attention so that we can become, instead of blank slates, stable human subjects, in the classroom, at dinner, or in psychology experiments.

The list of techniques used to stabilize the human subject is long. For stabilizing subjects in space there is the bite board, the chin rest, the eye tracker, the fixation point, the firm request to hold still, the foam pads in the fMRI, and the table. For stabilizing subjects in time there is the tachistoscope and the computer, both focused on reaction time. The length of this list is a testament to the difficulty of ensuring that human subjects, with all their variability, can be studied under controlled experimental conditions. But from the perspective of an anthropologist trained in participant-observation, the most important, and ubiquitous, technique used by experimental psychologists for stabilizing subjects is the mundane use of a chair and table.

7

Gazing Technologically

Vision is the most developed and the most important of our senses, and much of our knowledge of the external world is gathered by using our eyes. Where you place your gaze and how you move your gaze is associated with what you pay attention to and can reveal how you behave, even what you think.

—TOBII.COM, 2020

SOCIOLOGIST MAX WEBER once made a striking claim. In his analysis of the ways modern forms of power regulate the details of everyday life in bureaucracies and impose the kind of planned order he called "rational," he pointed to the limits of "rational" control: "The calculation of consistent rationalism has not easily come out even with nothing left over." Over the years, this statement has sent me on numerous explorations of schemes that are meant to completely order people's lives or to collect complete sets of data about them, but that inevitably produce "leftovers." The leftovers are a kind of gap between the numerical measure produced by something like a performance metric and the more subtle, qualitative understanding of what people are doing.

In the history of music, there is an example that illustrates the concept of leftovers within rational schemes. Pythagoras, the early Greek philosopher, devised scales of musical notes based on harmonics, essentially mathematical ratios of vibrations per second. In time, this method produced an error, called the Pythagorean "comma," and it still plays a part in piano tuning. Therein lies a tale.

Pythagoras was enamored of whole numbers and of ratios of simple whole numbers. He had found that tones on the lyre sounded most harmonious when the ratio of string lengths formed a simple whole number fraction. For him, ratios of simple whole numbers represented harmony in music and in the universe beyond. Accordingly, he favored easy fractions that resolved in whole numbers. For example, a geometric theorem credited to Pythagoras states that in a right triangle, the sum of the squares of the two sides equals the square of the hypotenuse, or $a^2 + b^2 = c^2$. A common example, $3^2 + 4^2 = 5^2$, results in whole numbers. Similarly, when the harpsichord was invented in the Middle Ages, the Pythagorean method could produce the entire scale that the key-board could play at intervals of "pure" fifths. (Certain intervals are called "pure" because the ratios of their frequencies are simple ratios of the small integers 1, 2 and 3.) The note A below middle C is 220 vibrations per second; A above middle C is 440 vibrations per second. On the harpsichord, the notes an octave apart (A above and A below middle C) formed a small-integer ratio of 2:1 and sounded harmonious to its listeners. But when the piano was invented in the seventeenth century, a keyboard tuned to an exact pure fifth through all its octaves sounded discordant to its listeners because of its larger range. Both then and today, piano tuners have adjusted for this by adding a few more vibrations per second to each "pure" fifth. The difference between the frequencies of pure fifths and adjusted fifths is called the Pythagorean comma. The idealized, pure ratios that Pythagoras perceived as harmonious on the lyre and in the cosmos do not fit the perceptions of Euro-American listeners over the larger range of octaves on the piano. A ratio that requires larger integers sounds more harmonious to them.

"The Eyes Don't Lie"

Toward the end of my fieldwork, a newly accessible technology, digital eye tracking, was introduced in Dr. J's lab, which led me to think again about Weber's leftovers and the Pythagorean comma. Made by the Swedish company Tobii, the Tobii Pro came with many online instructions and in-person workshops. During my fieldwork, many of the workshops were open and free on the web. Their website provided ample testimony from numerous companies that have used eye tracking to improve how they market products: Facebook, Toyota, Google, Unilever, and more. Tobii eye tracking technology evidently could improve performance in marketing, athletics, factories, websites, mobile platforms, games, and software. According to Tobii, there is no "gap" between their eye tracking data and the world. Repeatedly they say, "The eyes don't lie," and "Eye tracking is part of our DNA." The computerized trace of a human eye focusing on an object shows directly and exactly what the person's retina is fixated on, for how long, how many times it arrives there, and by what path.

Capturing what the fovea of the retina fixates on is taken to be direct evidence of what the person is perceiving visually. In turn, the measure of time a person spends looking is supposed to indicate something about the person's cognition such as attention, interest, or attraction. Naturally, I was a little dubious about the lack of any gap, any "comma."

In the Lab with the Eye Tracker

During a lab meeting, we got the news that Dr. J had purchased eye tracking equipment at considerable expense. I asked Randall if he would show me how it worked. I had been following Randall's research on repetitive negative thoughts (RNT) for some time. He had already done behavioral research and EEG research: eye tracking was to be his final research method. He took me to the booth where the equipment was set up, looking like nothing more than a monitor, keyboard, desk, and chair, but with an especially large computer tower. Just outside the booth was another table and chairs with another monitor and keyboard. That is where I sat with Randall. With apologies for the glitchy nature of the new system, Randall led me through a video recording of a grad student trying out the new eye tracking experiment. "So, what you're looking at here is the graphical user interface of the screen that the person was seeing in the booth. And this software, Tobii Studio, is able to superimpose eye tracking data onto the image that the student was looking at. I can virtually see what they were looking at," he said. He showed me how circles represent spots on the screen where the subject's eyes fixate, and how the circles grow larger as the subject's eyes linger in one spot. Straight lines show how the eyes move from one spot to another. What are called "gaze maps" can be static images of these circles and lines or videos of circles and lines developing over time.

"This is somebody's attention, so to speak, their focus?" I asked.

"Yes, she's reading instructions, and you can see where she's actually looking, and now she's doing a practice session, practice questions, in a general knowledge test." As we watched the video, her test question appeared: "What is hot molten or semifluid rock that erupts from a volcano or fissure?" She typed "lava." Randall explained that we could see how she was actually looking at the spot where she was typing "lava," "because the circle around the word "lava" grew larger as she remained fixated on that particular spot. As soon as she moved her eyes, you could see a line going to that new spot. "And a small circle will appear, and the circle will grow as she stays fixated on that spot. So, it's really cool." I agreed with Randall that the technology is a marvel. He elaborated, "It's such an elegant way to study attention, and very easy, nonin-vasive, nonobtrusive." From my later experience of being a subject sequestered in the booth, I can report that the experience is noninvasive (compared to an fMRI) and easy (the instructions are clear to a fault). Whether it is nonobtru-sive I am not so sure. The latest eye trackers accommodate a large range of head and body movement. As a subject, you can move around in your seat or even shift the position of your chair, so Tobii seems less confining than EEG or fMRI. But the eye tracker could alter the experience if the subjects were ever to watch their own gaze maps. When I did a trial run of reading with Tobii tracking my eyes and then saw my gaze map, I was astounded and slightly hor-rified. Did I really move my eyes around the page that much? Did I look at words and paragraphs out of linear order and revisit the same words repeti-tively? I did not think I came across as a very efficient reader, and that doubt has stayed with me.

The video recording of the student's session had a timeline along the bot-tom of the screen, and Randall had programmed the software to place time stamps when there were "events of interest," such as the appearance of a ques-tion or a fixation point on the screen. Similar events could then be viewed comparatively, and their numerical scores could be averaged. Then different subjects could be compared: for example, those who had experienced an "induction" or manipulation to cause distraction and those who had not. From previous experiments, Randall knew that the induction for distraction would make some subjects less able to correct errors. When there was a dis-traction, this gave subjects a chance to dwell negatively and repetitively on previous negative feedback from wrong answers, which are programmed to happen more than half the time. But with Tobii he could go a step further, "to try and understand why they didn't correct those errors. You want to capture the mechanism of what's going on for RNT, not just the behavior. We want to try and understand the patterns of thinking and attention, and these sorts of things that may cause or mediate that effect." Where the sub-ject's eye is focused is a clue to complex psychological states like attention, and hence this technology could potentially add a new dimension to his previous research.

I said, "That is just astonishing," and Randall agreed, "It's very cool in con-cept." But the technique is not without difficulties. "Practically speaking, how to extract data, taking the data and converting it all to numbers, and being able to leverage this visual data and use it to say something is going to be a challenge." Randall showed me how the "areas of interest" he has programmed are visualized by Tobii. "Tobii tells me how often they spend time in this rectangular space versus that rectangular space. So, I've actually got to program an 'area of interest' or a hot spot, such that when the eye goes there the counter starts counting." How to determine the area of interest is not obvious. One metric Randall showed me was "first fixation."

> How long did it take to deploy? And then once they got there how long did they stay with their first fixation? Maybe they went all over the place and came back. Well, on average how many times did they go to this place? And overall what's the total sum amount of time that they spent on this area if they left and came back? And maybe they fixated on it four times? Well, you could also generate the average fixation time per fixation. There are a lot of different things you can do, which is great. And it is a challenge at the same time.

There seemed to be no known correlation between any of these innumerable possible measures and any particular mental state, brain state, or personality trait. Taking this in, I said, "It seems somewhat overwhelming!"

Pointing to the video recording, Randall illustrated the extent of detailed data that could be harvested. "This is the center of the screen. So, the student stayed on a word at the center of the screen for a half a second. And then she deployed her attention up to the top of the word, up here. After she was done up here at .28 seconds, it took her another .08 seconds to get up to the top of the screen. And then she stayed on that spot for .3 seconds."

Listening to himself recite the bewildering numbers, Randall sighed, "Well, so that's maybe not that interesting." Moving on to something that does matter, Randall got to the main point: "But what about total fixation? Okay, well in the end she actually fixated on this word at the center three times. Her first fixation was only for a third of a second. But she actually fixated on that word three times. And in total she stayed there 3.6 seconds." Randall's challenge was to figure out what patterns mattered and then to write a program that would "plug in and in some way extract these patterns from the data." He showed me a moment in the video recording when the subject seemed to look steadily at one spot. But Tobii reported the subject fixated at three locations, not one. "So now we have a problem, because visually it looks to me like they looked at one spot. So, what do I do?"

"Yeah, what do you do?"

"Right, it's a good point. If it doesn't really matter, why do I need to go down the rabbit hole? You know? I guess it's a good question. I don't know if it matters to be honest."

But then Randall introduced the black box: "There is some algorithm by which this system decides." He suggested we both focus on the cursor hovering at the center of the monitor.

> Now whether we know it or not, we would love to report to one another that we have not deviated from looking right there [indicating the cursor on the screen]. But you know that your eyes are just accustomed, whether by habit or just general physiology, to sort of deviate from that spot, especially the more I tell you don't move your eyes from that spot! So now imagine I'm asking you to focus right in the middle of the spot. Well, this system uses some algorithm to say, "Okay, if they're within this circle I'm going to call that the same fixation. If they deviate at all from a certain radius from the center point I'm going to call that a brand-new fixation." You see what I'm saying? And that radius could be arbitrary, but they don't let it stay arbitrary. It starts off as an arbitrary default, but then you or I as the experimenter can reset that. We can set it as this circumference, or [pointing to a larger area] as this circumference. Of course, the default is probably the best thing, because they've done enough research to suggest that your eye is going to have some jitter and fluctuation to it. And it's okay to consider that a fixation.

Randall's dilemma was how to determine what to choose as the limit of a single fixation. Should he go with what Tobii set as the default ("they've done enough research"), or is he supposed to change it? He led me back to the video recording of the student's session.

> Between you and me, this person is not even looking at the word "atheist." I mean, they're looking *above* the word "atheist." Or are they? What is the extent to which they would actually report they're looking right at this word, but the eye tracking data is saying that they're looking above the word? So herein lies another issue that I can't make sense of. I can't draw an area of interest that's literally right around the word because that jittering data won't get captured. So maybe I should make my [area of interest] a lot larger to allow for some error or variability in this data. So that's one issue, but another issue is why the heck is there variability? Isn't this system you know, the perfect $50,000 system that costs so much money that it's going

to be accurate? And I'm just learning that it's not as accurate as you want it to be. But it is close, you know.

We were looking at the gap between the inscrutable signals from the apparatus and Randall's attempts to make sense of them. Tobii says "the eyes don't lie," but Randall was realizing that Tobii had decided beforehand what the eyes will say and that the responsibility of changing Tobii's default falls on him.

Slightly lost in the gap, I said, "I report to you I'm looking at the word 'atheist.' But the software and the whole apparatus says that I'm looking *above* the word. Are you saying there is something wrong with the program? Or that my self-perception is off?"

"I'm saying that there is something wrong with the program, something wrong in that the eye tracker is unable to accurately represent where the person is actually looking," Randall said. "And there is reason to believe that most eye trackers are like this. When you are designing areas of interest, it's more ideal to choose areas that aren't wed too tightly to the word."

At a workshop offered by Tobii, another difficulty became clear. As Randall reported, "they said that the calibration procedure isn't always perfect. And that you may have to recalibrate. Tobii tries its best after a recalibration to accurately pick up the person's eyes." Calibration can be thrown off by many things: "There are droopy eyelids, there are squinting eyelids, mascara, long eyelashes, beautiful long eyelashes. There is coloration of the iris. There is wearing glasses, the lighting in the room." Whatever the perturbations, "The eye tracker needs to pick up two things. It needs to notice my pupil, the size of my pupil. And it also needs to notice a light—a glint—bouncing off my cornea."

Not sure what to think, I asked, "With all those sources of error, can the instrument still provide accurate data? Or is it our fault that we don't have the instrument set up properly?" Randall replied,

> I literally finally got the answer to those questions out of the mouth of one of the Tobii guys on the phone. He said, "You basically discovered that there are some people for whom you are just not going to get good data from the eye tracker." So, I was like, "Okay, just thank you for telling me." It's not a problem on our end. You're going to have to throw away some data. I'm like, "Okay, all right. I can breathe. I know that my work here is done." You know, I don't need to make the thing perfect.

Once he has confirmation that the problem lies in the abilities of the instrument, he can relax and enjoy Tobii as a kind of playmate. "It is really cool. I feel

FIGURE 7.1. Gaze map produced by an eye tracker. The size of the circles indicate how long the gaze rested in each spot. Image by Tobii AB.

like a little boy who is doing a science project in fifth grade and trying to test out whether the plant will survive in Coca Cola. It feels that way."

What Randall was showing me is that when he uses the eye tracker, he must make many decisions that seem arbitrary (the size of an area of interest) and accept the ground rules already built into the device (the algorithm for fixation). The device is not perfect at tracking the glint from the cornea because of normal variation among subjects or their environment. Randall relaxes when he finds out the device manufacturer admits the machine is fallible. Many gaps have opened up between a precise measurement of the path of the subject's gaze and what Tobii can actually do. There is clearly a gap between the subject's visual perception and what Tobii measures. When he found out that Tobii's abilities are less than perfect, Randall had to lower his expectations accordingly. According to Tobii, there is no "gap" between their eye tracking data and the world; the eye tracker is like a computerized human eye. Both see the same thing the same way, and the Tobii eye tracker has the added benefit of generating a digital readout of what it sees. But Randall found that the Tobii eye tracker was not a perfect proxy for human vision. The eye tracker needed Randall's help to set its parameters and direct its attention.

Randall's realization led me to a slightly different question. The gap between perception and the tracker's measurement made me wonder whether what is measured, accurate or not, could be related to more than "looking"? Randall wants to find the mechanism, the cognitive operations going on, like paying attention or being distracted. Attention could certainly be defined (somewhat arbitrarily) as a fixation of a certain duration. But what about why the subject is paying attention? Is the word on the screen attractive, repulsive, desirable, nostalgic, familiar, strange? I was still left with the question of how psychologists identify any of these psychological states *without* asking the subjects what they are actually experiencing.

Manipulation or Induction in an Eye Tracking Session

A few months after Randall instructed me on the Tobii, he had devised an experiment on RNT using eye tracking. This time I was watching the duplicate monitor outside the booth while an undergraduate participant carried out experimental tasks inside the booth. At first, as in my own instructional session, it was jaw dropping. I saw her eyes moving along the words on her screen, forward, back, forward, and so on. But I also saw the massive swings of her visual focus up and down. Where she held her focus still, the dot grew bigger and bigger. This was a general knowledge task, so her answers were coded red or green for right or wrong:

What is the longest-living species of mammals?
What is the highest mountain on earth?

She was in the first group, which meant she would only be given a task along the way that was neutral, not one that was intended to elicit emotion or repetitive negative thinking. Participants in the second group would get a task also, but one that was intended to elicit RNT. Both groups were asked to describe a day they could recall in some detail, but the first group was simply asked to describe a neutral day, while the second group was asked to describe a day when something happened that was unresolved, like a conflict or dilemma that was left hanging. The idea was that recalling a neutral day would not change the subject's learning performance; recalling an unresolved event would change the subject's learning performance.

So, midway through the experiment, Randall turned the eye tracker off and instructed the student to recall a neutral day.

> Now I want to ask you to describe a day, just the events of an ordinary day you recall in detail, not the emotion of the events, just the factual sequence of events. Is there a day in the fairly recent past when you can remember what you did pretty clearly?

Since I could see the student plainly through the now-open door, I could see her eyes, face, and gestures; I could hear the tone of her reply. In a little while, Tobii would again continue tracking her eyes, but of course without the information I gathered about her emotional state by looking at her face. In answer to Randall's question, she responded, "Oh yes, I remember that day." She said this with an expression of dismay in her voice and on her face. "June 6. I certainly remember, it was my birthday." I immediately envisioned a birthday everyone forgot, or one where a close friend stood her up, or one where she was given a present that she found inappropriate. Randall accepted her selection of that day as an ordinary one, despite the counter evidence I had just observed, and gave her some examples of a neutral day's recall written by others. She then wrote out her memories of the day. Randall checked what she had written to make sure she had followed the instructions, and then she returned to the eye tracking session. Her data was logged as a subject in the "neutral day" condition.

What popped into her mind was a recent day she remembered in detail. Randall was careful to prompt her to recall a neutral experience and to write down just the details of what happened. His induction was rightfully neutral and was meant to elicit a neutral set of memories. That is all any experimenter could say and all any experimenter could notice. But I did wonder whether, if Randall had been able to ask her, she would have said it was one of her worst days. This single case could not have significantly affected the experimental outcome, since such perturbations are washed out, unnoticed, by the large numbers of people who no doubt would have remembered an ordinary boring day. But the incident opened a way for me to see the gap that lies between what the technology can capture and the many layers of what the subject is experiencing. Of course, it is true that the eye tracker would probably have recorded accurately the kind of data expected of a participant remembering a negative event, even though by the experimental protocol, this data would have been logged in the "neutral" category, adding noise to the data. Whether the problem comes from the eye tracker or the experimental protocol, the gap lies in the way the participant's experience was classified to fit the protocol.

Leftovers Redux

There is a gap between what the psychologists wish the eye tracker to record and what the subject is experiencing. The ideal is clear: the subject understands the instructions, wishes to follow them, and does follow them. But the rules cannot cover every eventuality, and, in that gap, things can go awry. This participant fastened onto an event she recalled vividly, but one that might have been very dismaying to her. The task was meant to be neutral, but her expression and tone of voice indicated she was thinking about a birthday when something went wrong.

I have put the emphasis on gaps the technology leaves between what the apparatus shows as the gaze point and what the experimenter understands to be a predictable focus for the subject's eye, given the task. We could call it the Tobii Comma. But unlike tuning a piano, minding the eye tracking gap involves conflating where the eye focuses and what the human subject is perceiving. Another graduate student in Dr. J's lab articulated this point. Ulla, herself working with EEG data, said eye tracking "is nonsense—you can't tell if the movements are covert or overt. You could be looking but your mind could be wandering. Could knowledge of being eye tracked affect your behavior?" Furthermore, she said the eye tracker produced "too much data!" With any numerical measure—including the data from EEG—the question is what part of the bewildering forest of data matters. Ulla thought eye tracking took this problem to new heights. Dr. J told me the amount of data you could gather is endless. Normally the tracker is set to gather data at a sampling rate of 30 or 60 or even 120 Hz (times per second). But you could set it to gather data as often as 300 times per second. (Newer—and more expensive—Tobii models can sample data at 1200 Hz.) After the experimenter chooses the sampling rate, Tobii's proprietary algorithm automatically calculates the eye's position and gaze point. Apart from describing it as a "sophisticated 3D eye model algorithm," Tobii's instruction manual does not give users information about how exactly the algorithm works. Randall has to take on faith that the algorithm is doing its job appropriately.

To be sure, despite all these hurdles in the use of the eye tracker, the technology does produce information that both psychologists and marketers find very useful. Some of these hurdles may be overcome by effective problem solvers like Randall and Ulla. In any case, the hurdles I observed do not perturb data enough to prevent statistically significant findings from emerging. Randall will go on to find important correlations between subjects who are asked to recall an unresolved condition and measures of their memory and learning. His research will shed light not only on how cognitive processes work, but also on how teachers could help students learn. No small accomplishment.

Marketers too find eye tracking useful. Marketing students learn how to use eye tracking by watching a video of people pretending to be shoppers wearing portable eye trackers while browsing the products on the shelves inside a staged replica of a shop, complete with a salesclerk. The eye tracker can calculate what shoppers are looking at and for how long. From these data, marketers can learn how to optimize the appeal of a product's size, color, position, packaging, and so on. Another remarkable accomplishment. But I noticed that they do not calculate how long the shoppers gazed at the female clerk or where on her body they fixated. These data are not deemed relevant to marketing questions, of course, because she is not for sale. Here, the eyes are not lying, but the data they produce greatly exceeds the specific information marketers want to use, another kind of anthropologically interesting "gap."

Wrap-Up

Over the last few chapters we have seen the incompleteness of the numerical measures and quantitative readouts of devices that detect human perception. Such technologies, including EEG, fMRI, and eye tracking, depend on a partnership with human researchers to make their data useful in experiments. Sometimes the partnership feels playful, allowing Randall, for example, to have some discretion about how he sets the parameters of the eye tracker. Sometimes the partnership puts the researcher in the position of a disciplinarian, requiring Dr. J, for example, to keep students from attributing too much power to the EEG. Sometimes the partnership requires researchers to place their trust in elements like an algorithm that is hidden as a proprietary secret, or in subjects who they depend on to admit when they are unable or unwilling to follow instructions. Nonetheless, the sheer number of devices used to make numerical calculations in psychology labs might lead one to think that results would pop out unproblematically, as if from a well-oiled machine.

But nothing in the lab happens automatically. Human judgment, social re-lationships, trust, and cooperation, with all of their vagaries, are the oil that is necessary for the machines to work at all. Human judgment, social relation-ships, trust, and cooperation flow along the conduits between the machine and the experimenter, making the machine's results unpredictable, but there-fore as complex and interesting as any social interaction. The training and methods of experimental psychology in the labs I studied consistently exclude introspection and even conscious awareness of subjects during the testing. It is as if their training and methods explicitly ignore the possibility of a Pytha-gorean comma.

8

Practicing Experimental Tasks

Not only rules, but also examples are needed for establishing a practice.
Our rules leave loopholes open, and the practice has to speak for itself.

—LUDWIG WITTGENSTEIN, ON CERTAINTY

A KEY to understanding how subjects become able to play their part in psychology experiments remained hidden in plain sight for me during a long period of fieldwork. This key was the small practice session I was given before each experiment. Why would practicing play any part in an experiment in a psychology lab? One might practice to learn a skill or to improve performance. Or one might practice to coordinate complex interactions, such as, for example, in the elaborate rehearsals for the technically intricate production of a play. Surely, however, there would be no rehearsal for psychology experiments, which, I thought at first, treated subjects as blank slates until the experiment began. But, as we saw in Wundt's lab, practice can serve to standardize different people so that their actions (walking, seeing, reacting) are comparable. In other times and places, practice served the purpose of creating standard measures. In mid-nineteenth century India, the colonial British India Survey trained Hindu spies from the Indian Himalayas to travel through Tibet, *surreptitiously* compiling measurements that would enable the British to map Tibet. The scheme was devised by Major Thomas G. Montgomerie of the Corps of Royal Engineers. He first trained the men "through exhaustive practice to take a pace of known length which would remain constant whether they walked uphill downhill or on the level."[1] This historical footnote makes us realize how variable humans are in size, height, weight, agility, perception, and so on, and how much effort is required to standardize their actions.

Discovering Practice

I begin with an incident from Dr. R's lab. Wade told me about an experiment he was thinking of doing that would build on earlier research. He said, "The earlier experiment didn't work, and one of the reasons that it didn't work is, they didn't train people. They just put them immediately in the scanner and tried to do everything at that time." So, Wade said, he was definitely planning to include a practice session in his upcoming experiment. Coincidentally, a few days later, in Dr. J's lab meeting, there was a long discussion of "test-enhanced learning." I learned that researchers have found experimentally that any form of practice before a test improves outcomes. Frequent practice tests about one topic can even improve students' performance in tests on another topic! Practice in answering test questions improves performance across the board.

At that moment, I felt shocked. Wade had just told me a few days before that lack of practice before an experiment was a factor in the failure of an experiment. But sitting there in the meeting of a different lab, I was learning that psychological research had demonstrated the power of the "practice effect" in improving performance. Only then did I realize that in almost all the experiments in which I had volunteered as a subject, I was trained before the experiment started. I certainly remembered the practice exercises. But I had thought of them as if I were a student who was being tested about whether I was an adequate subject, not as a form of training that would affect my performance in the experiment. After the practices, I couldn't help asking the experimenter, "How did I do?" None of the experimenters ever answered that question, except to say "fine" with a smile, as if my question really didn't have an answer. Nor were my experiences unusual: the dozens of textbooks on experimental method I have consulted recommend the use of practice trials to allow the performance of subjects to "stabilize before the experimental conditions of interest are introduced."[2] Besides such commonplace instructions from textbooks, manuals for the normalized scales discussed in chapter 3 also describe practice sessions held while they were being developed. From the International Affective Picture System (IAPS) manual:

> In addition to the 60 IAPS exemplars rated in each Picture Set, 3 practice pictures are viewed prior to the experimental ratings. These pictures provide subjects with a rough range of the types of contents that will be presented, as well as serving to anchor the emotional rating scales. Common

anchor points used to date are: 4200 (woman at beach), 7010 (basket), and 3100 (a burn victim).[3]

It is easy for the eye to skip over the "3 practice pictures are viewed prior to the experimental ratings" in this manual, just as it was easy for me to be oblivious to the routine practices before experiments. Perhaps one reason for the invisibility of practice is that it becomes obscured as we gain expertise. Wittgenstein remarked that once we know how to perform a skill, our "training may of course be overlooked as mere history."[4] Practicing before experiments trains subjects by "structuring and modifying the behavior of the learner. That structuring is never fully eliminated though it is rightfully obscured from view in the behavior and judgments of those who have mastered a practice."[5] Practice may be obscured, but as anthropologist Don Brenneis observes, it is "signally in moments of practice and pedagogy that theory is articulated, negotiated, transformed, and made audible."[6]

I was surprised about the ubiquity of practice in experiments because practice might pose a threat to the value of objectivity. Objectivity is a goal my interlocutors mentioned frequently. In some ways, objectivity seems straightforward: many of the scientists in the labs I studied were trying to discover how the brain works—where neural events are located and how they are connected functionally. When this is the goal, the subjective experience of human participants is not relevant. The cognitive processes being measured are assumed to be unknowable to the subject. Under ordinary circumstances we do not know what we remember best, what we react to most emotionally, or what enables us to read or spell. We certainly do not know what parts of the brain may be processing these cognitive operations. In this endeavor, experimenters need not take account of "subjective" experience. The experiment can rightfully produce "objective" findings. But with the standard inclusion of practice sessions before experiments in mind, I began to wonder: what do the terms "objective" and "subjective" actually mean?

Objectivity versus Subjectivity

A useful framework is Lorraine Daston and Peter Galison's historical overview of the concepts of "objectivity" and "subjectivity." They set out three phases of scientific knowledge over the centuries, from "truth-to-nature," to "mechanical objectivity," to "trained judgment." They call these "epistemic regimes."[7] For my question, the contrast between "mechanical objectivity" and "trained judgment" matters most. On the one hand, the epistemic virtue of "mechanical objectivity" strives to "capture nature" while eliminating any intervention on the part of the researcher. Scientific photographs of snowflakes show that they are actually somewhat asymmetric, despite the common belief that each of them is perfectly symmetric. The photos show that scientists can capture nature without interference from their preconceived ideas. The more recent epistemic virtue of "trained judgment," on the other hand, can include the scientist's intuitive or aesthetic judgments. One of Daston and Galison's examples of trained judgment shows an image of the magnetic field of the Sun, "produced by sophisticated equipment but with a 'subjective' smoothing of data—deemed necessary to remove instrumental artifacts."[8]

Where do psychology experiments fit into these categories? How does what psychologists call "practice," a short session that is conducted with participants in an experiment just before they begin the tasks in the experiment, fit into these epistemic regimes? The "practice" before an experiment is a small event, but it involves relationships between experimenter and participant that prepare the ordinary person to become an adequate psychological subject. Practice sessions occur so commonly that they seem inextricable from the proper conditions of the experiment. Practice trains the participant's subjectivity, but it is not there by mistake. Historian Steven Shapin has noted that in accounts of how knowledge is made, subjectivity is often described in opposition to objectivity. Subjectivity is the "evil twin" of objectivity; it "pollutes" objectivity in the sense that it is "grit in the knowledge-machine." Such accounts imply that this "grit" could be identified and removed, or at least ignored.[9] Following this pattern, psychologists sometimes insist that subjectivity has no role in experimental cognitive psychology. But perhaps the production of knowledge through the psychological experiment *necessarily* depends on subjective elements that lie inside the formal properties of the experimental model itself and yet do not, as psychologists hold, invalidate the "objectivity" of their findings.

Once I tuned into the ubiquity of practice sessions, I could see them in my field notes, wrongly described there as assessments of my qualifications to be a subject. On one occasion, as I described in an extract from my fieldnotes in chapter 4, I had volunteered to be a subject in an fMRI study of spelling and reading. Given the expense of booking the fMRI machine and the time required to get there (on another campus a bus ride away) it seemed completely expectable that I would need to pass muster before being booked for the experiment itself. A few days before the fMRI session was scheduled, I showed up at the lab and sat at a seminar table in the main room. Liz, the lab adminis-trator, then gave me a spelling test: there were about thirty words of increasing difficulty: car, book, dairy, argon, fibrous, and so on. Then I was shown into an adjacent room where I sat at a computer. On the screen were previews of what I would see in the fMRI machine. I saw the word "spelling" on the screen while hearing a different word in my earphones. I then saw various single letters and was told to indicate with a key press whether that letter was in the word "spell-ing" or not. As I would be told again in the fMRI itself, Liz cautioned me to ignore the spoken word.

Then I saw many words in English, strings of consonants, and checker-boards. Liz told me, "Just look, don't say the word in your head, don't think about it, let your brain do the work. Don't read the word to yourself!" Next, I saw pictures of faces (many different expressions, but all were White men or women) and then pixelated faces. Then I saw houses, followed by pixelated houses. Liz gave more directions, "Do not get involved, I mean do not do what one person said he did—he gave the faces names! Afterward he told me, 'Oh. that one I called Bob.' The most important request is do not fall asleep!"

Though I still thought I was being tested, the session seemed logical to me for practical reasons. The experimenters wanted subjects to behave consis-tently, under the same instructions. They wanted the instructions to be clear. They wanted some control over the mental processes to which the subject attended: do not give names to the faces, do not try to read anything. But I now have no doubt that this was a practice session, not a test: I was being trained to be a subject.

To be sure, there is a way in which psychologists can understand the use of practice before an experiment as contributing to objective results. Dr. S explained,

> There's certainly a component of practice that is very general, providing familiarity with the apparatus (the monitor, where the buttons are, what the buttons feel like when you press them, etc.) and the task (what the tim-ing of the trials will be, where things will appear on the monitor, how big they will be, how hard the task will be, etc.).

He continued, "The bottom line argument for why practice trials are kosher is simply *efficiency*." Dr. S explained that if you were to omit the practice trials, which are not analyzed or recorded, the necessary "practice" would just take place in the experiment proper. Subjects would still need practice in perform-ing the task—they would need to be "stabilized"—but it would happen in trials that get recorded and analyzed. The early experimental trials would then be noisy because of the lack of practice, and the experimenter would have to run many more trials to escape the noise from the lack of practice. "The more trials you run," he explained, "the less effect those practice trials will have because almost all of the practice effects happen at the beginning. So, in most cases, practice trials are 'benign' and have the benefit of reducing noise." This way of looking at the experiment helped me see how practice can remain invisible. If you are going to test the performance of a race car's engine, you would certainly allow the engine to warm up before you started the assessment. For the sake of efficiency and accuracy, allowing the engine to warm up before you start assessing its performance makes common sense. But when a human subject is to be tested instead of an engine, the role of practice is more interesting.

Demand Characteristics

As a volunteer subject I misidentified practice trials: I saw them as a performance—am I a good enough subject? Moreover, I failed to see that practice is both for the subject's *and* the experimenter's sake, in the sense that the experimenter's goal of achieving an *effect* might be said to have intervened in the experiment. Psychologist Martin Orne identified this as a potential problem in the 1950s. In his internal critique of his discipline's methods he called the problem "demand characteristics." The worry was that the researchers' "demand" could affect the subject's data.[10] The idea of demand characteristics opened up a rush of new inquiries. Some researchers, such as John Adair and Barry Spinner, gathered data on how subjects regarded experiments: How difficult were they? How personal were they? How scientifically important were they?[11] Having now explored the concept of normalization, we can understand the limitations of these inquiries. The subjects were queried about their views, but only within the set terms of standard scales—in this case the standard scales were called The Experimental Description Checklist and the Affect-Behavior Checklist. In a circular way, both of these scales were developed for the purpose of the Adair and Spinner study.[12]

The moment in history when "demand characteristics" were taken seriously in psychology is well known by contemporary researchers who make good faith efforts to heed Orne's warning. Orne called attention to the ways a psychological experiment is a social interaction in which the subject "will behave in an experimental context in a manner designed to play the role of a 'good

subject' or, in other words, *to enable validation of the experimental hypothesis.*
Viewed in this way, the student volunteer is *not* merely a passive responder in
an experimental situation, but rather he has a very real stake in the successful
outcome of the experiment."[13] The experimenter is implicitly or explicitly "demanding" cooperation and patience from the subject in order to reach his
goals. The subject willingly complies with these "demands" and so may play
an unintended role in the experimental results.

How do demand characteristics relate to the issue of objectivity? Psychologists might generally accept the virtue described by Daston and Galison as
"mechanical objectivity," which refers to "capturing nature" while avoiding
interventions by the researcher. Following that principle, any form of objectivity would have to avoid the effects of demand characteristics. But one kind of
intervention is apparently an exception: training for subjects, which experimenters design, which happens routinely *as a part of the experimental protocol.* We could ask whether another of Daston and Galison's virtues—"trained
judgment"—is playing a role here, but we would have to realize an important
difference: for Daston and Galison, it is the *experimenter* whose judgment is
trained; in the labs where I did my fieldwork it is the *human subject* who is
trained. How can a subject who is trained by the experimenter play a part in
producing objective scientific knowledge?

When I started admitting to my interlocutors the many unintended consequences I created and perverse opposition I fomented during experiments,
they were of one voice in saying they would throw my results out if they had
known. So, there must be a basic level of competence required of subjects. As
an anthropologist, I needed a way to understand the logic of practice or training sessions right before the data are collected. The puzzle is—how is it allowable in searching for objective data that the *subject* can be trained through
instruction and practice?

The research process of experimental psychology, taken as a whole and
considered over time, actually enfolds and depends on complex subjective
experiences. Those lively subjective experiences in the lab—and indeed in the
experiment itself—are part and parcel of even the most quantitative descriptions of isolated individuals. They are not so much "grit in the knowledge-
machine" as they are grist for the knowledge mill. There is overlap between
this point and something sociologists of science have called "tacit knowledge."
Harry Collins and others have astutely pointed out that even the simplest operations in scientific labs depend on socially learned habits. Drawing on Ludwig Wittgenstein's comments about following a rule, the argument is that rules

do not contain within themselves the rules for how to apply them. If you asked a child to continue the series 2, 4, 6, 8, . . . , the child would continue reciting more even numbers (10, 12, 14, . . .) only if the child knew from parents or teachers that the series would conventionally be continued with the subsequent even numbers. The social environment provides the understanding of how to "go on." Otherwise, many ways of "going on" would be possible. The child might continue, "who do we appreciate?" As Collins puts it, "There is no mathematical inevitability about the right way to continue a series, and therefore what counts as the correct way to carry it on is conventional."[14] So "practice" could be called a setting that teaches tacit knowledge.

In the past, numerous publications, including my own, have argued that neuropsychological experiments simplify the complexity of human experience. Now, I am finding that the experimental setting is not simplified; in at least one way it is extremely layered and complex, but its complexity is hidden in plain sight. As a subject, I took the practice training to be an evaluation of my worthiness as a subject who could produce objective data, and in this way my understanding of the complexity of objectivity and experimental method in psychology was flawed. What I was participating in was in some ways like Wundtian training or like anthropology's "living rough." The practice of living rough hopes to lead the anthropologist into thinking like Torres Strait Islanders, while practice prior to a psychology experiment attempts to lead the subject into thinking like a psychologist.

My original puzzlement arose from a too-simple understanding of objectivity. I suggest we need to add a step to Daston and Galison's epistemic scheme. In addition to mechanical objectivity and trained judgment, we need "trained participation." Even undergraduates, let alone members of the general public, need to be trained to be subjects: they have to be trained to sit still in a chair at a table, to pay attention selectively, to look at the screen, to use a keyboard, to choose appropriately, to stay awake, to remain until the end of the experiment. James Cattell said, "It is usually no more necessary for the subject to be a psychologist than it is for the vivisected frog to be a physiologist."[15] But human subjects are not frogs, and in a certain way, in order to produce objective data, subjects do have to become psychologists, at least to the extent of conforming to the explicit and implicit requirements that psychologists expect of their subjects.

Pulling things together, I think that in psychology, practices from a previous epistemic regime (where conscious introspection was central) persisted into a new one (where unconscious responses are central). "Practice" was required for Wundt's students and for the Cambridge anthropologists in order to make the introspective experience of subjects comparable. But practice then became submerged in today's experiments alongside the knowledge that "practice" of any kind can dramatically affect the outcome of tests and the insistence that interventions by the researcher in the process of capturing nature are undesirable. Practice increases the chances of achieving the goal experimenters seek: a statistically significant, objective "effect." Since all subjects receive the same training, the objectivity of the results remains intact. Subjects are not trained in order to validate any particular hypothesis (that would be both unscientific and unethical) but to enable experimenters to gather data with less noise and more efficiency than otherwise.

The apparently narrow concept of the experiment with its controlled variables takes place in a larger setting: one could say the experiment is preceded by a foyer or entrance hall in which the volunteer is trained to be a good subject. In my fieldwork I was sometimes told that my subjective experience had to be left behind at the door, but it would be more accurate to say that inside the door there lay an anteroom—a waiting room—where training would take place and where some elements of subjective experience would necessarily linger. These lingering elements of subjectivity are what historian Betsy Bayer described as the "phantoms" that have supposedly been eliminated from psychological research but actually continue to haunt it.[16] I would not call them phantoms—dead and unreal—but vital spirits, because they are *necessary* for the researcher to harness training to the experimental model.

To be sure, in their practice sessions participants in psychology experiments do not learn what the results of the experiment are hoped to be, but rather what behaviors and attitudes are necessary to produce measurable results. More generally, language itself can be seen as something that arises out of practice. To capture this idea, Wittgenstein used the German noun *ein Abrichten* or the verb *abrichtung*, translated into English as "training." *Ein Abrichten* can be applied in German to both humans and animals—it designates clear, simple orders and responses practiced many times until a pattern is learned, such as teaching or training a child to bring different building materials, teaching or training a dog to sit on command, or breaking in a horse. In other words, "Here the teaching of language is not explanation, but training."[17]

So, we could say that subjects in psychology experiments undergo *ein Abrichten*—sitting in a chair, pressing the correct keys, paying attention, following directions, making good faith efforts for each task, giving honest responses, and so on. Inside the experiment resides a tiny moral economy that is repeatedly taught anew.

I was originally inspired to look into the world of experimental psychology by something that happened when Wittgenstein was an undergraduate at Cambridge. He was reading moral sciences, for which psychology was required. At the time the psychology lab was headed by C. S. Myers, the very same veteran of the first anthropological expedition to the Torres Straits. At a meeting of the British Psychological Society, Wittgenstein carried out a demonstration for a psychological experiment designed by Myers, which was about rhythm in music. Young as he was, Wittgenstein was not impressed. In 1912 he wrote a letter to Bertrand Russell saying that the paper he had to write for the demonstration was "*most* absurd."[18] Much later he restated this point, writing that psychology is a science whose "problems and methods pass one another by." As this book demonstrates, exploring why he said this became irresistible to me.

It is the circularity of this system—explicitly training people to become subjects who can emit data that can be measured numerically—that I think explains Wittgenstein's assessment that the experiment he demonstrated was "absurd." Whatever subjectivity a participant brings to the experiment, it is trained up like a dog, broken in like a horse, so the subject can emit objective data. The problem of interest (a subject's cognitive experience) and the method (experimental control) do seem to "pass one another by," as Wittgenstein put it.[19] Specifically, the method includes training that ensures the subjects' responses will speak to the problem. Problem and method pass one another by in the sense that the method circles around the problem while selecting findings that are statistically significant.

9

Envisaging "Productive Thinking"

The basic thesis of gestalt theory might be formulated thus: there are contexts
in which what is happening in the whole cannot be deduced from the
characteristics of the separate pieces, but conversely; what happens to a part of
the whole is, in clear-cut cases, determined by the laws of the inner structure
of its whole.

—MAX WERTHEIMER, *PRODUCTIVE THINKING*, 1920

IN MY JOB as an academic anthropologist I have given many departmental
guest lectures at universities other than my own. This kind of lecture is unlike
any other. Typically, guest speakers come from the same discipline as the department, and they appear as guests because a committee of the department,
often including graduate students, has chosen them. So, these events are hon-
ors of a particular kind: the invitation means some other department in your
field is interested in your work. The kicker is that the audience is likely to be
very well informed, in the way of experts with their own opinions. Department
guest speakers expect hard and probing questions much different from the
broad speculations of a general audience. This background might explain my
near terror when the Department of Psychology where some of my major
interlocutors were based invited me to speak at their department seminar.
I was certainly honored but also nervous. Not only was I *not* a psychologist,
but I was to lecture on my ethnographic research *about* psychologists *to* psychologists. Explaining my ethnographic research to psychologists who were all
experimentalists was a prospect that made me quake in my boots. I sought protection for myself by limiting the historical period I would discuss. I announced
that I would start with Wundt's lab in nineteenth-century Germany and the

Cambridge anthropological expedition to the Torres Straits in 1898, moving through Titchener's introspection in the early-twentieth-century United States, and ending with Watson's clarion call for behaviorism in 1913. The talk was solidly historical, so I would only have time to hint at some continuities between contemporary psychology and its origins in the nineteenth century.

Although the audience seemed interested and pleased, afterward I learned that my talk left at least one member of the audience feeling somewhat disappointed. "If that is the history of psychology," Dr. S said, "what does that say about my work for the last thirty years?" Because I knew that his current research in psychology was influenced by the European tradition of Gestalt psychology, I guessed that he was referring to the fact that I had not even mentioned the contributions of the Gestalt psychologists. I later realized that I had failed to appreciate the importance of another landmark event in the history of psychology that occurred at virtually the same time as Watson's announcement of behaviorism in 1913. Just a year earlier, Max Wertheimer launched the Gestalt movement in psychology with the publication of his investigations of the *phi* phenomenon, a subjective experience of motion in static images induced by presenting them sequentially like successive frames in a movie film. Together with his primary colleagues, Wolfgang Köhler and Kurt Köffka, Wertheimer pioneered an approach to psychological theory and methodology that was, in important ways, the antithesis of behaviorism. Like behaviorism, it rejected Wundt's method of trained introspection as fundamentally flawed, but unlike behaviorism, it embraced the primary role of subjective experience in psychological inquiry. Rather than focusing solely on Wundt in Leipzig and the advent of behaviorism, I should also have drawn on historian Mitchell Ash's work on Gestalt theory in German culture and considered the contributions of Christian van Ehernfels in Prague, Oswald Külpe in Würzburg, and Carl Stumpf in Berlin. It took me a while to realize the import of what I had missed.[1]

Right after my talk, I had a conversation with two of my main interlocutors, who of course had been in the audience. Dr. S said, "I don't recognize my own work in the history you told." I was a bit defensive, reminding him that I had stopped in 1913. I added that I hoped the planned book would bring my account up to the present and that it would deal in detail with Gestalt psychologists, as well as other critics of Wundtian methods like Sol Sternberg. But, I explained again, I had stopped short in the early twentieth century for lack of time. Despite my explanation, Dr. S was mildly offended, especially because Gestalt psychology had begun in Germany at virtually the same time as behaviorism in America. This was the beginning of my education in the history of Gestalt psychology.

In my talk, I had overlooked an important fork in the road in the history of psychology. Brought to its flowering in Germany in the early twentieth century, the Gestalt approach formed a vocal counterpoint to the method of trained introspection stressed by Wundt and his students and also to the anti-subjective strictures of behaviorism. How could I have not included this important approach? The clues about how different this approach was from the mainstream story of Wundt should certainly have already occurred to me.

Historical Fork in the Road

Thinking afresh about my research, I did know that in late nineteenth- and early-twentieth-century psychology and anthropology, tensions between experiment and experience were not necessarily considered to be a problem. As we have seen, psychologists shared experiences in labs and anthropologists shared experiences in villages. Shared experience allowed experimenters to be researchers one day and subjects the next. Experiments included individual experience, which they called introspection, and that introspection determined the beginning and end of timed reactions. I also knew, as I described in chapter 2, that Wundt limited the usefulness of experimental methods to restricted domains, calling the facets of human experience that lay outside experimental knowledge "folk psychology." The Cambridge anthropologists similarly used experimental methods to study perception, but ethnographic methods to study everything else.

I also already knew that after the 1898 expedition, C. S. Myers began to take the field in new directions. As I described in chapter 2, in 1912 he founded the Cambridge Laboratory of Experimental Psychology, which focused on aural perception in music and rhythm. Throughout his career, well into the 1930s, Myers stressed that the aesthetic aspects of music and rhythm had to be understood comparatively in different cultures. By paying attention to unfamiliar music from different cultures, people could come to regard incomprehensible music as meaningful. As Myers summarized: the ethnographic goal in understanding unfamiliar music is to "banish to the margins" of awareness our habitual focus of attention and make the incomprehensible meaningful through "much familiarity" and "faithful description." Consistent with the methods of the Cambridge Expedition, Myers thought both psychological experiments and qualitative aesthetic descriptions were necessary to understand musical form.[2]

I failed to realize that Myers provided a step toward a different branch of psychology, which was a direct revolt against the methods and assumptions of both Wundt and the subsequent behaviorists like Watson. I now realized that Myers was aware of Max Wertheimer's work and that I should have paid more attention![3] Given my training in anthropology, I should also have recognized sooner the kinship between the beginnings of Gestalt psychology and the beginnings of my own field. First of all, as Dr. S soon told me, "introspection" and "subjectivity" are not the same thing. I had blurred them in my thinking. The slightest acquaintance with these early Gestalt psychology texts would have shown me that something very different from Wundtian experiments was afoot. Even the validity of introspection as a tool of psychological inquiry was in question. Classical introspection was aimed at separating subjective experience into its primitive elements and analyzing those elements and the relations among them. In contrast, Gestalt theorist Max Wertheimer claimed, "There are wholes, the behavior of which is not determined by that of their individual elements, but where the part-processes are themselves determined by the intrinsic nature of the whole. It is the hope of Gestalt theory to determine the nature of such wholes."[4]

I was now very curious. I wondered what "the whole" meant in Gestalt theory. According to Gestalt pioneer Wolfgang Köhler's 1925 observations in Tenerife, the key is "the handling of forms." Köhler showed a chimpanzee that there were bananas on the other side of a fence. From one position the chimp could reach the bananas with a stick, but from that position he couldn't pull the bananas under the fence. However, if the chimp pushed the bananas farther away from himself with the stick, he could move to another position along the fence and pull the bananas within his reach. Köhler called this a "roundabout" method because the chimp's first move taken by itself would seem to put him farther away from his goal. Köhler concluded that there must be a whole "form" in the chimp's mind because, "the beginning of the procedure, taken separately, contains no trace of a solution, but seems rather to prevent one, and so cannot arise as an isolated part." There may have been an "aha!" moment when the chimp realized the solution to the puzzle. Or to put it another way, the first roundabout act has to be conceived within the structure of the whole sequence of acts as a Gestalt form in the chimp's mind. "Actually, a whole is required, after that, which will, as it were, legitimize its 'parts'—if such procedure as described could be intelligently accomplished. The theory of shape recognizes wholes which are something more than the 'sum of their parts.'" In another experiment, Köhler tied a rope to one end of a stick and a ring to the other. He slipped the ring over a nail. The chimp needed the stick to reach the bananas. Hence the chimpanzee had to grasp the arrangement "ring over nail" in order to slip the ring free and then use the stick to fetch the prize. The "fundamental importance for a technical consideration of the organism is the degree in which the handling of things is determined by a clearly grasped structure of forms in space."[5]

Along similar lines, in his final work Max Wertheimer introduced a description of forms of thinking that differ from mathematical logic, inductive logic, and associationism. He called this "productive thinking." In one example, children were asked to solve a geometry problem about the area of a parallelogram, but they were given no instructions. The observer recorded what they did and said. The children came up with axioms from their play, such as that cutting the parallelogram into parts and rearranging them does not change the area of the parallelogram. Wertheimer noted that although these axioms may seem trivial, they are not. They are not true by necessity because "worlds are possible in which they do not hold."[6] These axioms could not have been learned from exactly comparable previous experience, because the situation was novel. "They are an outcome of the structural way of working of our mind and brain rather than of blind associations." [7] Still, experience played a role. The personality of the individual (having the confidence to propose answers), the social atmosphere the child was experiencing (working at home or in the classroom), all contributed to the child's ability to think productively.

Wertheimer's overall term for this aspect of productive thinking was "envisaging."[8] He gave the example of a badminton game in which the more skillful player changed the rules to "how many hits can we make in a row" to keep a less skilled opponent playing with him. This was engaged, situational, creative thought in action. Wertheimer's emphasis was on the practical consequences of how we see things subjectively, on taking the whole context into account instead of staying withing the rules. Alongside this "envisioning," he also called attention to "centering—the way one views the parts, the items in a situation, their meaning and role as determined in regard to a center, a core or radix—is a most powerful factor in thinking."[9] These insights are worthy of admiration from an anthropologist. They seemed akin to approaches in anthropology that treat cultural practices as if they were themes in a literary text. Like Clifford Geertz and many others, one could follow the roundabout ways in which central themes in cosmology or kinship, for example, appear in different guises in different cultural contexts.[10]

Gestalt Theory 101

Not long after my department talk, Dr. S and Dr. B gave me a gentle tutorial in the ways some contemporary psychologists were following Wertheimer's Gestalt-oriented path rather than the reductionist one started by Wundt and then narrowed by Watson. First of all, I learned I had partly misunderstood Watson. As Dr. B explained, "Watson didn't only kill subjectivity, he killed mechanistic thought. He killed coming up with mechanisms." Dr. S agreed: "In pure behaviorism you weren't supposed to have to think about what's inside the mind. It was a black box–ology kind of notion that the mind has inputs and outputs, a stimulus and a response framework." Dr. S and Dr. B explained that subjectivity was just one aspect of what happens in the black box, and it was disallowed by Watson's behaviorism along with all other theoretical mechanisms. "You deprived the animal of food for so many hours and measured how many times they pressed the bar to get food. But *hunger* as a subjective experience was not an allowable concept in strict theoretical behaviorism. Not until George Miller's work in the 1960s did we know that the concept of hunger was essential." Miller argued that "you cannot make any sense of behavior" unless you address subjective experiences, such as intentions, plans, or desires like hunger.[11] He called for combining qualitative accounts of subjectivity and quantitative measures of behavior to account adequately for human intelligence.

Second, though I knew about well-established claims in the history of psychology that subjectivity had been ruled out of psychology by twentieth-century behaviorism, I had been misled, and was quickly set straight. Dr. B began,

> We all (meaning the two psychologists in the room) believe that we are always dealing to some degree with subjectivity. I may have somebody push a button to indicate some aspect of their internal experience so that I have an objective behavior to measure it with, but we've always done that to deal with the subjectivity that lies behind the behavior.

(I noted that by "objective behavior" he meant reaction time.)

"Dr. B and I and all kinds of other people often start out with subjectivity," Dr. S added.

I notice something, I notice for example that in photography if I'm taking a picture of something and I focus on one edge because it's closer, it's sharp and the farther one is blurry. The blur is a cue to how we perceive figure-ground. That was a phenomenological observation on my part. But then we go further to ask how can you demonstrate that empirically? We are not dealing with the psychology of Martians. Since we are all humans and we know each other as humans, there is no reason I should not take our observations of each other to inform my experiment. In the kind of cognitive psychology that I do, I start with my introspection about my own experience then translate it into a paradigm of some sort that I can use to demonstrate to others that this is the case, so they don't just simply believe this without any evidence. There's two kinds of evidence that you can use. One kind of evidence is fundamentally subjective, which is just asking people which surface looks like it is closer to you: the one on the left or the one on the right? There's no right answer. This is not an objective fact; it's purely subjective. Then it's a matter of doing the introspective experiment statistically on a bunch of people and showing that everybody sees the one that's got the sharper focus as being closer. You are getting what is called "objective evidence," but remember that it still relies on subjectivity. At the bottom of all this stuff is subjectivity. You can't get away from it.

Here's an example that began with me noticing something interesting about my conscious experience. I was giving a lecture in my perception class about Gestalt grouping, which is the fact that when we see the world, some parts of what we see get organized together in groups. I showed an overhead transparency illustrating an array of dark gray and light gray circles, some spaced at closer intervals and some at farther intervals. The array tends to be spontaneously perceived as pairs of circles, grouping the ones that are closer together and have the same lightness. Then, I said to the class that this didn't need to be true, and I illustrated what I meant by drawing ellipses with a magic marker around the adjacent circles that were farther apart and had different lightnesses. I was startled to see how completely the ellipses had changed the organization of the array: the items inside the ellipses were now very strongly grouped together, even though they were farther apart and different in lightness. But this grouping factor of enclosing contours, which I later called "common region," had never before been described or studied experimentally.

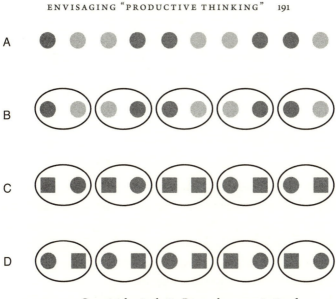

FIGURE 9.1. Grouping by similarity. Personal communication from
S. E. Palmer. Redrawn by Kara Healey.

Dr. S. continued,

In the kind of experiments I do, I often start with this kind of introspection
about my own subjective experience and then translate it into a behavioral
experiment that demonstrates this to others. There are two kinds of behavioral evidence that you can use: direct and indirect. Direct evidence comes
from behavior that's fundamentally based on subjective experience itself.
The simplest way to do this is by asking people to report what grouping
they experience when looking at ambiguous displays in which both factors
are present but predict opposite groupings. For example, in the illustration
I made [reproduced in Fig. 9.1], you could ask them whether the groups
have the same lightness (grouping by lightness similarity) or different lightnesses (grouping by common region). Notice that there's no objectively
"correct" answer here. That's because perceived grouping isn't an objective
fact about the external world; it's a purely subjective fact about the observer's internal experience of the external world. Then it's just a matter of
doing the subjective report experiment with a bunch of subjects and showing that a lot of people report seeing the groups defined by common region
even though they have different lightnesses. So, you're getting "objective
behavioral evidence" because you're measuring observable behavior in an

experiment, which other experimenters can replicate, and that means it conforms to the requirements of methodological behaviorism. But it's behavior that directly reflects the report of subjective experiences. I call this kind of evidence "direct" because it's as direct a measure as you can get of a purely subjective phenomenon.

Feeling like I had reached the mother lode of insight about neo-Gestalt psychology, I asked, "Is there also an indirect kind of evidence?"

There are other ways of measuring common region using a task where there is a verifiably *correct* answer. I call these "indirect" measures because they don't actually measure perceived grouping itself, but something else that might be systematically influenced by perceived grouping. Here's an example for common region. Diane Beck and I developed a reaction time task that we called the repetition discrimination task. We showed our subjects arrays of alternating squares and circles in which one shape is repeated once: either two adjacent squares or two adjacent circles. Their task is to press the "square" button if the repeated items are squares and the "circle" button if the repeated items are circles, and we ask them to respond as quickly as they can while keeping their error rate at or below 5%. Notice that in this task there *is* an objectively correct answer because there's only one repeated pair per trial and it's always either a pair of squares or a pair of circles. So, we measure two aspects of each button press: whether it's correct or not (accuracy) and how many milliseconds it takes to make (reaction time). The ellipses that define the common regions are technically irrelevant to this task, but it is an independent variable because on some trials the target pair is inside the same ellipse [a within-group trial, as in Fig. 9.1C] and on other trials it is inside two different regions [a between-group trial, as in Fig. 9.1D]. If the speed of detecting the shape of the repeated element is facilitated by seeing them within the same group, and if the ellipses influence perceived grouping, then subjects' responses should be significantly faster on the within-group trials than on the between-group trials. This is exactly what we found. And we also showed that these reaction time effects were strongly correlated with other subjects' subjective reports of grouping in similar displays.

I asked, "Is there is a preference in the field for indirect evidence versus direct evidence?"

Modern experimental psychology very much favors objective tasks in which responses are either correct or incorrect. I think that's because the behavioral accuracy measures provide a way to know whether subjects are actually doing the task you're asking them to do. If their accuracy is below, say, 90 percent correct, you throw out their data and only analyze the reaction times from subjects who get 90 percent correct or better. In the subjective report task, subjects just say what they see, so there is no correct answer, which means that you can't really tell whether they're doing what you asked them to do. But when you analyze their responses, you *can* tell whether what they're doing is *systematic* with respect to your independent variables and whether it's *consistent* with what the other subjects are doing. And that's usually all you need to convince reasonable readers of your conclusion. Where it's possible, I actually prefer to get both direct and indirect measures that are highly correlated. The direct ones make sure your subjects are reporting about what you're trying to study, and the indirect ones make sure that their subjective data is consistent with the objective task data that gives you an accuracy criterion. To me it's odd that more researchers don't bother to get direct subjective report data, but if the phenomenon is really obvious subjectively when readers look at the stimuli, it may not really be needed. In fact, my first journal paper about the common region grouping effects had no data at all! It was just a series of phenomenological demonstrations in which the readers of the paper were serving as implicit subjects in an experiment. That's actually how Gestalt psychologists usually did things— just a series of very compelling phenomenological demos.

Dr. S started to go on, "In those cases where you are trying to understand what the neural correlates of consciousness are—"

"—consciousness comes first," Dr. B finished his sentence. "Yeah. It's the ground of all of this stuff. It's the thing—like Descartes said—it's the primal thing."

Dr. S continued,

If you rule out subjectivity as an object of study, as behaviorists tried to do, because they demanded that experiments have to be completely objective, that rules out all kinds of interesting and important questions that simply cannot be answered—including everything that I've been doing for the last ten years of my career, like what colors people experience as most aesthetically pleasing. There's obviously no objectively correct answer, but you can certainly get people to press a button to indicate whether they like this color more than that or whether they like that color more than this. And then you can get statistics about which colors people like most and which they like least, and you can even test theories about why they like the ones they do. So, you can measure purely subjective experiences using solid behavioral measures. It sure looks like science. You have some hypotheses derived from a theory, you're collecting data, and it's reproducible because it's measuring objective behavior. And yet it's a topic that you can't even study if you believe that subjective experience isn't an appropriate topic for scientific psychology.

Letting me have it, Dr. S asserted, "Here is the deal, Emily. You changed [...] the word that John Watson used to put down Titchener mostly in the United States, which was 'introspection.' You kind of substituted in 'subjectivity.' That substitution is not a good equation."

Noticing that despite this terminological distinction, all of three of us had kept on using "introspection" and "subjectivity" interchangeably, I went for the basics: "How would you define subjectivity?"

"Anything we have consciousness of is subjective," Dr. S said.

"Why is it confused with introspection?" I asked.

Introspection is an historical technical term from Wundt and his followers. He thought you could discover the underlying primitive elements and processes of the mind by using your own mind to inspect itself. Sort of a reflexive thing. Subjectivity is just reporting your experience. Introspection is a theoretical term that has to do with those primitive mental concepts and processes. It failed because there were different schools of psychology and different theories about what the primitive stuff was. The problem with introspection was that the subjects were students trained extensively in the introspective methods of their own professor before giving their introspections. So, not surprisingly, Prof. X's students found X's elements, Prof. Y's students found Y's elements, and Prof. Z's students found Z's elements. Subjective reports by naive observers don't have that problem because there's no training phase to influence what they say. You just ask untrained people to report on some aspect of what they see, like whether this tomato is redder than that one.

For Dr. S and Dr. B, once the misleading role of introspection is removed, the field has breathtaking reach, amply qualified to deal with the subjectivity that lies behind behavior.

Other wrinkles in the history of psychology I had missed were experiments that directly contradicted Wundt's use of reaction time. We already met Saul

Sternberg in chapter 5, where I discussed his exploration of conscious experience in experiments. But now Dr. B laid out explicitly how Sternberg had improved on Wundt's approach to reaction time.

> What Sternberg did was to bring a very formal, logical approach to testing theories of mental processing by measuring reaction times. He did this initially for memory rather than perception. He would give subjects a memory set of, say, four items, that could be letters, digits, or whatever. So, let's say there're four letters—A, Q, Z, P—and he would tell you, "please remember those four." And then because you remember the set, as he named random letters, you would say whether they were in the set or not—yes or no—as fast as you could.
>
> He found that reaction time increased linearly as a function of the number of items you had to remember in the list. It was as if you went through your internal memory list one item at a time. And you didn't stop even when you found the one that you were looking for, but you kept searching until the end of the set. When you got to the end, you answered. So, your reaction time to find an item in a list of two items was fast, but with four items it was a little bit slower, and with six items a little slower, and with eight items a little bit slower still. His theory set up a series of stages for comparing the test item to your list in memory and predicted just the kind of linear increase that showed up in the reaction time data. And it was very successful.

Sternberg thus added thought-provoking complexity to Wundt's simple reaction time.

Going even further beyond Wundt, also in the 1960s, George Miller held that psychology should no longer try to analyze a perception into its "basic atoms." Rather it should try to "discover the transformations that a perceiver can impose upon the information he takes in." Dr. S urged me to read a passage in Miller's book, *Psychology: The Science of Mental Life*, which displays the absurdity of Wundt's approach:

> Imagine that you are visiting a psychological laboratory—probably around 1915. As you walk in, a psychologist comes over and, without waiting for introductions, asks what you see on the table.
>
> "A book."
>
> "Yes, of course it is a book," he agrees, "but what do you *really* see?"
>
> "What do you mean, 'What do I *really* see?'" you ask, puzzled. "I told you that I see a book. It is a small book with a red cover."

The psychologist is persistent. "What is your perception *really*?" he insists. "Describe it to me as precisely as you can."

"You mean it isn't a book? What is this, some kind of trick?"

There is a hint of impatience. "Yes, it is a book. There is no trickery involved. I just want you to describe to me *exactly* what you can see no more and no less."

You are growing very suspicious now. "Well," you say, "from this angle the cover of the book looks like a dark red parallelogram."

"Yes," he says, pleased. "Yes, you see a patch of dark red in the shape of a parallelogram. What else?"

"There is a grayish white edge below it and another thin line of the same dark red below that. Under it I see the table—." He winces. "Around it I see a somewhat mottled brown with wavering streaks of lighter brown running roughly parallel to each other."

"Fine, fine." He thanks you for your cooperation.[12]

For Miller, this sketch served to illustrate Wundt's assumption that our perception (I see a book) is composed of elementary sensations (I see a patch of dark red in the shape of a parallelogram). And it gave him an opportunity to say that psychology no longer assumes this: "The notion that perceptions are built from sensations the way a wall is built of bricks is now generally recognized to be unsatisfactory."[13] Dr. S brought this up to the present: Miller's scenario was "part of trained introspection. That kind of training is still outlawed, the idea that you can tell people *what* to say when you ask for a subjective report. Still it is entirely plausible that I might do an experiment in which I ask people to say whether a given shape on the computer screen is rectangular or trapezoidal and show that under certain contextual circumstances, people would be slower in saying that it's trapezoidal than that it's rectangular. I am sure that this would work. I could do that experiment. And that would be allowed. I don't train, I just tell participants what the task is and what the various possible correct answers would be, and then I measure their performance and it turns out there is this systematic difference in the perception of shapes." As an anthropologist I took note of the assumption that subjects were constrained by the "various possible correct answers" in the experiment. Constraining answers is part of what makes an experiment possible, even in the subjectivity-rich world of Gestalt psychology.

In 1966, a few years after Miller's work, a different method for measuring subjective perceptions objectively was developed. Dr. S explained,

FIGURE 9.2. Drawing of a rectangular block
showing that the top appears to be the shape of a
trapezoid. Drawing by Kara Healey.

David Green and John Swets proposed a systematic theory and experimental method called Signal Detection Theory that allowed researchers to measure a person's subjective impression of stimuli under different payoff conditions that strongly influenced their behavior. Let's take an auditory discrimination task of detecting very faint tones in noise as an example. Subjects were asked to press a "tone-present" button on each trial if they heard a tone embedded in some background noise and a "tone-absent" button if they heard only background noise. Sometimes the tones were loud, sometimes soft, and sometimes in between, but all were heard with the same level of background noise. The most important independent variable was the way subjects were paid for their performance. In some blocks of trials, they were paid, say, $10 for each time they pressed the tone-present button when there was, in fact, a tone present (that's called a "hit") and were docked, say, only $1 for each time they pressed the tone-present button when there was, in fact, no tone present (called a "false alarm"). But on other blocks of trials the experimenter gave them opposite payoffs, rewarding them only $1 for a hit and docking them $10 for a false alarm. Perhaps not surprisingly, subjects pressed the tone-present button much more often in the first payoff conditions than in the second payoff conditions, even when the tones were physically identical. How can this be? A purely behavioral approach based on button presses clearly implies that payoffs strongly affect people's subjective experiences of the tones.

Trying to repress how confused I might have felt in such an experiment, I wondered to myself, "Does this experiment depend on subjects actually needing the money they are earning?"

Dr. S continued,

Signal Detection Theory manages to tease apart two different components, both of which affect behavior. One is an early sensory component that depends only on the loudness of the tone. The other is a later decisional component that depends only on the payoffs. Together, these two components work together to explain the different data in the experiment. The sensory signal reflects how loud the tone is within the noise, if there is a tone at all. When hits are rewarded more than false alarms are punished, the subject uses a very lax decision criterion for deciding when to press the tone-present button, pressing even when the signal is barely louder than the noise. When false alarms are punished more than hits are rewarded, they press the tone-present button only when the signal is very clearly louder than the noise. Signal detection theory is a mathematical theory that turns out to give very stable estimates of the perceptibility of the tones in noise even when the listener's detection behavior differs dramatically due to different payoff conditions. And the payoff conditions don't have to be monetary either. The reinforcements and punishments attached to hits and false alarms can be social or political or emotional or whatever. The same analysis would apply!

Dr. S said that made good sense of how subjective reports relate to underlying sensory and decisional processes in a very rigorous way. He summed up: "You can't always take perceptual reports at face value. Underlying factors, including the decisional consequences of different kinds of responses, work together to determine what behavioral response people give."[14]

Structure and Process

It turns out that not everyone has such a rosy view of the scientific value of subjective reports in scientific psychology. I told Dr. S and Dr. B about an incident that happened several years earlier at a conference on interdisciplinary approaches to cognitive science. One of the speakers began her talk with a simple observation from everyday life. "Why," she asked, "do we notice the bright red envelopes above all else in a pile of mail?" This was the start of her experiments on perception and color. Returning from this conference to a lab on the East Coast, I asked Dr. R whether most cognitive psychology experiments began with a phenomenological observation. Perhaps because of the awkward way I phrased the question and my use of the term "phenomenology," she replied, "Absolutely not!" Somewhat horrified, she instructed me that experiments are "seeking cognitive structures, looking for the grammar of cognition, finding patterns in what makes the mind work." The idea that you could start with phenomenological experience was perfectly acceptable, but the goal of experiments lay much deeper for her. She explained with passion,

> For people who really like their science, I think there is something really exciting when you see structure. There is just something that is exciting about that and it doesn't even have to be the most amazing discovery. Obviously the bigger, maybe the more exciting, the better, but there is still, for me at least, always something really exciting when you are collecting all these data points people are making, all these boring decisions, and then you see structure to it. It is like, "Oh it really does have structure!"

She continued,

> Because we researchers live in such doubt about whether what we are doing makes any sense, confirmation that the methods we are using really are capable of revealing something about the structure of cognition or what mental representations are like is very important. For me, every time I see that kind of structure I feel the excitement of "yes, there really is structure!" We can go through these murky waters and find something, some hidden pearls lying there.

For Dr. R, hidden pearls are to murky water as structure is to boring decisions. The self-reports of subjects are "slippery." But the controlled input from subjects in an experiment, restricted and confined as it is by the demands of the experimental method, once it has been sorted and measured, can reveal the hidden pearls.

Although Dr. R thought individual introspection could legitimately spark an idea for an experiment, something was alarming to her about too large a role for phenomenology in psychology experiments. But later, what Dr. S and Dr. B were telling me suggested otherwise. In response to my report about what Dr. R said, Dr. S explained,

> Her feelings about finding structure reflect the goal of her research. They don't seem to have much to do with the process of coming up with ideas about doing the research, at least for her. But for us, it's different. We really do get insights into things that are interesting to study based on our

subjective experiences. Her view would imply that we could be just as good at studying visual perception if we were blind as if we were sighted. That seems highly unlikely because so much of what we study is, in fact, driven by phenomenal perception.

Dr. B added that the phenomenology of ninety years ago would be useless today because "you only got phenomenology and stopped there." He stressed the importance of individual introspection in developing an experiment.

Since I do have vision, why not use things I notice visually to come up with ideas? Suspicion about phenomenology might be coming from a reaction against introspection, but introspection can be used in two different ways. It could be used in the way William James used it. He wrote these two long volumes about what he felt when he woke up in the morning, what got him out of bed, but we don't know if that's what really got him out of bed or not! That's one kind of introspection. The other kind is Wundtian. That kind held that you could get a special understanding of the world just by learning how to observe things about your own experience and how to express those introspective experiences. We tell undergraduates that this is not what we do as scientists anymore.

But nonetheless, he agreed with Dr. S: how subjects perceive the world—their subjective experience—is a central part of many experiments.

Going back to George Miller's discussion about the red book, Dr. S pointed to the role of training.

Suppose the people from Wundt's lab got the parallelogram result, but people in the Wertheimer lab got the book result. What was there in their instructional training that caused this? Well, it turns out that in Wundt's lab, if the subjects said "book," Wundt was scowling, and if they said, "red parallelogram," he was smiling. In Wertheimer's lab, whatever they said was fine, but everybody would probably say "book." So, there's something about the training that these two sets of subjects had that was different in the two labs. That was the reason you got different results. That's entirely reasonable, it seems to me. Training in the Wundt lab was antithetical to how people naturally experience the world, whereas Wertheimer allowed people to say what came naturally.

Dr. S referred back to a topic I had stressed in my talk to the psychology department, the role of training in Wundt's lab. He said, "It's possible to think within that framework about why Wundt couldn't get reproducibility across labs. In your way of framing the problem in your talk, you showed that Wundt had a different system of training with very long instructions." Dr. S thought that Wundt's elaborate training regime could have produced unique (and hence not comparable) conditions.

The two of them then made my day: Dr. S said, "It would be good for somebody (maybe you're the right person) to understand the difference between the kind of introspection that is allowed to influence and, in some sense, drive scientific perceptual psychology vs. the kind that is not." Dr. B encouraged me: "I think it would be a service if you did put this in your book, but you don't have to." That service would be to correct the misperception that psychology has eliminated subjectivity. I could do that by insisting that psychologists actually do depend upon the kind of subjectivity involved in introspection that accompanies people's everyday engagement with the world (including participating in psychology experiments), but not upon the artificial kind of introspection that Wundt demanded of his subjects.

The Ether of the Field

Pushing one step further, I asked them both whether any psychologists pay attention to what subjects have to say about their phenomenological reactions *after* they have been in an experiment. Dr. S told me, "You put your finger on the 'ether' of the field: we *don't* study what subjects say after experiments. It would give us too much feedback and that's not good." At this moment, I thought about Wittgenstein's remarks on psychology: what you ask depends on what you want to find out.[15] This seems too obvious to mention, but Wittgenstein points to a subtle line between disciplines. Not asking about how the subjects experienced the experiment is a choice *dictated* by the goals of psychology; in contrast, deliberately asking about their experience would be the chosen role of an anthropologist *dictated* by the goals of anthropology. On the one side the question is whether there is too much data for a psychologist to handle quantitatively; on the other the question is whether there is enough data for the anthropologist to turn into a finely grained description.

Why Gestalt Psychology Was Rejected

Now seemed a good time for me to ask why Gestalt approaches are no longer in the mainstream of cognitive psychology. Dr. S said,

Gestalt psychology was rejected, but perhaps for the wrong reasons. One of their basic tenets was what they called the principle of isomorphism: the idea that perceptual processing and the underlying physiological representation must be highly correlated. For example, in the phenomenon of grouping, the isomorphism principle suggests that the brain representation of the closer dots with similar lightnesses would interact more strongly with each other to form the pairs seen in my illustration [Fig. 9.1B]. Wolfgang Köhler proposed that this happened because the brain was a "physical Gestalt," a complex system that worked by neurons generating electrical brain fields, and the dynamic physical behavior of these fields was isomorphic with the unfolding perceptual experience. Its equilibrium was upset by neural stimulation arising from new sensory input, but it then achieved a new state of equilibrium that incorporated the input and settled back into a minimum energy configuration.

This set me wondering whether EEG measurements could provide evidence for the brain as a physical Gestalt. Dr. S explained,

The existence of electrical brain fields and the measurement of EEGs provided some evidence potentially supporting Köhler's field theory. However, prominent physiologists Karl Lashley and Roger Sperry conducted experiments to test the theory and found it wanting. Lashley attempted to disrupt the fields by laying electrically conductive gold foil over and inserting gold pins into monkey brains, neither of which had any effect on their perceptual behavior. Sperry made a further attempt by putting electrically insulating strips into the brain, and they too had no effect. This was taken as compelling scientific evidence that Gestalt ideas about there being a physical Gestalt within the brain were wrong.

Dr. S put this in context:

But, in fact, it only showed the idea of *electrical brain fields* was wrong, and that isn't the only way in which the brain might be a physical Gestalt. In the 1980s and 90s, another Gestalt-like theory was devised by physicist John Hopfield and others based on computational models using computer simulations of neural networks. They discovered that when certain kinds of connected neural nets interact to process information, they indeed settle into minimum energy states, much like the electrical brain fields Köhler proposed. If such global dynamic neural networks were the substrate of Gestalt phenomena rather than electrical brain fields, they would not be disrupted by the experimental manipulations used by Sperry and Lashley. But these global dynamic neural network models are complex and not easily reconciled with current views of neural processing as divided into different regions of the brain, as present theories propose.

Since all human experience must have a neurological origin, Dr. S thought that "the interesting questions are how particular cognitive and perceptual experiences arise in the brain: how perceptual forms are organized, envisioned, or centered." This question is especially interesting when perceptual forms must arise from different regions of the brain.

The Vigor of the Experimental Method

There is one more reason I was thrown off the track and missed the early Gestalt theorists. During my initial fieldwork in Dr. S's lab, I listened to discussions in lab meetings about how to set up experiments. Clearly, as I had learned from Dr. S and Dr. B, even the most Gestalt-friendly topics, like aesthetics, were being studied by means of rigorous experimental methods. Even though topics derived from Gestalt thinking were often discussed in lab meetings, the basic tenets of the experimental method were honored. Quantitative measurement of behavior was taken for granted, for example, though more often by having subjects make direct quantitative ratings of their aesthetic experiences than by indirect reaction time measures. Control of experimental conditions was also a paramount concern, especially precision in the stimuli they studied. In one lab meeting a graduate student worried over the discovery that the computer monitor was not showing accurate colors in an ongoing experiment, but because of the need to keep conditions comparable across subjects, the group decided not to change anything midstream.

Somehow this fidelity to experimental requirements led me to pay less attention to a purely Gestalt-like discussion in the same lab meeting about the "affordances" of various objects and animals. "Affordance" is a concept developed by a pioneering ecological psychologist, James Gibson, in strong sympathy with the forbearers of Gestalt theory.[16] It refers to the way objects in a given world interact with the perceptions of the inhabitants of that world. For example, if inhabitants of some culture have the habit of placing things on tables, then a physical object that is horizontal, rigid, flat, extended in space, and somewhere between knee-high and waist-high might have the affordance of holding an array of small-to-medium sized things and could be perceived as a table. Its properties are not the abstract physical properties of height, length, and weight; they are only table-like if they fit into the habits of the people in question. A structure at hip height might have the affordance of holding plates of food for people who eat while sitting on chairs, but not for people who eat while sitting on the floor. I could now see that the long discussion in the lab meeting about how to represent objects and animals in an experiment about affordances reflected a sophisticated neo-Gestalt sensibility. What images of dogs, for example, should we present? A photograph of a living dog? A drawing of a dog? A painting of a dog? Which posture, mood, breed, size, age? Too specific an image might evoke idiosyncratic associations: What if one subject grew up with a small, friendly lapdog and another grew up with a gruff, muscular guard dog? The decision was to generate images using computer graphic software in which they could rigorously control the position of the object within the rectangular frame and the perspective from which it was seen. It was the complex cultural associations with an image that they needed to consider, a most anthropological concern! These aspects of the image mattered the way things matter to anthropologists: things are significant because they are embedded in and function within contexts in which they come to have some meanings and not others. Anthropologists want to relish and describe idiosyncratic associations; psychologists want to control them for the sake of comparable results.

I failed to take seriously the important role these subtle aspects of the "affordances" of objects played in the lab's research. The experimental method and the quantitative measurement of people's aesthetic experiences were the end result, and for me that blotted out what came before. I was paying attention, as it were, to the rules of badminton, not to the way players could creatively disregard some of the rules in order to keep playing.

Although Gestalt ideas played an important role in my fieldwork because of Dr. S's interest, I would have been hard pressed to find many other labs using Gestalt theory. Generally speaking, the moves crucial to a Gestalt approach fit uneasily into the experimental model, and that model is the only reliable route today to publications and grants. It will be no surprise that Gestalt approaches were also inimical to the historical development of computer technology. Historian David Bates has shown that Gestalt theory made an appearance in the early history of computers, noting "the rather surprising fact that ideas about the intrinsic, foundational unity of creative, insightful thought framed some important discussions of mind and brain at exactly the same time as the first electronic computers were being developed—and along with them, the first modern concepts of machine intelligence."[17] But the idea expressed by Köhler was also soundly rebuked by one of the founders of cybernetics, Norbert Wiener, who said that "if a phenomena can only be grasped as a whole and is completely unresponsive to analysis, there is no suitable material for any scientific description of it; for the whole is never at our disposal."[18] Bates concludes that "the machine analogy, so important for cybernetic theory and the earliest forms of artificial intelligence theory, was therefore antithetical to these holistic approaches."[19] In other words, the Gestalt approach was fully available to the founders of cybernetics, but they rejected it because something that has to be grasped as a "whole" is not amenable to scientific analysis. By and large, Dr. S's interest in Gestalt theory is still very unusual in the field. As an ethnographer, I felt very comfortable during discussions involving Gestalt theory because of its engagement with how people creatively move around rules and structures, something Wertheimer characterized as "productive thinking" and explained in a nutshell in the epigraph for this chapter.

10

Moving beyond the Lab

To-day we know scarcely a single realm of the mental life into which with rich success experiment does not dare to go. Who shall set the limit? To show the significance of the experimental method for the highest and most complicated phenomena of mental life, has come to be to-day exactly the goal of our labors.

—HUGO MÜNSTERBERG, *THE NEW PSYCHOLOGY*
AND HARVARD'S EQUIPMENT FOR TEACHING IT, 1893

TOWARD THE END of my research I began to realize that the methods of experimental psychology have become deeply involved in daily life beyond the laboratory. My realization occurred as I took stock of how my interlocutors and I were handling my anthropological way of describing their field. At the beginning of this research I certainly felt like a fish out of water. As I began to make sense of the landscape I was in, however, I began to fall into the malady Marx describes when people are actively involved in conflicting elements in their daily lives and cease to notice them: they grow accustomed to moving about among them and feel not the slightest mystery as they do so. They feel "as much at home as a fish in water."[1] Experimental protocols had begun to seem familiar rather than strange to me. I needed to find out whether my interlocutors also felt "as much at home as a fish in water" among their experimental methods. I recalled how disconcerting it was for Dr. B to think of leaving the world of tables, flat and still in their single plane. Returning to that conversation again, Dr. B went further. Remarkable for his wide imagination, he told me in detail how ambivalent he was about the taken-for-granted assumption that reaction time was a central indicator in experiments. He told

FIGURE 10.1. A Gabor filter, once used as the
stimulus in experiments. Image by AkanoToE,
CC BY-SA 4.0.

me, "Reaction time determines what problems you can model, in particular
brief reaction time. Why always depend on brief exposure? What would happen if we lengthened the time the stimulus was exposed?" This was a disturbingly revolutionary idea to me. I had worked hard to accept the importance
of using brief reaction time as a measure of the early steps of cognitive
activity.[2]

Dr. B was undaunted by my discomfort: in experiments, he said, "We have
to use boring stimuli, we have to overcome the really interesting questions
based on everyday scenes in order to get to more fundamental processes." He
exclaimed, in a sudden insight, "*Experiments deconstruct everyday elements!
They don't occur to you. No one notices everyday elements like the table.*"
Over his career, he went on, what is allowed to serve as a stimulus in an experiment has gotten more and more restricted:

> Early in my career, I used letters. It was a big deal to go from letters to words.
> But people in vision science believed they had to use these Gabor filters,
> modulated sine-waves, because somehow that's the only stimulus that they
> believed in. But you can totally ask many of the same questions that aren't
> restricted to that. And I think a lot of really interesting things haven't been
> asked because of restricting questions.

"Restricting questions"? I felt like I was talking with another anthropologist.
Speaking impatiently about his discipline, he complained,

They're so into the table, the computer screen, the fixation point, and the brief exposure, that nobody has the guts to do it without the table, without the fixation point, and without the brief exposure. And if I go, "Colleague, if you're really concerned about that, why not go out to a coffee shop, get your subject looking for somebody, and have them wave their hand or not wave their hand." And maybe in fact *we've kind of beat the phenomenon out of our subjects by I guess four things, the table, the fixation point, the brief exposure, and the repeated many, many trials to average out error.*

I felt like he was summarizing the conclusions of my research for me. Then he went beyond me. He remembered I had told him about Wade's desire to interact with his subjects, which his lab had essentially forbidden. Dr. B said,

So treating the subject as a machine—some people do this, they'll put the subject in the booth and treat them like a machine. I'm with that graduate student [Wade] who wanted to chat with his subjects—don't tell the professor [Dr. R] that I said that! Some psychologists will take the subject and say sign here and then go in the booth and press a button in the center and instructions will come up. That's all the interaction there needs to be.

Bringing the point home, Dr. B continued, "I did that for forty years. I don't think it's necessarily wrong, but *I think subjects are now a different kind of human being. You've optimized the machinery as much as you possibly can.*"

I was sympathetic with those forty years of research and reflexively defended the discipline I had tried hard to comprehend, so I replied, "I mean there are totally legitimate reasons why you'd want to treat the subject as a machine, because you're trying to get out a readable signal." At this point, hearing my own words, I was overwhelmed by the realization that Dr. B was willing to articulate something I had not dared to say: that psychological experiments, spread across the contemporary landscape, have made people into a "different kind of human being." The "optimized machinery" of the experiment would directly affect only experimental subjects, of course. But it dawned on me that a great many of us perform exercises like rating the quality of a commodity or a service, filling out questionnaires, or checking our status on Facebook. These exercises are not necessarily part of an experiment but, like experiments, they involve choices determined in advance by others and outcomes analyzed statistically.

Dr. B was showing me that he was assessing the larger influence of his discipline on society in general. At a minimum, Dr. B meant that subjects are optimized to fit the requirements of the experimental apparatus. This insight was what eventually led me to see the significance of practice sessions held before experimental trials. Dr. B led me to see a way the experimental method demanded a certain kind of human subject, one that was trained to operate like a sort of "optimized machinery," familiar with the tasks to be carried out, attentive, focused, calmly sitting or lying down, and willing to participate until the experiment's end. The method of practice, the foyer to the experiment, enlisted both subjects and researchers in producing useable results.

Somehow Dr. B's astute anthropological take on his own field galvanized me to think beyond the lab. He is a practitioner of the discipline I had struggled to get inside of, yet he is remarkably able to crack open the boundaries around the discipline's assumptions. I had thought my research was almost finished. However, news reports and congressional hearings about social and digital media were happening at the time, and inspired by Dr. B's insights, I began to listen with a keen ear. Were users on social and digital media acting like the subjects in experiments who were "optimized machinery"? Was this convergence enabling the manipulations on social and digital media that were then coming to light? I began to wonder whether the underlying paradigms of the discipline of experimental psychology were making the operations of social and digital media possible. Those paradigms, embedded deep in the assumptions of the discipline and central to its practices, began to visibly materialize in my awareness as the *engine* of social and digital media. Donald MacKenzie argued that, "Financial economics . . . did more than analyze markets; it altered them. It was an 'engine' [. . .]an active force transforming its environment, not a camera passively recording it."[3] I wanted to explore how experimental psychology might be serving as an "engine" propelling social and digital media.

Exploring this question led me away from my laboratory field sites. While I was doing fieldwork, the world of social and digital media and internet design seemed to occupy a far distant planet. Only once in my fieldwork was there a tiny bit of contact between these worlds. Dr. S reported excitedly that the CEO of Pinterest had called him to ask the same question I had asked him recently: Do you know what it is like for subjects to experience your experiments? The CEO had heard that Dr. S's lab was doing research on the aesthetics of sound and color and thought his lab's findings might help the company design more aesthetically appealing web pages. Beyond this incident, in the labs where I did fieldwork, neither the PIs nor the grad students had any role in internet companies; but the underlying paradigms of the discipline they practice might have helped create the operations on which digital media is built. I began to realize that those paradigms, embedded deep in the assumptions of the discipline and central to its practices, were appearing in real time as the mechanisms underlying the operations of digital media.

Ergonomics

When I mentioned this idea to my interlocutors and other colleagues, they were skeptical. But there is an earlier case, ergonomics, in which experimental psychology certainly helped to transform our everyday environment. Returning to the history of ergonomics, whose reliance on experimental psychology has been well documented, foreshadows my argument about digital media. The inspiration for the science of ergonomics occurred during World War II, when errors in American military operations began to be understood as a result of faulty design in technological devices that led human operators to make mistakes.[4] In one case, the engineer in a B-29 airplane on the way from Canada to Marrakesh, North Africa, was seated facing backwards. There were four engines on the plane. The no. 1 engine began to fail and needed to be shut down. If the engineer had been facing forward, he would have been aware that the engines were mounted on the wings in order from left to right. The no. 1 engine would have been on his left and so would the no. 1 engine control. Facing aft, he would have been aware that the no. 1 engine was now on his right. However, the engine controls in front of him had simply been swiveled around and left in their original positions, so the engineer now faced them in their original order from his left to his right. Believing the no. 1 engine to be on his right, he pulled the rightmost engine control and inadvertently shut down no. 4, the wrong engine, leading to a dangerous emergency.[5] During the latter years of the war and afterward, ergonomics relied on psychological experiments of exactly the sort I have described earlier in this book to improve the design of military technology. In 1947, "most research on equipment design belong[ed] to the field of experimental psychology."[6] Human capacities were measured in experimental settings to determine reaction time for motor and cognitive tasks.[7] Often, simple feedback loops were built into equipment so performance could be monitored, and equipment could be redesigned as needed.

By the 1960s, ergonomic research had expanded greatly to include systems engineering for such things as space flight and began to make some inroads into civilian consumer products. Psychological experimentation continued to provide the basic research that informed redesign.[8] No matter how improved the ergonomic design of complex systems, like controls for nuclear reactors or airplane cockpits, their human participants always required extensive training in how to use them correctly. This training was like an amplification of the routine practice session that would have been part of prior lab experiments.

Today, the applications of ergonomic research are ubiquitous, playing a part in the design of computers, writing instruments, keyboards, appliances, chairs, and tables. Consumers can purchase and use these devices without any awareness of the role of psychological research in designing them. But it is very much there. Current textbooks on ergonomics contain many pages of material that could just as well be found in textbooks for experimental psychology: consider the chapter titles "How the Mind Works" and "Human Senses" in *Ergonomics: How to Design for Ease and Efficiency*.[9] So all the ease of use we take for granted in our desk chairs and computer keyboards is based on now hidden early-twentieth-century experiments in psychology. These ideas, now considered elementary, have been built upon in so many ways and have become so embedded in our lives that we no longer notice them.

User Friendly Design

An important descendant of ergonomics is "user centered design," also called "user experience design." In 1988, Donald Norman published a book titled *The Psychology of Everyday Things*. Later editions were retitled *The Design of Everyday Things*.[10] In the book, Norman calls on behavioral experiments and observations to test the advantages of different designs of door handles, water faucets, stove burner controls, and other ordinary objects. He also appeals to the concept of affordances, related to Gestalt theory as I described in chapter 9, to encourage thinking about how devices interact with users in particular cultural contexts. More recently, in *User Friendly*, Cliff Kuang and Robert Fabricant trace the origins of the design thinking behind the shape, color, and arrangement of icons and buttons we now take for granted on our iPhone screens and keyboards. They explore the history of the idea that all devices should be, as the title suggests, user friendly, designed to fit the habits and capacities that most humans find intuitive. They argue that there was a "great chain of ideas" that spawned the notion of being user friendly, a "steel cable, buried but already in place" that stretches back to the last world war.[11] Control panels for nuclear reactors like Three Mile Island and cockpits for tank operators were once illegible without extensive training for each operator. Faced with emergencies like planes that crashed and reactors that almost exploded, the "ethos of user-friendly design" slowly came into play.[12] Buttons whose functions were related would be placed closer together; controls would have different colors and shapes to differentiate different functions, and data would be collected about where human bodies, hands, and fingers could most easily reach and manipulate controls.[13] In our daily lives, as we enjoy the comforts of user-friendly design, we usually do not realize how those comforts came to be. Ease of use, whether for keyboards or chairs, rests on the invisible transfer of sciences like ergonomics and user-friendly design into daily life—sciences that themselves arose from methods at the core of experimental psychology.

The Playbook

The logical next step for me was to consider whether a similar case can be made for the role of the methods of experimental psychology in creating social and digital media platforms. If the basic methods of experimental psychology have helped create the platforms by which digital media operate, then they are situated (as is user-friendly design) like a "steel cable, buried but already in place" underneath digital media platforms. As I described in earlier chapters, there is a large toolbox of practices that form the core of research in experimental psychology. The reward for understanding these tools is that we can grasp the links between the tools used in scientific labs and the ways the same methods are being deployed for very different purposes in our digital lives. As with design thinking, seeing the origins of the elements of our digital lives in experimental cognitive psychology will enlighten us about digital media's great powers and unintended consequences.

This toolbox, every item of which we have met in some detail in previous chapters, is summarized in box 10.1, which connects experimental psychology labs and digital media platforms. I will take the points up one by one.

1. Discoveries from Psychology Lab Experiments Were Used to Build the Platforms of Social and Digital Media

Moving from experimental psychology experiments to social and digital media "experiments" felt to me like passing through the looking glass. I could easily recognize familiar practices from psychology labs, but I could also see that their purpose had been inverted. Most apparently, designers of social and digital media used research from experimental psychology to create an addictive desire to engage with social media platforms. I cannot stress enough how

Box 10.1. The playbook

As in the lab, so also in social and digital media:

1. *Discoveries* from psychology lab experiments were used to build the platforms of social and digital media.
2. Data is produced by *individual* subjects or users.
3. *Data* is numerical, *digital*, and is often guided by *algorithms*.
4. The *experimental model* is fundamental for both psychology lab researchers and social and digital media designers.
    - Both subjects and users are *manipulated* through inductions, priming, or persuasive technology.
    - Subjects and users must be *stabilized*.
    - Subjects in the lab and algorithms used in social media must be *trained through practice* to produce usable data.
5. Subjects and users *willingly* provide data in labs and on social and digital media.

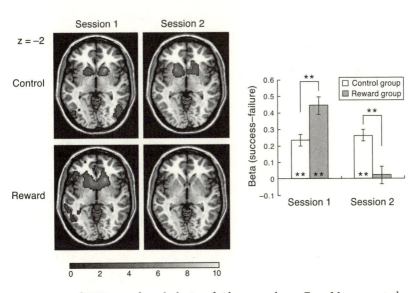

FIGURE 10.2. fMRI images from the brains of video game players. From Murayama et. al. (2010), figure 2.

closely related the laboratory methods I have described in this book are to the methods used by social and digital media. The path to the media companies' primary goal was laid by research in experimental psychology that showed how to harness the production of dopamine. In figure 10.2, the fMRI images at the top show the brains of video game players (the controls) who were not paid, but whose brains activated in the neural striatum, where dopamine neurons are located, when they scored a point in the game. The bottom fMRI images show players in two different sessions.

On the left is the first session, where we see subjects who were rewarded in the game with money, and whose brains then strongly activated in their dopamine-producing areas. On the right is the second session with the same subjects a while later, where no rewards were offered, and the subjects' activation of their dopamine-producing areas has stopped.[14] This is the germ of the notion that the possibility of a reward always needs to be present to keep the dopamine flowing. You know that addictive feeling you get when checking Facebook, Twitter, or Gmail again and again? Whenever you return, the possibility (though not the guarantee) of another reward will always be there.

The focus was on production of dopamine from the start. Sean Parker, a Facebook founder, said, "The thought process that went into building these applications, Facebook being the first of them . . . was all about: 'How do we consume as much of your time and conscious attention as possible?'" He continued, "And that means that we need to sort of give you a little dopamine hit every once in a while, because someone liked or commented on a photo or a post or whatever. And that's going to get you to contribute more content, and that's going to get you . . . more likes and comments. It's a social-validation feedback loop . . . exactly the kind of thing that a hacker like myself would come up with, because you're exploiting a vulnerability in human psychology." All this was not a happy accident: "The inventors, creators—it's me, it's Mark [Zuckerberg], it's Kevin Systrom on Instagram, it's all of these people—understood this consciously. And we did it anyway."[15]

Regret over having deliberately designed such a system is common. For example, there have been recent alarms about Cambridge Analytica, its parent company SCL (Strategic Communication Laboratories), and Alexander Kogan's GSR (Global Science Research), all of which worked with the University of Cambridge's Psychometrics Centre to deliberately manipulate users on Facebook. Several former Facebook IT employees and executives, now working elsewhere, are expressing remorse at what they designed Facebook to be.[16] One of them, quoted in *The Guardian*, slammed the "short term dopamine-driven feedback loops that we have created."[17] According to Silicon Valley consultant Nir Eyal, these technologies "have turned into compulsions, if not full-fledged addictions," just as their designers intended.[18] Not only are they claiming that psychological research was used to design Facebook, they are showing how our behavior on social media can be used to manipulate us, via the traces left there by our behavior, but also via questionnaires we agree to fill out on Amazon's Mechanical Turk or the ones on Facebook itself, such as "Mypersonality" or "Thisisyourdigitallife." It might be shocking to discover that "short term dopamine-driven feedback loops" designed to turn users' actions into compulsions and even addictions were affecting the experiences of Facebook's more than two billion active users. Those responsible have, with hindsight, expressed regret at what they designed. The whistleblower Christopher Wylie, formerly of Cambridge Analytica, has repeatedly acknowledged the devious nature of manipulations on social media: he came forward in order to come to terms with what he had created. Of himself he said, "I should have known better."[19]

We could have been forewarned by the powerful analysis in *Addiction by Design* by anthropologist Natasha Dow Schüll, who demonstrated how the design of digital technology in casinos meticulously steers gamblers' addictive engagement with machine play.[20] She describes the elaborate user design built into the architecture of machine gambling operations in Las Vegas. The machines, including monitors, chairs, and cubicles, and the sensory environment, including sound, color, and space, are deliberately designed to thrust users into a tight and enduring relationship with the game. She found research showing that the psychological manipulation in machine gambling works much like cocaine addiction, producing a "cycle of affective peaks and dips."[21] Subsequently, Schüll commented to a journalist that "Facebook, Twitter and other companies use methods similar to the gambling industry to keep users on their sites." The user gets drawn into repeated cycles of "uncertainty, anticipation and feedback—and the rewards are just enough to keep you going," she explained.[22]

Even Facebook designers who have begun to have doubts about what they did make it clear that psychological research on "variable rewards" was explicitly used in designing the app. Research on variable rewards has a long history in psychology, going back to B. F. Skinner's work with pigeons. If a pigeon is rewarded every time it makes a correct response, it rapidly stops trying. But if the reward appears only after some unpredictable number of correct responses, the pigeon keeps trying. Skinner called this "variable ratio reinforcement."[23] As we just saw, Skinner's work has been brought up to date with work on brain imaging in humans.[24] The key is to make the possibility of a reward ever present, but never guaranteed for any particular response.

Facebook has the power to run human experiments on an unprecedented scale [. . .] The experiment took the form of a deceptively simple new feature called a "like" button. Anyone who has used Facebook knows how the button works: instead of wondering what other people think of your photos and status updates, you get real-time feedback as they click (or don't click) a little blue-and-white thumbs-up button beneath whatever you post.[25]

Users are essentially gambling every time they post a photo, web link, status update, or comment. Sometimes you can feel rewarded if enough friends "like" what you post; but the risk is that you can feel humiliated if no one is impressed enough with your post to "like" it.

Tristan Harris says, "The most seductive design exploits the same psychological susceptibility that makes gambling so compulsive: variable rewards. When we tap those apps with red icons, we don't know whether we'll discover an interesting email, an avalanche of "likes," or nothing at all. It is the possibility of disappointment that makes it so compulsive." This explains how the pull-to-refresh mechanism, whereby users swipe down, pause, and wait to see what new content appears, rapidly became one of the most addictive and ubiquitous design features in modern technology. "Each time you're swiping down, it's like a slot machine," Harris says. "You don't know what's coming next. Sometimes it's a beautiful photo. Sometimes it's just an ad."[26] Although some former Facebook designers are regretful about these deliberate efforts to addict Facebook users, others have made a virtue out of necessity. Nir Eyal's book *Hooked: How to Build Habit-Forming Products*, contains instructions about how to design products using variable rewards and has an accompanying workbook to spell the lessons out.[27]

2. Data Is Produced by Individual Subjects or Users

I have argued previously that in labs, the individual subject produces data about cognitive processes in particular settings, which are putatively independent from others, but actually dependent on elaborate social relationships among lab members. Social media is called "social" because it allows people to communicate with friends and colleagues. Social media produces a large network across which messages, photos, videos and so on pass, but the nodes of the network are almost always occupied by single individuals. Is there any kind of collective social ethos operating in social media? There is not likely to be anything like Dr. J's insistence on collaboration, Dr. R's tenderness toward her injured subjects, or Dr. S's skills in creating sociality.

Users may have collaborative goals, kind emotional feelings, or sincere desires for social connection as they post content and respond to the content of others. But it is all too easy to reduce the feelings of others toward you to a numerical count of "likes," followers, or retweets, a translation that drains away the nuances of what others feel and leaves you with a quantitative score. And of course, organizations like schools and colleges, political parties and candidates, or grass roots initiatives of all sorts, can post with a collective voice. But all too readily the responses organizations get will be reduced to a digital quantity—How many likes? How many followers?—a numerical tabulation that makes a collective appear as a single individual. And there is a larger related issue, which is the focus of a vigorous debate over whether social media promotes new and vigorous forms of sociality or an impoverished sociality. In whatever way this debate is resolved in the future, individuals are sure to be at the center of interactions in social media, as they are in cognitive psychology experiments.[28]

Individualism is an old problem—many scholars have stressed the centrality of the concept of the "individual" for modern capitalism. Recently, Leith Mullings has explained how individualism facilitates racism:

> This [. . .] racial ideology is integrally related to the hegemonic project of neoliberalism, which is about unrestricted open markets, flexible labor, the diminished role of government, [. . .] productivity as the measure of an individual's worth, and personal responsibility. It incorporates older notions but speaks the language of individual merit, freedom of choice, and cultural difference. Like neoliberalism, these contemporary explanatory frameworks facilitate the denial of racism and conceal the inner workings of the social system by attributing contemporary inequality to individual culture or meritocracy.[29]

That is, the focus is on individual actions, and not the social systems those actions depend upon. Perhaps there could be something of a remedy: when we come across media coverage from experiments in psychology, we could remember the rich sociality behind the apparent individuality of the findings. Surprisingly, given its role in promoting the individual, experimental psychology could be a beneficial model: if its social nature were made evident, it could carry with it beyond the lab a vision of human capacities as necessarily arising out of social relationships and not out of the actions of autonomous individuals.

3. Data *Is Numerical,* Digital, *and Is Often Guided by* Algorithms

Expanding on the role of numerical tabulation, "data" today is a collection of numbers or a collection of materials that can be represented numerically.[30] Numbers have come to seem necessary for locating people, figuring out what they like or dislike, who they interact with, how well known they are, and a myriad of other things. Numbers are necessary for digital engineers to build algorithms and for consumers to register approval of a purchase or service. Although numbers seem to be the epitome of objective truth, lacking any judgment about what is valuable, when numerical measures are put to work in databases or algorithms, they can carry with them very particular human cultural biases about, among other things, gender, race, age, and income.[31] Careful studies have shown how the databases used to build algorithms that track recipients of welfare benefits electronically can target the poor with mor-alistic and punitive strategies that increase the stigma of their position.[32] It is important to avoid taking the value of "data" for granted, and to ask instead about the difference between a numerical scale representing emotion or bias and a description in which people are seen as part of a social context that bears far more thought and feeling than can be captured by a numeric measure.

Operations on computers are not only numeric—they also require binary distinctions.[33] Every point of decision produces either a 1 or a 0. What could be more straightforward—except that we may doubt the fiction that anything meaningful for or about complex living beings could be easily sorted into just two states ("is" (1) or "is not" (0)), even if such points of difference were mul-tiplied many times. It is in the gap between the 0 and the 1 that living beings make decisions, love others, fight for recognition, enjoy their pleasures, and a million other things.[34] Numerical measures abound in psychology labs and in social media, and pointing this out is another way of seeing both the com-mon elements between them and the stripped down nature of the data they work with.

The numerical tools of social and digital media resist the effort to label them as beneficial or harmful because they are now ubiquitous and (to most of us) invisible. Today we meet algorithms on every side, as they select the news feed we see in social and digital media, the things we are likely to buy online, or the movies we'd like to stream. Nonetheless, a great many accounts have emerged recently that try to specify when such tools as algorithms work to people's advantage and when they do not. A major report from the Pew Foundation is called "Pros and Cons of the Algorithm Age," while the Nuffield

Foundation calls its report "Ethical and Social Implications of Algorithms, Data, and Artificial Intelligence." Books like *Algorithms to Live By* or *The Ethical Algorithm* analyze how to develop algorithms that are accurate and fair. Organizations like *AI Now* and *Data & Social Research* run symposia and fund research exploring these questions.

Sometimes algorithms decide matters of life and death. Lucy Suchman has shown in a devastating account how the assumptions behind the United States military's algorithm-driven drones are filled with blind spots. The assumptions behind the algorithms promise accuracy and precise identification of the enemy. The conclusions that are used in directing drones to target enemies are derived from training on huge datasets of video captured previously—also by drones. The conclusions appear pure and clear, allowing us to deploy instruments guided by logic alone and incapable of error. In reality, they articulate "racialized and gendered bodies." There are culturally specific patterns—assumptions about race, gender, and culture—that inform the databases that algorithms are trained on. For one thing, the humans who coded the data did so with their own cultural biases intact, which they inadvertently taught to the algorithm in training. For another thing, the databases themselves were already problematic because they included people previously labeled as suspect, rather than people who could be verified as constituting a threat at the present time.[35]

An algorithm is a particular kind of tool. Basically, it is simply a set of instructions for computers to follow. But its use raises worries about both privacy and profit making, as happened when Google recently gobbled up millions of health records in the Ascension hospital system as training for its algorithms.[36] This raised alarms about the urgent need for government regulation of this kind of data collection, the ethics of building a dataset that included identifying information, and the ethics of extracting data without either requesting permission or giving notice. It also raised alarms about the ultimate purpose of the dataset. Would it be used to predict health outcomes? To target susceptible individuals with ads for products that prevent illness or enhance health? To lead insurance companies to refuse coverage or raise the price of coverage on the basis of newly identified risks? To nudge or "prime" individuals toward greater awareness of health risks?

To my mind, the deepest matter of concern in the use of algorithms is common to any numerical measure, and that is the process of *abstraction* intrinsic to producing "data." I learned about the power of abstraction from Marx's account of how the concept of value arose with the development of capitalism.

Labor of different kinds—hoeing the ground, running a machine, crafting furniture, writing an essay, picking produce, digging for minerals—involves different skills for each task: different muscular movements, different parts of the body, and different kinds of knowledge are called upon. As capitalist relations developed, all forms of labor came to be compared according to the amount of time the laborer worked. The details of radically different jobs were erased as the abstract concept of labor as time worked became the measure of the value of labor. Historically, this allowed wages to be calculated on the basis of time worked, not on the basis of the quality of work, or on the basis of payments that were traditional for specific kinds of work.

Derek Sayer called this aspect of capitalism "the violence of abstraction," after Marx, because abstraction involves forcibly stripping away the specific characteristics of the infinitely varied kinds of human effort and replacing them by a numerical measure of time.[37] This violent and powerful process of abstraction operates in machine learning and in the algorithms it uses. Although an algorithm can be simply defined as a "finite sequence of steps used to solve a problem," the most common algorithms used in digital media today involve mathematical calculation, and mathematical calculations invariably involve abstraction.[38] When Google identifies a set of people who might be interested in buying new shoes and places ads accordingly, its algorithm is ignoring the specifics of each person's situation—one person is required to buy a certain kind of shoes for a new job, another needs to replace shoes that were lost in a flood, and yet another just wants to wear the latest style. Google may gain profit for the shoe company with their advertisement, but at the cost of stripping away from people everything except the likelihood they will spend money on shoes, which is all that matters to an algorithm.

Some business practices are made easy by the simplicity of mathematical calculations: algorithms on Facebook can simply count the number of "likes" a given post is awarded to calculate where it should appear in a newsfeed. Others depend on human intelligence to encode (tag or label) items before an algorithm can work. This is where what are called "human intelligence tasks" (HITs) come in, often via crowdsourcing marketplaces like Amazon Mechanical Turk. Human workers are paid very small wages to mark images or articles according to their emotional valence, or to label images with the name of the object depicted.[39] For example, a worker might view an image of an animal and create the label "dog." Once human intelligence has created an abstracted valence or label, an algorithm can then count, trace associations, and calculate an outcome. Why do I say abstracted? Because nearly all such sorting tasks only allow for a subset of possible descriptions, reducing the total possible responses.

For instance, the *New York Times* used Amazon Turk to assign HITs that would tag the emotions evoked by their articles. This was in the service of a project called Project Feels, which in turn placed ads for products near the article that would get more clicks because of the associated emotional valence.[40] Amazon Turk workers had to choose six emotions from eighteen possibilities. So, let's imagine an article about a family whose lost dog traveled hundreds of miles to find them again. Out of the list of eighteen choices, I would pick: optimistic, inspired, adventurous, love, hope, happiness—six words. But if I had been allowed fully to express the emotions the article evoked, I might have wanted to add sadness at the grief suffered by the family while waiting in limbo, anxiety about finding out what physical and mental condition the dog was in after its travel, suspicion over the family's carelessness in losing the dog, admiration for the individual dog, awe at the canine species' loyalty, and much more. The six words allowed represent a small selection, an abstraction from the full gamut of emotional responses I might have. One might argue that the six words I could choose from the available options were the essential, or that they represented the core emotions evoked. But from *The New York Times'* point of view, it is more likely that they would simply wait to see if Project Feels worked: if the ads it placed got more clicks. The algorithm would be judged on whether it increased profits for the newspaper and its advertisers. But, more tellingly, *the abstraction it employs entails the loss of the great complexity of human emotions.*

4. The Experimental Model *Is Fundamental for Both Psychology Researchers and Social and Digital Media Designers*

We have seen previously how the experimental model provides the framework for cognitive psychology labs. In *The Age of Surveillance Capitalism*, Shoshana Zuboff makes the parallel to social and digital media clear. She cites a former Facebook product manager:

> Experiments are run on every user at some point in their tenure on the site. Whether that is seeing different size ad copy, or different marketing messages, or different call-to-action buttons, or having their feeds generated by different ranking algorithms ... The fundamental purpose of most people at Facebook working on data is to influence and alter people's moods and behavior.[41]

In psychology labs, the goal is to understand how cognitive processes work in a general sense: Is learning enhanced or encumbered for most people by a certain induction? There is no attempt to manipulate subjects into acting differently after they finish the experiment. In social and digital media, the whole purpose is to move people toward specific actions in the world more than they would have moved otherwise. In the psychology lab, the effort is to describe, as it were, the psychic laws of cognition. In social and digital media, the effort is to deploy the psychic laws of cognition to influence behavior in specific ways. In sociologist Shoshana Zuboff's words, Facebook's behavioral modification "is aimed at solving one problem: how and when to intervene in the state of play that is your daily life in order to modify your behavior and thus sharply increase the predictability of your actions now, soon, and later."[42] Toward this end, their efforts bear down on every detail, from the size of fonts to the color of icons.[43]

Successful algorithms can predict behavior. A leaked document from Facebook described by Zuboff explains: "The idea is that these predictions can trigger advertisers to intervene promptly, targeting aggressive messages to stabilize loyalty and thus achieve guaranteed outcomes by altering the course of the future."[44] Perhaps most tellingly, the Facebook "experiment" happens without subjects being aware they are in an experiment. They are given no monetary rewards, sit in no special place, sign no consent form, and receive no directions. Nonetheless the grammar of the experimental method is alive and well. Thus, experimental psychology is like an engine that propels the operation of social and digital media. Its methods and findings have provided the underpinnings of how social and digital media works. The engine works, even without the ethical guidelines of the labs, and, alarmingly, no matter what motivates those running the experiment.

Further, all the component elements of the experimental model are alive and well in social and digital media. Social and digital media users are manipulated, stabilized, and trained, just as subjects in experiments are.

BOTH SUBJECTS AND USERS ARE MANIPULATED THROUGH INDUCTIONS, PRIMING, OR PERSUASIVE TECHNOLOGY

As we have seen, the experimental method can require inductions or priming. Randall's induction for his experiment on repetitive negative thoughts illustrated the technique. The engineers of social and digital media rely instead on what is called persuasive technology or persuasive design. The idea that psychological research could be applied to social and digital media platforms largely began at the Persuasive Technology Lab run by psychologist B. J. Fogg at Stanford University. Fogg focuses on "methods for creating habits, showing what causes behavior, automating behavior change, and persuading people via mobile phones."[45] Gradually, the influence of this lab's methods on social media designers has come to light through acknowledgements of the social media designers who were Fogg's students.[46]

> A decade ago, Fogg's lab was a toll booth for entrepreneurs and product designers on their way to Facebook and Google. Nir Eyal, the bestselling author of the book *Hooked: How to Build Habit-forming Products*, sat in lectures next to Ed Baker, who would later become the Head of Growth at both Facebook and Uber. Kevin Systrom and Mike Krieger, the founders of Instagram, worked on projects alongside Tristan Harris, the former Google design ethicist who now leads the Time Well Spent movement. Together, in Fogg's lab, they studied and developed the techniques to make our apps and gadgets addictive.[47]

Fogg's textbook, *Persuasive Technology: Using Computers to Change What We Think and Do*, has been available since 2003.[48] Looking back at its content now is slightly shocking, knowing as we do how its *ideas* have been used and how long they have been available. In 2003, Fogg looked forward eagerly to growth in mobile technology, and explained "why mobile and connected devices can be so effective in persuading people to change their attitudes and behavior."[49] To be sure, many of the ways Fogg imagined people can be motivated and influenced involve worthy, health-related goals: quitting smoking, increasing exercise, and the like. He provides many pages of discussion of the ethics of building persuasive technology into computers and makes it clear that his own research requires approval of Stanford's IRB, which is always alert to preventing harm to research subjects.[50] But at the same time, he acknowledged that "some companies" do not have research approval systems, and that individual designers should find a way to assure the kind of protections for subjects that an IRB provides. I agree, but there is little evidence that this has happened. If digital media companies did institute an IRB, perhaps they would have to seriously assess the harm caused by the spread of conspiracy theories or fake news compared to the benefits of easy communication among friends or rapid dissemination of urgent news.

Many people have become aware that our behavior on social and digital media can be used to manipulate us via the traces left there by our behavior, but also via questionnaires we agree to fill out on Amazon, Google, or Facebook itself. Even more seriously, the manipulation has gone far beyond enticing us to buy products and has entered fully into the realm of swaying political elections. When the scandal over Cambridge Analytica and its allies broke, the whistleblower, Christopher Wylie, testified before the United States Senate Committee on the Judiciary and the British Parliament.[51] Of the many accounts of this scandal in *The Guardian* newspaper and elsewhere, Wylie's own statement to the Senate Committee remains among the most powerful:

> CA [Cambridge Analytica] did not operate in elections to promote democratic ideals. Oftentimes, CA worked to interfere with voter participation, including by weaponising fear. In one country, CA produced videos intended to suppress turnout by showing voters sadistic images of victims being burned alive, undergoing forced amputations with machetes, and having their throats cut in a ditch. These videos also conveyed Islamophobic messages. It was created with a clear intent to intimidate certain communities, catalyse religious hatred, portray Muslims as terrorists and deny certain voters of their democratic rights.
>
> I am aware that CA clients requested voter suppression as part of their contracts. CA offered "voter disengagement" as a service in the United States and there are internal documents that I have seen that make reference to this tactic. My understanding of these projects, which I did not personally participate in, was that the firm would target African American voters and discourage them from participating in elections.[52]

Fomenting religious prejudice, promoting fear to discourage voting— although Cambridge Analytica filed for bankruptcy in May 2018, their actions still stand as a nadir in the damaging kinds of manipulation that can happen.

Less nefarious manipulations can be disturbing simply because they make clear that from an application designer's point of view, the proper role of a user is to conform unquestionably to the design of the application. This was explained to me by a young tech worker in New York City. She said that her company's CEO would never look at any of the customer feedback about their app, which she was tasked with collecting and organizing. Instead, he told her that she should find a way to manipulate the customers to love the app *just as it was*. Now the app is calling the tune that the user must dance to.

It is as if the experimental model described in my ethnography was turned on its head by digital media. In my fieldwork, experiments were devoted to what researchers considered "basic science": individual subjects emit data that psychologists can process to understand how we think or remember, daydream or forget. According to the ideals of basic science, the researchers are not seeking any particular outcome, let alone any practical application of their results. In accord with this ideal, while researchers build predictions into their experimental design and they look for statistically significant results that add to our knowledge about human cognition, they do not consciously try to nudge subjects in any particular direction. However, it is actually just a small step to introduce a specific nudge. Internet companies could harness findings from basic research for a baseline understanding of how cognition works, and then they could redeploy the knowledge of how to get inside cognitive processes to influence them in a particular direction: buy these shoes instead of those shoes; vote for this person instead of that person.

All these forces are likely to intensify. Recently, a new facial recognition app produced by the company Clearview AI began to raise alarms. The app is based on a "database of more than three billion images that Clearview claims to have captured (or 'scraped') from Facebook, YouTube, Venmo and millions of other websites," writes tech reporter Kashmir Hill in *The New York Times*. "Without public scrutiny, more than 600 law enforcement agencies have started using Clearview in the past year, according to the company," enabling law enforcement to identify anyone in a public place—at a demonstration, or just walking down the street. "You take a picture of a person, upload it and get to see public photos of that person, along with links to where those photos appeared."[53] It is a sure bet that more news of powerful facial recognition algorithms will be coming and that cries for more public regulation will increase. Canadian authorities have recently declared that the operations of Clearview are illegal in Canada and that the company should delete the faces of Canadians from its database.[54] Already, in the face of protests against racial discrimination by the police, Amazon has instituted a one-year pause on allowing the police to use its facial recognition technology, fearing it could lead to unfair treatment of African-Americans.[55]

One consolation for the anxious public might be that as people begin to realize that they are being subjected to the manipulation common in the experimental methods used by social and digital media, they might also begin to realize that they can experience the experimental method in many ways: as a serious test, a fun game, a painful ordeal, or a suspenseful drama. Perhaps the chameleon-like nature of the experiment will make the data it gathers seem less like the key to objective truths. At the same time, data is often used for blatant marketing efforts, and those are hard to experience as anything else: when people buy tea online and then find ads for tea pots popping up on their social and digital media accounts, they are meeting an algorithm pressuring them like a salesman.

SUBJECTS AND USERS MUST BE STABILIZED

Of course, digital experiments running on social and digital media cannot count on tables or any of the other means of stabilizing the laboratory subject in time or space. People engage with social and digital media while eating, riding the subway, talking with friends, listening to lectures, and many other daily activities. They may be paying some attention in spite of noise, smells, vibrations, interruptions, crowds, rapid motion, and spotty internet connections.

Perhaps what might compensate for the lack of a stable setting is appreciation of the power of big data. Marc Rotenberg, director of the Electronic Privacy Information Center, refers to regard for big data as "'digital scientism' [...] an unwavering faith in the reliability of big data."[56] The sheer size of their sample may give confidence to developers and operators, since the magnitude is hard to comprehend: a "petabyte" (10^{15} bytes) is a common unit used to measure big data, and one petabyte equals 500 billion pages of standard typed text. Perhaps these dazzling amounts of data convince analysts to believe their findings must be meaningful because the dataset is taken to represent the *entire* universe of responses. A *sample* from the dataset could be biased, but if you are analyzing data that represents *everyone's* response, how could you go wrong?

Similarly, when the engine of the psychology lab experiment is put to work in the digital world, extremely large numbers are readily at hand. One report of an experiment on Facebook is titled, "A 61-million-person experiment in social influence and political mobilization."[57] The subjects were simply users of Facebook who accessed the site on the day of a United States congressional election. The sample of subjects was divided into those who received an induction (information about voting)—more than sixty million were in this group—and those who served as controls—over 60,000—who did not receive the induction. The results revealed modest effects toward greater political engagement from those who received the induction. Without the large numbers, the modest effects might not have been detectable. The machine is empowered by its large numbers, but also by its ability in the social and digital media context to track subsequent off-line behavior—namely, voting. The experimenters were able to track off-line behavior by matching their sixty million subjects to publicly available voting records.

When big datasets are readily available, the public cannot anticipate their future uses in order to guard against applications that are illegal, unethical, or simply distasteful. Classically, Martin Heidegger said that technology "puts to nature the unreasonable demand that it supply energy that can be extracted and stored."[58] Even a simple technology, like a scythe, "demands," so to speak, that the grain field "supply energy" in the form of sheaves of grain that can be extracted and stored. A cell phone "demands," so to speak, that servers supply enough energy to extract and store information about our interactions and locations. What is the "energy" stored in big data? Heidegger's description of technology as "on call for duty" impels us to ask: What duty is big data on call for? At this moment we are realizing some nefarious ways big data has been used. But it is not too late to address head-on whether or not big data can be used responsibly.

Recall that even when Randall chose the standard setting of 60Hz for eye tracking, he would still use only a small portion of the data collected at that wavelength. What happens to the rest? It is donated to the UK Data Service, a repository for data funded by the European Economic and Social Research Council (ESRC). The plethora of excess data is preserved for unknown researchers and purposes. Do depositors into big data repositories like this anticipate how it will be used or envision any limits to its use? The question should be answered cautiously. Researchers can set time limits and impose permission to access data. But big data might be called the apotheosis of making human activity into numerical measures. As Ian Hacking observed, "Enumeration demands kinds of things or people to count. Counting is hungry for categories."[59] Hence, we should not be surprised to see this kind of data used for new purposes. The recent scandal over Cambridge Analytica, SLC, and AggregateIQ's use of massive amounts of data from online sources—including but not limited to Facebook—have raised the issue of the unfortunate consequences, in which attempts are made to manipulate users' behavior, including how they vote.

SUBJECTS IN THE LAB AND ALGORITHMS USED IN SOCIAL AND DIGITAL MEDIA MUST BE TRAINED THROUGH PRACTICE TO PRODUCE USABLE DATA

Surprised as I was to find that practice sessions were routine for subjects in psychology experiments, I was even more surprised to discover that the embodiment of the experimental subject in digital technologies, the algorithm, is also developed through training. Artificial intelligence programs designed to perform like natural language, such as Google's Bidirectional Encoder Representations from Transformer (BERT), analyze large amounts of textual material—like reams of digitalized books and Wikipedia articles. The textual material is the training set for the algorithm. "Since they are optimized to capture the statistical properties of training data, they tend to pick up on and amplify social stereotypes present in the data as well."[60] For example, BERT learned from its training data to assume that computer programmers are men. By now, one can easily find emphatic statements about the bias likely to be carried by algorithms. Dudley Irish, a software engineer, said,

> All, let me repeat that, all of the training data contains biases. Much of it either racial- or class-related, with a fair sprinkling of simply punishing people for not using a standard dialect of English. To paraphrase Immanuel Kant, "out of the crooked timber of these datasets no straight thing was ever made."[61]

Other datasets would be no less likely to contain biases that algorithms would learn during their training: Google used data from its news coverage to develop algorithms for searching text and categorizing emails, data that one assumes would contain a certain amount of opinion.[62] Natural language machine learning systems have been trained on a large database of over 600,000 emails generated by 158 senior executives from Enron, data that would, one assumes, teach the algorithm responses that are biased by what wealthy, white, mostly male corporate employees emailed to each other. Training pulls subjects and algorithms into particular social worlds. Focusing on what any of us are trained to do provides a powerful clue to the sources of circularity and bias in digital algorithms.

Oddly, a way to fix this kind of bias is something social and digital media engineers could have adopted from experimental psychology, but by and large did not. That is the technique of normalizing datasets. Recall the trouble Dr. J went to in renormalizing the International Affective Picture System (IAPS) responses to reflect the population of her public university? This ensured that the dataset reflected as accurately as possible the worlds her student subjects lived in.

Training in a psychology lab contains within it the goals of the experiment: practice helps subjects notice cues that matter to the experimental hypothesis being tested. Training sets for algorithms also contain within them the goal of the training: creating a standard based on how people in certain rather privileged positions (employees of Enron, users of Google) talk and interact. The algorithm, through the repetitive feedback loops of machine learning, learns what its designers need it to learn. This is the core of the problem with the bias carried into the determinations algorithms make. Whatever the makeup of the training set—whether it is predominately white people, middle-class people, people of color, or young people—it will shape the optics through which the algorithm sees the world. Algorithms are *value-laden propositions* that can enact biased outcomes based on, for instance, racist assumptions.[63] This is why job search algorithms have been found to shortchange people of color; why Apple's health data from the Apple Watch has been found to privilege problems of the well-off; why facial recognition algorithms misidentify people of color; why algorithms have shown bias in favor of whites entering high-risk health management programs; why algorithms played a role in the expansion of high-risk subprime mortgages before 2007 and then in the denial of mortgage assistance to those homeowners who most qualified for it.[64] As these and more problems come to light, biases can be corrected, but as long as bodies of data containing historical inequities are used to train algorithms, these kinds of hidden biases will persist.[65]

5. *Subjects and Users* Willingly *Provide Data in Labs and on Social and Digital Media*

Users of social and digital media, including myself, yield a river of data for the world of interested corporations and governments. Why do we give away such a valuable resource? The insights of Dr. B are worth repeating here: "*we've kind of beat the phenomenon out of our subjects by I guess four things, the table, the fixation point, the brief exposure, and the repeated many, many trials to average out error.... I think subjects are now a different kind of human being. You've optimized the machinery as much as you possibly can.*" The habits that were modeled in the 1893 World's Fair exhibit, carried into the multitudes of experiments by researchers in psychology, and replicated in the single subject pressing keys on a phone or tablet, provide a template for the subject as the "optimized machinery" of the engine of psychology. It is clear that the data we willingly produce can be used for good but also questionable purposes.

When people willingly answer online quizzes and the like, they produce data that can be silently brought back around to influence them. A complete answer to why people do this awaits ongoing and future research projects, especially ones in which users are asked and given a chance to explain why they so eagerly provide data to Facebook and other sites.[66] But some preliminary guesses about imminent changes in our willingness to provide data are possible. For one thing, there has been a slow dawning about the ways in which such data can be used to manipulate our behavior. One need only listen to the testimony Christopher Wylie gave to the US Congress and a British parliamentary committee in 2018 to hear how unaccustomed elected officials were only a short time ago to the most basic aspects of online data, how it is collected, and how it can be used. Their ignorance was a wake-up call for how much the public needed to learn about the manipulation of their online data. Today the learning curve is still steep, but routes to effective knowledge are proliferating. Scholarly analyses such as Shoshana Zuboff's *The Age of Surveillance Capitalism*, recent government initiatives such as the EU's privacy mandates, and widespread attention to data scraping and surveillance in various media have all gathered together to make the informed public more aware that the data they willingly provide is anything but innocent. Mainstream media is growing more and more blunt about the implications. As *The New York Times* summarizes the situation: "Social media platforms use color and sound to reward engagement, which humans naturally seek out. Comments and likes are presented like a set of diamonds clicking into place on a slot machine. That delivers a little dopamine boost, training us to repeat whatever behavior wins the most engagement."[67] Acknowledging that social media includes deliberately engineered designs to create addictive behavior is causing alarm in some quarters.

Alarm is particularly warranted when networks develop on social media that spread misinformation internally. There has been much public attention to this issue, which has been blamed for increasing political polarization in the United States as well as for allowing floods of misinformation about such matters as political candidates' qualifications, public health measures, or vaccines' efficacy. Sometimes the spread of misinformation is powered by bots, which add to the apparent popularity of posts and increase their spread irrespective of the validity of the content.[68] Facebook and other social media platforms' executives are well aware of this problem and are seeking to modify the algorithms that determine how posts are ranked in news feeds so that they place more weight on the quality—that is, the veracity—of news. There is a worry that such measures might reduce the number of users, which would negatively affect corporate growth.[69] It is deeply troubling when addictive consumption of false information is tied to the bottom line.

For another thing, participating in clever questionnaires might seem like a case where language is "idling," or at least a case where users are "idling" rather than working. Most people turn to social and digital media as a break from their daily routine or work schedule. It is confusing to realize that a leisure activity meant for a relaxing break in the routine is actually working on us. This may be an example of the kind of confusion that Wittgenstein characterizes as arising "when language is like an engine idling, not when it is doing work."[70] When we face a judge in a courtroom, the language spoken there would definitely be doing work: we might be ordered to pay a fine, or worse. But when we are playing around—idling—on social and digital media, it is confusing to be confronted by words or images that merchants or political organizations intend to act on us like a judge's order.

Where language is apparently "idling" but in reality producing powerful effects, it can be bewildering. So many of the questionnaires we are offered on social and digital media seem like innocent fun: Which Star Wars figure, which Muppet, which character from *The Hunger Games*, Harry Potter, or Disney am I most like? Who do I find attractive? What kind of sexuality, intelligence, or personality do I have? All are fun and seemingly harmless exercises that yield an immediate insight into one's identity that a user can share or (perhaps) keep private. The confusion here is that individual portals to social and digital media appear to belong to the individual user, but in reality they belong to the corporation behind them. They are susceptible to being turned into numerical data that can be compared to other individuals or groups and used to compose posts intended to change users' behavior and profit from it.

In foregoing chapters, we have seen how well-established methods in experimental psychology labs are being deployed for very different purposes in our digital lives. Just as participants in psychology lab experiments must practice before producing data that can be used, so social and digital media users have been practicing unaware for years, until these tiny online exercises seem innocuous. This is partly a result of our training to be subjects: we have been trained to sit still in a chair at a table or hold a device where we can see it, to pay attention selectively, to look at the screen, to use a keyboard, to choose appropriately, to stay awake, to remain there indefinitely.

Public audiences have long been accustomed to take for granted that their participation in psychological research is a good thing: from the 1893 World's Fair exhibit where, in the not-too-distant past, the American public was explicitly taught to participate in psychology experiments, to the large numbers of undergraduate students who take introductory psychology classes, passively sitting at a table with a computer monitor while answering questions that produce quantitative data, users have become like devices, propelled by the engine of experimental psychology, who now generate data without the need for

FIGURE 10.3. A facial recognition graphic. Image from Vectorstock,
https://www.vectorstock.com/royalty-free-vector
/facial-recognition-system-3d-face-vector-19888747

a laboratory setting. Only by taking a hard look at the full process of producing data online can we learn the full implications of what we are being asked to do when we complete a fun questionnaire on Facebook or Twitter.

My goal is not to condemn the increasing presence of digital forms of data, algorithms, machine learning, artificial intelligence, and the rest, but to focus on how to describe what is different about these forms of representation. Some of the differences may make work easier and more efficient, travel swifter, learning more accessible, or relationships more understandable. Political movements of all sorts, from Black Lives Matter to the Three Percenters, can use social media to build a following and call their followers to action. Grassroots political movements have benefitted from social media's rapid communication in many countries around the world. And of course people can find each other more easily: long-lost kin; newly discovered kin; others who share a diagnosis, an experience, or a political perspective. Like any tool, social media can be put to many uses, and there is hope that one day its valuable uses might outweigh its negative uses.

But some of the differences may be repellent and require a serious effort to regulate their effects. The goal of this book is neither to tar digital technologies with a heavy brush nor to welcome them with naivety. It is to help in the effort to better describe what difference they make. Digital incursions into daily life are riding in on an older set of technologies: the experiment, normative scales, training, the extraction of data from subjects. This book first followed that set of technologies in research labs, where they flourish in the enterprise of attempting to describe normal human cognition. These technologies have now been put to a different use, to manipulate our decision-making and to replace analog representations with digital approximations. This is an important difference! Compare a photo of John Lennon by Annie Leibowitz with a schematic used for facial recognition. The photograph captures, as it were, the soul of one unique person and cannot usefully be compared to anyone else. We see emotion or apathy, age or youth, grace or awkwardness, strength or weakness, the signs of a relationship between photographer and subject. Instead, the facial recognition schematic shows a mathematical set of relationships between chin and cheeks, eyes and nose. It is immanently for the purpose of comparison—did that unique set of ratios go in a store and steal something? Hurt someone? Help someone? The *keyhole* through which such data looks into a person's life is very small, as Lucy Suchman says, and it serves very particular purposes.[71]

Experimental psychology's methods also look at human cognitive capacities through a small keyhole, though Dr. B has shown that a wider vision is possible. As I mentioned earlier, he acknowledged that none of his colleagues "has the guts to do [experiments] without the table, without the fixation point, and without the brief exposure." He could envision leaving the lab environment without the playbook and moving the experiment into daily life to collect data about how people recognize other people. The engine experimental psychology has provided to propel digital media recreates small, laboratory-like settings in daily life. It may be difficult to see these small experiments for what they are, but it is important to understand their power—and their limitations.

11

Entering Social and Digital Media

For, whereas the ideal psychological experimenter is an immaculate perceiver of an objective reality, the real psychological observer is, to a far greater extent than has been suspected, very much like his counterparts in the other social studies. He too is a *participant-observer.*

—NEIL FRIEDMAN, *THE SOCIAL NATURE OF PSYCHOLOGICAL RESEARCH,* 1967

AT THE BEGINNING of this research project, I wanted to understand why findings from experiments in cognitive psychology flow so easily and frequently into major news media. I wondered what it was about the findings of the field that made them so intriguing. I mentioned in the introduction that media accounts about psychological research are often appealingly presented in the form of useful tips about solving practical problems in daily life. In addition, in light of my ethnography of psychology labs, perhaps it is also intriguing that their findings are believed to be about universal qualities all humans share: how all people learn, remember, read, or spell; how all people perceive shapes or sounds, judge beauty or ugliness—not to mention the locations in peoples' brains where those psychological processes are happening. The psychologists who were my interlocutors do not divide subjects by race or nationality for the most part, though they sometimes do by gender. Hence their findings are meant to shed light on human cognitive capacities in general. But, as my interlocutors were well aware, not everyone has the same opportunity to learn, remember, perceive, judge beauty, read, or spell as a college student or an Amazon Turk worker. Structural forces of poverty, racism, or misogyny profoundly affect many people around the world, preventing them from entering

234

the pool of subjects who produce data in psychological experiments. Perhaps it is fair to say the experiments are appealing because they measure the awesome cognitive capacities of human beings under the controlled conditions that enable them to carry out experimental tasks successfully.

In contrast, my own field of cultural anthropology moved away from the kind of experiments on perception that Haddon and his colleagues did in the Torres Straits Islands, although there are robust fields of cross-cultural psychology and cognitive anthropology that describe universal human capacities in a comparative framework. But many cultural anthropologists have given up the quest for universals in favor of describing and analyzing rich historical and cultural specificities—spurred by a conviction that universals are inextricably linked to culturally specific contexts. Along with the quest for universals, we anthropologists seem to have given up the particular media-friendly frisson that comes with describing cognitive abilities all humans are thought to share.

But there is a cost to cognitive psychology's search for universal cognitive characteristics. The experimental setup depends on an individual subject who, tightly controlled in time and space, produces data that is used to formulate claims about universal characteristics of cognition, free of any context outside the lab. In my fieldwork for this book, I found it necessary to constantly bear this goal in mind in order to follow the logic of lab practices. But at the same time, as I have shown, the lab is a very specific kind of site, produced in the context of a particular historical trajectory. Erasing these specific characteristics of the lab's existence impoverishes our understanding of the cultural setting in which the lab is embedded and on which it depends. Many elements of experiments, as we have seen, carry with them conventional cultural assumptions: what the basic emotions are; how discrete basic emotions are; what attention consists of; what distraction consists of; what practice is necessary, and so on. Although these elements are culturally specific, they are translated via experimental models that are thought to produce universal findings.

Whatever the reason for the appeal of universal claims, the main point of my research is to show how *social* the production of findings in cognitive experimental psychology actually is. A great deal of social activity—learning by collaborating with others, relying on others, celebrating with others, competing with others, feeling delighted or annoyed by others, eating and drinking with others, disagreeing and arguing with others—necessarily lies behind scientific findings in experimental psychology. Some of this activity may be painful, some pleasurable, but it all adds up to a kind of sustained and dedicated work that depends on social relationships in specific settings, where psychologists build scientific knowledge using trusted participants and following proven methods.

The sociality of psychological research even extends to the subjective experience of participants. During our discussions of the role of subjective experience in psychology experiments, Dr. S emphasized its crucial importance. He explained that even in the most elaborate machinery for reading activity in the brain, like the fMRI,

> subjects in the scanner are being shown "emotional" pictures that have been previously rated by other subjects as "being emotional" (or even as specifically producing "anger" or "fear" or "joy," etc.) and those ratings are just behavioral reports of people's subjective experiences! Think about what the same experiment would look like without anyone ever considering people's subjective experiences on looking at them. There'd be no distinction between emotional pictures versus landscapes versus sporting events, etc., so how would the researchers be able to decide what parts of the brain responded to emotion versus landscapes, etc.? They'd have no idea how to interpret the fMRI data at all. So, the so-called objectivity of the fMRI results rests on a very important foundation of subjectivity.

Perhaps, Dr. S thought, another reason for the appeal of psychological research to the mainstream media is that "psychology largely hides the subjectivity underlying its methods and results, whereas anthropology wears it proudly as an important conclusion." As an appeal to generally accepted standards of truth, the claim to have both universal and objective conclusions is hard to beat.

Uncovering Subjectivity

An important place where we have seen that psychology "hides the subjectivity underlying its methods and results" is inside the experimental method itself. By means of practice sessions, subjects are enlisted in a cooperative venture to produce reasonably clean data. The subjects' role is to enter the small, ephemeral, social world of the experimental trial. There, the subject is trusted to pay attention, sit still, follow directions, answer honestly, and return for further trials if needed. This tiny world is ephemeral, but subjects may still be asked to preserve its integrity into the near future so that other subjects can participate naively. Researchers hope that they can trust participants to keep their secrets because their academic degrees, grant applications, and jobs may depend on it.

The subjectivity of participants not only plays a central role in experiments; it also acts as a focal point of researchers' practical concerns. As I have shown, researchers take care not to unduly bore participants (Rob) or to tire them unnecessarily (Ulla). When possible, they offer friendly conversation (Wade) and empathic appreciation of participants' unique contributions to research (Dr. R). These mundane ways researchers attend to participants leads us back to literary scholar Amanda Anderson's worry that cognitive psychology's "punctual" time, which we have met as "brief reaction time," might prevent participants from engaging in moral considerations. Because of their complexity and interrelationship with many social domains, moral considerations need "slow time" to emerge. My interlocutors would agree that experiments must narrowly isolate very particular aspects of perception or learning in order to yield the desired result. Demanding slow time in an experimental setting seems doomed to failure because of the conventions that hold the experimental form in place as the gold standard of scientific evidence. Maybe it will be of some comfort to literary scholars to know that slow time is there in the psychological science of my fieldwork, but it lies in the passages through which the experiment experimental results are processed before being published and embraced by the media. Faculty and graduate students have to juggle multiple constraints and opportunities: stay home with a sick child or attend a lab meeting; take up a distant but prestigious postdoc or continue contributing to one's PhD advisor's research; satisfy the IRB; take time away from one's own work to help junior colleagues or let them flounder. In these slow passages of collective work lie multitudes of moral considerations. The moral is social: we should help each other because we will also need help someday; our individual inconvenience should be set aside for the sake of building strong social relationships. Lab members learn they are expected to contribute time and effort to shop and cook for a potluck lunch; to give up sleep to travel to the site of an experiment; to take the time to answer the questions of a curious anthropologist and thereafter to edit her manuscript with a fine-toothed comb. In addition to all this, there is a shared commitment to the value of scientific knowledge: helping fellow psychologists with their work and sharing ideas about and critiques of their methods and findings will increase the chances that the field can make new advances and discoveries about human cognition.

At its heart, my argument is simply that the path to producing universal psychological findings is eminently a social one. Groups of lab members, students, professors, and subjects collaborate in the arduous work of planning and conducting experiments. This science is a collective endeavor that could (if its work were better understood) carry with it into mass media a vision of the shared human activities it depends on. Then we could realize that the solitary human is *never* the default condition, even in psychology experiments. The deep sociality of the field means that experimental cognitive psychology entails a generous moral frame, one that becomes far more apparent as its findings move beyond the lab. This frame does not say what *should* be or what *must* be; it is what anthropologist Michael Lambek calls "ordinary ethics." Ordinary ethics are "relatively tacit, grounded in agreement rather than rule, in practice rather than knowledge or belief, and happening without calling undue attention to itself." [1] Such a moral frame depends on humans working together collectively—not always harmoniously, but in attentive relationship to each other. [2]

The collective social activities involved in producing psychological science are a clarion call to a moral world to which we can aspire, and they demonstrate that the most powerful investigations of humans by humans are built on social relationships. If the social cooperation that lies behind the research findings of psychology experiments were made more obvious, perhaps we would be unwilling to tolerate uses of those findings that have nefarious social effects. The dark side of experimental psychology, which I mentioned in the introduction, from historical support of eugenics to more recent collaboration in interrogation techniques, depends on laboratory findings that are held to be universal and context free. I have argued to the contrary that the experiments themselves are a highly specific site of knowledge production that depend on social relationships unique to each site.

The Gaps

Throughout this book, we have encountered many gaps between the pure models of how cognition works on the one hand and the practicalities of living experience on the other. First, there was Cattell in Wundt's lab with his lip key, which overcame his inability to produce the ideal reaction time between stimulus and response. He thought the lip key bypassed his impairment and filled the gap with a direct numeric measure of brain activity. But when numeric measures filled the gap, they helped establish the convention of relying only on numerical data, which obscured the complexity of human responses. Then there was the gap between digital ones and zeros, in which the subtleties of ambivalent or uncertain responses disappear; the gap between the data eye trackers can capture and the emotional expressions it cannot capture and must ignore. There was the gap between the subject as a blank slate and the subject after being trained in the foyer of the experiment, which hides the dependence of the experimental method on the need for subjects to practice in order to master the conventions experiments depend upon; and the gap between the formal model of the experiment and the many different ways experiments can be experienced. The engine of psychology is powerful, but some of the technologies it depends upon reduce living experience to abstractions that leave behind the immensely subtle and complex nuances of human expression. A "gap" sounds like a place where something is missing, a dangerous emptiness like the void between the train and the platform or a missing step on a ladder. We have seen that all these gaps are far from empty, and in fact are filled with what we need to know to understand how formal models like the experiment function at all. In short, we should "mind the gap"—not to avoid it, but to pay attention to what happens in it, because it is there that numerical measures and formal models live their social lives.

Data and Individuals

Digital big data lends itself to predictions and manipulations that are potentially informed by very particular and questionable political goals. At its worst, judgments can be racialized, or elections can be thrown. Obviously, my research focused on the backstory of digital big data—the experimental psychology lab—not on the inside story of how internet technology companies use digital data in harmful ways. We are far from knowing the full reach of these manipulations. As I write this, it has just come to light that life insurance companies have been harvesting people's social media patterns to calculate the risk of offering them a policy.[3] There will doubtless be more revelations. As the methods and findings of experimental psychology escape the lab they have opened a remarkable Pandora's box!

My interlocutors' research in cognitive experimental psychology might in some ways promote a concept of the individual: single, isolated persons press keys and carry out predetermined tasks in small booths; researchers aggregate individual scores into averages and norms that represent the typical psychological subject. This would matter because seeing persons as individuals is a necessary component of contemporary free market capitalism. Every single person is to be an entrepreneur whose goal is to maximize his or her assets in a competition with others. Such individuals appear to have no social encumbrances or supports; they are not nurtured or endowed by parents or siblings; they are not transported on trains or highways paid for out of national budgets; their individual talents, if good enough, will carry them through barriers of race, gender, or class. And if individuals appear to not be good enough, they are relegated to the rank of the poor and disenfranchised.

But none of these are individual accomplishments or failures. We are only alive to be entrepreneurs because of public health regulations that give us clean water and vaccines; federal regulations that keep food safe and edible; public transportation agencies that build roads and run trains; housing regulations that keep buildings standing; civil and human rights legislation that enables large open markets across the world. In accord with this, the science of cognitive experimental psychology depends on a complex social world: trust in other researchers; trust in subjects; trust in technology as a product of past human uses; empathy for subjects; attention to subjects; cooperation and contestation with other researchers. When we come across media coverage from experiments in psychology, we can now remember the thick sociality behind the apparent individuality of the findings. We can think of research in experimental psychology as a journey up a staircase built with the help of many carpenters along the way and secured by many handrails. And we can also remember that access to the staircase is only through a foyer in which subjects are asked to practice how to behave as good psychological subjects.

If psychologists have "beaten" psychological data out of subjects, as Dr. B suggested, that means that subjects have been trained to submit data in particular kinds of ways. The training has appeared in this book in various guises. In part we are trained by the ubiquity of media coverage about psychological experiments, which, as we have seen, depend on the training of participants. In part we are heirs to the exhibit in the 1893 World's Fair, which first introduced the public to psychological questionnaires. In part we participate in pervasive opportunities to register our individual opinions online within strictly limited options (like choosing among four smiley faces on a HappyOrNot terminal). We are far from autonomous in these settings.

Commodification

There is an increasing awareness of the inescapable monitoring of our opinions, but most of the pushback focuses on *privacy*. I think the concern with privacy is important but somewhat off the mark. Privacy is an individual thing.

FIGURE 11.1. HappyOrNot terminal in Stockholm Arlanda airport, Sweden. Photo by author, 2019.

Monitoring is a social thing. In the digital world of New York City, where I live, my daily activities—my purchase of an e-book, my time reading the book, my decision to order takeout food, my travel with a metro card, iPhone in hand, while passing by many surveillance cameras to meet with a group of friends to discuss the book—become something else. The flow of my purposeful activity is transformed into discrete acts: separable into things that can be measured and monetized, and also separated from the purpose that gave them meaning in the first place. My purpose of putting time and effort into a gathering of friends and colleagues with whom I want to engage is erased. Marx taught us that capitalism rests on extracting the surplus value of commodities. Now our thoughts, plans, likes, and wishes are being commodified. They are gathered, put into a different form, and sent into the world as a force no longer at our behest, transformed into numbers that can guide product development and deployment. As Marx insisted, we need to follow the commodities of data and big data into the "hidden abode of production."[4] This is something we can think about when we are encouraged to push a "HappyOrNot" button terminal. Are we acting as unpaid consultants to corporations? We might imagine we are improving services or products for other consumers, but I doubt our feedback would be collected if it decreased profits for corporations.

Marx said that nothing, not even "the bones of the saints," can withstand being swept up in the circulation of commodities.[5] Similarly, with our digital lives, translating experience into numerical measures facilitates their circulation as commodities. Algorithms trained on masses of data readily generate numerical results that beg to be bought or sold: what to buy on Amazon, what to rent on Netflix, what to order on Seamless. More and more spheres of life are subjected to this transformation. Behind it all we can now see the circulation of the psychological subject, who appears in the lab as a blank slate of sorts, but who is then trained up in the foyer of the experiment to fit its demands for attention, focus, and patience. The terms of the experiment circle around the subject, draw him or her in, and generate experimental data. We are being optimized for generating numerical data inside the lab and out.

Looking Ahead

How can anyone help avoid the deleterious effects of having the value of our lives extracted and commodified? Ideally, we would work to make internet media corporations like Google or Facebook part of the public trust instead of privately owned. While we wait for that chance, we can support actions like the Google walkout, the formation of the research center AI Now, or the Algorithmic Justice League, founded by Joy Buolamwini.[6] We can sign petitions like the one at Daily Kos to protest the fact that Amazon's database provides "the technological backbone for ICE's operations to track, identify, and hunt down immigrants and markets new technologies to further help ICE."[7] We can join journalists in following the effects of specific content in social media in particular times and places. Despite the presumption of internet neutrality, called the "raceless imaginary" by sociologist Jessie Daniels, we can track invidious distinctions like racism on digital media: who has access to infrastructure and devices, who is affected by bias in algorithms or facial recognition.[8]

We can reject the conclusion that internet technology is an unmitigated disaster. In an op-ed, historian Jill Lapore says the digital machine is on fire! "The [digital] machine [. . .] has no brake, no fail-safe, no checks, no balances. It clatters. It thunders. It crushes the Constitution in its gears. The smell of smoke wafts out of the engine room. The machine is on fire."[9] Another dire diagnosis is in the recent *New York Times* "Privacy Project":

> We in the West are building a surveillance state no less totalitarian than the one the Chinese government is rigging up. But while China is doing it with government, we are doing it through corporations and consumer products, in the absence of any real regulation that recognizes the stakes at hand.[10]

Instead of imagining the digital machine self-destructing and taking us along with it or becoming a totalitarian monster, we can advance open questions about the digital, as many are already doing. We can do fieldwork, look into unintended consequences, understand the operations of power, see a variety of motivations not only for profit, but for creativity, innovation, preservation, sociality, and grassroots organizing.

We could be helped in this task by remembering the common beginnings of experimental psychology and ethnography. When I turned back in time to the standardization required by the Wundt lab, with its demand for endless practice trials inside the lab and engagement in comparable living and exercise routines outside the lab, I was reminded of the way the Cambridge anthropologists trained themselves to participate with the "minds" of Torres Straits Islanders and of the expedition's aim to make subjects comparable through experience of—and training in—the same environment. I realized that, in the Torres Straits, their routines entailed literal immersion in the physical surroundings and social life of the islanders. Recall the photo of the anthropologists with a family of Islanders who were their friends and interlocutors, "living rough." They were barefoot, their clothes were dirty and rumpled, their posture and position relative to the islanders were rather nonhierarchical for their time, albeit still within the overarching tenets of colonial power.

In the late nineteenth century the fields of anthropology and psychology were both operating from similar assumptions. Their goals were to discover the universals of the generalized mind for the Wundtian psychologists and the universals of human sensory capacities for the Cambridge anthropologists. Subsequently, cultural anthropology mostly dropped the experimental aspect of its early program but kept the participation and introspection aimed at understanding other human minds. "Living rough" entails a kind of equivalent of Wundt's endless practices to get in sync with others—practicing speaking another language, eating strange food, using unfamiliar tools, handling different weather and climate—in order to open a way to the minds of people from another culture. Living rough—participating by adopting the daily living conditions of others—became a criterion of good fieldwork. It was the only way to experience how people in other cultures lived, and it came to be called participant-observation. Anthropology was moving toward a more deeply contextualized kind of qualitative methodology. Of course, these beginning steps would falter, as I noted in the introduction. Some of these sentiments were tainted by colonial attitudes, and some would be harnessed to the ends of invidious and violent actions drawing on racism.

Meanwhile psychology moved away from Wundtian introspection and greatly developed the objective experimental aspect of its early program. Psychology too was at times harnessed to invidious practices that reproduced the assumption of Euro-American superiority. Perhaps something would be gained by finding new paths *between* these disciplines in their contemporary form, especially since both anthropology and psychology have mounted extensive efforts to make critical reflections on their histories a central part of their disciplines.

The engine of experimental psychology powers the prevailing perception that users of social and digital media take actions and make choices as *individuals*. This power relies on the strength of traditional technologies—the experiment, normative scales, training, and the extraction of data from subjects—to create spaces in the experimental psychology laboratory that are apparently occupied only by individual actions. And digital media, as we have seen, simply put this old wine in new bottles. In the context of the internet, the power that arises by way of extracting data from individual actions is formidable. There is hope for greater public awareness of both the benefits and the costs of this power: numerical data can help us predict when and where heavy traffic will grind to a halt or a dangerous epidemic will spread; but biased numerical data can also strengthen damaging distinctions based on race, gender, age, or class. On the one hand, businesses can sell numerical data for a profit or can loop predictive data back into social media for the sake of selling more commodities or electing more candidates favorable to business interests. On the other hand, the weakness of such data, since experimental methods in the lab or on social media can only capture rather superficial aspects of the complexity of human life, might actually limit how successfully users' decisions can be monetized. In the end, the weakness of such data might make us yearn for a richer description of human life. Ironically, we have seen that the apparently individually wielded tools of experimental psychology depend on a luxuriant set of social relationships in the laboratory that are necessary to achieve the collective effort that experiments require. Experiments with individual subjects rely upon subjectivity, practice that trains subjects in experiments, and habits that bring members of labs into a shared world. I hope taking serious account of these elements in this book will enable the development of an anthropological view of the social world from which experimental psychologists have launched the engine of their science.

NOTES

Preface

1. (Dwyer, 2020)

Acknowledgments

1. (Latour & Woolgar, 1986; Lynch, 1985; Traweek, 1992). Among the journals that I have found invaluable are *Isis, Science in Context, Science, Technology and Human Values, History of the Human Sciences, Science as Culture,* and *Social Studies of Science.*

Introduction

1. MacKenzie's work draws on classic studies of economics in its cultural contexts: (Callon, 1998; Knorr-Cetina, 2009; Latour, 1999; Mackenzie, 2008, p. 12).

2. (James, 1918[1890], p. 192)

3. (Mcdermott & Simpson, 2017, p. 21)

4. (Slater, 2005)

5. (Morawski, 2015, p. 572)

6. (Richards, 2002, p. 8)

7. (Lave, 1988)

8. (Cohn, 2008)

9. (Jack & Roepstorff, 2003)

10. This characterization holds for contemporary experimental psychology but not for the separate subdiscipline of "abnormal psychology." It is worth remembering that in the earlier history of the discipline, according to Nikolas Rose, "psychological knowledge of the individual was constituted around the role of abnormality." According to Rose, psychology "sought to establish itself by claiming its ability to deal with the problems posed for social apparatuses by dysfunctional conduct." The discipline focused itself on behavior and practices that needed regulation for the sake of smooth social functioning (Rose, 1985, p. 5).

11. (Saunders, 2008)

12. (Rose, 1998, p. 87)

13. (Laber-Warren, 2019)

14. (Project Implicit, 2011)

15. (Smith et al., 2017, p. 1)

16. (Tversky & Kahneman, 1974)

17. (Brooks, 2018, p. 2). Another version, from editorialist Margaret Renkl, reads, "Prejudice is endemic to humanity itself. Human beings are tribal creatures—we trust the familiar and are drawn to it; we distrust the unfamiliar and keep our distance . . . we are hard-wired to recognize difference and to view it as an aberration" (Renkl, 2018).

18. (Smith, 2014)

19. (Anderson, 2018, p. 31)

20. (ibid., p. 18)

21. (ibid., p. 96)

22. Many of the issues I discuss for cognitive psychology are addressed for the psychology of emotions in important work by Otniel Dror, which focuses on the history of the numerical representation of emotions (Dror, 1999, 2001).

23. (Open Source Collaboration, 2015; Stanley, Carter, & Doucouliagos, 2018)

24. (Jarrett, 2017)

25. (Braun, 2014; Carson, 1999; Pettit, 2007; Richards, 2012; Spiro, 2009; Stocking, 1968)

26. (Stark, 2012) gives useful insight into the way IRBs actually work.

27. (Morawski, 1994)

28. (Richards, 1997, p. 417). Capitalization in the original.

29. (Goff et al., 2008; Mullings, 2005). A number of psychologists have recently called for an appraisal of how a preponderance of subjects who are WEIRD, which stands for white, educated, industrialized, rich, and democratic, limits the universality of findings in psychological research (Henrich, Heine, & Norenzayan, 2010). There are a plethora of critical accounts of the history of anthropology focused on its legacy of colonialism and its assumptions, which once ignored the importance of diverse experiences. For some starting points, see (Asad, 1973; Baker, 1998; Stocking, 1968).

30. (Comaroff & Comaroff, 2003; Fanon, Sartre, & Farrington, 1963; Howitt, Owusu-Bempah, & Owusu-Bempah, 1994; Mama, 2002)

31. See (Brigham & Yerkes, 1922) and (Galton, 1891) for nineteenth- and early-twentieth-century efforts to promote eugenics, and (Danziger, 1990; Richards, 1997; Rose, 1985; Spiro, 2009) for historical analyses of eugenics and racism in the history of anthropology and psychology.

32. (Forte, 2011; Price, 2011)

33. In recent years, the APA has passed a series of resolutions that restrict "the role of military psychologists in detention sites that are in violation of the U.S. Constitution or international law" (American Psychological Association, 2018)

34. There are some illuminating analyses of gender (Behar & Gordon, 1995), colonialism (Comaroff & Comaroff, 2019), the Cold War (Price, 2016), and racism (Baker, 2010) in relation to anthropology.

35. (I. Parker, 2007; Teo, 2015; Walkerdine, 2002) are good starting places from which to explore this field. See also journals such as *International Journal of Critical Psychology* and *Theory & Psychology*. The "Critical Social/Personality Psychology" program at the Graduate Center of the City University of New York and the "Historical, Theoretical, and Critical studies of Psychology Program" at York University are examples of programs devoted to critical psychology.

36. (Helmreich, 2001, p 613)
37. (Boellstorff, 2013)

Chapter 1: Doing This Ethnography

1. (Ingold, 2013, p. 5). Emphasis in original.
2. (Miller, 1962, pp. 13–14)
3. (Rose, 1998, p. 13, 63)
4. (de Waal, 2019, p. 234)
5. Morana Alač provides an account complementary to mine in her ethnography of an experimental psychology lab studying olfactory sensations. She describes the embodied experience of psychologists and their subjects by focusing on what participants experience in real time experiments considered as a "shared environment of interaction" (Alač, 2020a; 2020b, p. 31).
6. I promised anonymity to the faculty and students in the labs where I carried out field work. I have devised various methods to keep this promise. First, of course, I use pseudonyms. Second, I keep the level of description to practices and concepts that are shared to varying degrees across the labs. Third, when I cite published articles, I do not identify which, if any, of them, were published by the labs I studied.
7. (Rhees, 1970, p. 50). My translation.

Chapter 2: Sensing the World

1. (Morgan, 1868)
2. (Feeley-Harnik, 2001, p. 75)
3. (Haddon, 1891)
4. (Coon, 1993, p. 770)
5. (ibid., p. 775)
6. (Boring, 1953, p. 172)
7. (Benschop & Draaisma, 2000, pp. 19–19; Cattell & Sokal, 1981, p. 89)
8. (Coon, 1993, p. 776)
9. (Benschop & Draaisma, 2000, pp. 58–59)
10. (Miller, 1962, p. 18)
11. (Dallenbach, 2013[1913], p. 469)
12. (ibid., p. 467)
13. (Diriwächter, 2004, pp. 96–98)
14. (Wong, 2009, p. 240)
15. (Bruner, 1986, pp. 32, 40)
16. Throughout the text, ellipses not in brackets are from the original source text, while any ellipses I have inserted are in brackets.
17. (Cattell & Sokal, 1981, p. 335)
18. (ibid., p. 99)
19. (ibid., p. 65)
20. (Cattell, 1886; Cattell & Sokal, 1981, pp. 334–35)
21. (Cattell, 1886, p. 41)

22. (Prochnik, 2012, p. 144)
23. (James, 1909, pp. 115, 119)
24. (Cattell, 1898; James & Cattell, 1898, p. 535)
25. (James & Cattell, 1898)
26. (Coon, 1992, pp. 149–50)
27. (Kuklick, 1998; Richards, 1998, p. 4)
28. (Kuklick, 2011, pp. 20-21)
29. (Haddon et al., 1935, p. 286)
30. (ibid., p. 14)
31. (Haddon et al., 1901, pp. 121–22)
32. (ibid., p. 142)
33. (Richards, 1998, p. 137)
34. (Haddon et al., 1901, p. 177)
35. (ibid., p. 152)
36. (Richards, 1997, p. 46)
37. (Barkan, 1992, p. 28)
38. (Jukes & Browne, 1871, p. 116)
39. (Taussig, 1993, p. 215)
40. (Haddon, 1901, p. 49)
41. (Grimshaw, 2009)
42. (Edwards, 1998)
43. (Freire-Marreco & Myres, 1912)
44. (Myers, 1909, p. 96)
45. (ibid., p. 97)
46. (ibid., p. 99)
47. (McGuinness, 1988, p. 127)
48. (Myers, 1907, p. 249)
49. (Myers, 1913, p. 582)
50. (Edwards, 1998, p. 17)
51. (Danziger, 1990, p. 183)
52. (Titchener, 1901, 1908)
53. (Boring, 1950, p. 413)
54. (ibid., p. 172)
55. (Blumenthal, 2001, p. 131; Kim, 2016)
56. (Danziger, 2001, pp. 111–12)
57. (ibid.)
58. (ibid., p. 112)
59. (Cattell, 1947, p. 65)
60. (Cattell & Sokal, 1981, p. 333)
61. (Cattell, 1947)
62. (Cattell & Sokal, 1981, pp. 334–35)
63. (Cattell, 1947, pp. 107–9)
64. (Cattell, 1897, p. 298)

65. (O'Donnell, 1985, p. 35)

66. (ibid.)

67. (Baldwin, 1895, pp. 264–67)

68. (Angell et al., 1896, pp. 246, 258)

69. (O'Donnell, 1985, p. 34)

70. (Buckley, 1989, p. 27)

71. (Watson, 1913, p. 169)

72. (Watson, 1913)

73. (Watson, 1919, pp. 12–13)

74. (Buckley, 1989, p. 98)

75. (ibid., p. 104)

76. (Kevles, 1968, p. 573)

77. (ibid., p. 578)

78. (Rose, 1998, p. 87)

Chapter 3: Experimenting Scientifically

1. (Morawski, 1998, p. 215)

2. (Bayer, 1998, p. 187; Danziger, 1990)

3. Danziger (1985) provides a history of the changing elements of the psychological experiment from Wundt's nineteenth-century laboratory to twentieth-century American practices, based on published experimental reports.

4. (Winston & Blais, 1996, p. 599)

5. See (Morrison et al. 2019) for a trenchant examination of the "task," and how it has been operationalized in experimental psychology.

6. A similar quandary occurs in large-scale survey research. Coding of interviews that can yield precise numbers is required for scientific validity, even though many relevant insights will be ignored. In survey research, "to ensure the standardization of the procedure, the interactivity of ordinary conversational processes is suppressed" (Suchman & Jordan, 1990).

7. (Kaplan, 2017)

8. (Libet, 1985)

9. (Wise, 1997, p. 3)

10. (Stam et al., 2000, pp. 365–82)

11. (Morawski, 1988; 2015, p. 592)

12. (Despret, 2017, p. 13)

13. (Frankenberg, 1997, p. 1)

14. (Bradley & Lang, 2007; Lang, 1995)

15. (Ekman & Friesen, 1971, p. 124)

16. Recently, the idea that there are a basic number of facial expressions that are universally interpreted as depicting a basic set of emotions has been criticized. Some researchers have found that "facial expressions vary widely between contexts and cultures" (Heaven, 2020, p. 502).

17. (Brenneis, 2008, pp. 162–63)

Chapter 4: Normalizing Data

1. In *Picturing Personhood: Brain Scans and Biomedical Identity*, Joe Dumit provides a detailed description of how "the normal brain" is identified from PET scans of the brain (Dumit, 2004, p. 60ff).

2. (Linstead & Pullen, 2006; Schulz & Mullings, 2005)

3. (Canguilhem, 2016, p. 212)

4. The debate is active within the field of psychology, where researchers wonder whether their sources of data are too "WEIRD," or Western, educated, industrialized, rich, and democratic, to be generally representative (Kupferschmidt, 2019).

5. (Morawski, 2015, pp. 567–97)

6. (Paolacci et al., 2010)

7. (Newman, 2019)

8. (Fourtané, 2018)

9. (Irani, 2015)

10. You can see the way this looks in table 3.2.

11. (Morawski, 2015, p. 570)

12. (Luck, 2014, p. 259)

13. (Jastrow, 1890, p. 99)

14. (Jastrow, 1930) quoted in (Shore, 2001, p. 72)

15. (Baldwin, 1901, pp. 384, 398–99)

16. (Jastrow, 1893, pp. 50–60)

17. (Benjamin, 2014, p. 51)

18. (ibid.)

19. ("Experimental psychology at the fair," 1893; "Where men's senses are tested," 1893)

20. (Danziger, 1990, p. 100)

21. (Wittgenstein et al., 1969, p. 122)

22. See (Suchman, 2007, pp. 66, 74, 118ff.) for insightful elaboration of the role of "normative categories" in the social sciences.

Chapter 5: Delimiting Technologies

1. (Watson, 1913, p. 163)

2. (Luck, 2014, pp. 13, 15, 19, 27)

3. (Bennett et al., 2009)

4. (BBC, 2011)

5. (Sparks, 2013)

6. (Carp, 2012, p. 149)

7. Lucy Suchman and Brigitte Jordan (1990, p. 240) argue that "Validity is not assured simply by having interviewers repeat the same words across different respondents. In contrast to a thermometer or other instrument of measurement, an interview, no matter how standardized, remains fundamentally a linguistic and interactional event. However successful the effort to improve the wording of survey questions may be, word choice will never eliminate the need for interviewers and respondents to negotiate the meaning of both questions and answers."

8. (Sternberg, 1966, p. 428)

9. (Sternberg, 2016)

10. (ibid., p. 2072)

11. (Kutas & Hillyard, 1980, pp. 99–116)

12. (Downing et al., 2001, pp. 2470–73)

13. (Haxby et al., 2001, pp. 2425–30)

Chapter 6: Stabilizing Subjects

1. (Hering, 1868)

2. (Cahan, 1993, pp. 143–47)

3. (Benschop, 1998)

4. (Cattell, 1886, p. 512)

5. (Sanford, 1888, p. 419)

6. (Banister, 1927, p. 52)

7. (Tinker, 1928, p. 478)

8. (Fisher et al., 1969, p. 112)

9. (Jacobs et al., 1989, p. 95)

10. (Liu & Arditi, 2001, p. 51)

11. (Latour, 1999, p. 38)

12. (Gell, 1996, p. 29)

13. (Bloch, 2009)

14. (Bowen, 1964, p. 4)

15. Plato says in *The Republic*:

> "Let us take any common instance; there are beds and tables in the world—plenty of them, are there not?"
>
> "Yes."
>
> "But there are only two ideas or forms of them—one the idea of a bed, the other of a table" (Plato 2016, pp. 257–58).

Marx says in *Capital*:

> It is absolutely clear that, by his activity, man changes the forms of the materials of nature in such a way as to make them useful to him. The form of wood, for instance, is altered if a table is made out of it. Nevertheless the table continues to be wood, an ordinary, sensuous thing. But as soon as it emerges as a commodity, it changes into a thing which transcends sensuousness. It not only stands with its feet on the ground, but, in relation to all other commodities, it stands on its head, and evolves out of its wooden brain grotesque ideas, far more wonderful than if it were to begin dancing of its own free will (Marx 2006, pp. 163–64).

Chapter 8: Practicing Experimental Tasks

1. (Hopkirk, 2006, pp. 330–31)

2. (Kantowitz et al., 2014, p. 269). David Martin recommends "practice trials" to "minimize warm-up effects," which he defines as "fast improvement" before "general readiness" (Martin,

2007, pp. 31, 152). In Breakwell's *Research Methods in Psychology*, "general tips" are provided that advise experimenters to use practice trials to make sure the performance levels off before you capture the "variability intrinsic to performance." Breakwell also states it will take a lot of practice trials before "performance stabilizes" (Breakwell et al., 2012, pp. 177–78).

3. (Lang et al., 2008, p. 4)

4. (Wittgenstein, 2014[1956], p. 336)

5. (Williams, 2002, p. 213)

6. (Brenneis, 2008, p. 156)

7. (Daston & Galison, 2007)

8. (ibid., pp. 20–21)

9. (Shapin 2012, p. 171)

10. (Orne, 1969)

11. (Adair & Spinner, 1983, p. 5)

12. (Adair & Spinner, 1983)

13. (Orne, 1969, p. 778)

14. (Collins, 2001, p. 118)

15. (Cattell, 1904, p. 180)

16. (Bayer, 1998, p. 187)

17. (Wittgenstein, 1953, para. 5)

18. In May and June of 1912, Wittgenstein worked in Myers' psychology lab: this we know from entries in the diary of his friend, David Pinsent. There were so many entries that biographer McGuinness says psychology was Wittgenstein's hobby (McGuinness, 1988, p. 128).This would not have been exceptional: according to Frederic Bartlett's autobiography, "all students reading moral science then did—or were supposed to—do four hours of experimental work weekly in the psychological laboratory" (Bartlett, 1936, p. 39). According to Monk, "it seems to have been his intention to investigate scientifically the role of rhythm in musical appreciation" (Monk, 1991, p. 49). Wittgenstein demonstrated an experiment for the meetings of the British Psychological Society, introduced by Myers, which was recorded in the proceedings of the British Psychological Society in July 1912 (Wittgenstein & Muscio, 1912). North surmises this was the rhythmograph (North, 2002, p. 44). Klagge and Nordmann (2003, p. 360) note that Moore described the experiments as being about rhythm. In any case, Wittgenstein called it a "most absurd paper on rhythms" in a letter to Russell (McGuinness, 1988, p. 128).

19. "The existence of the experimental method makes us think we have the means of solving the problems which trouble us; though problem and method pass one another by." (Wittgenstein, 1953:xiv, p. 232e)

Chapter 9: Envisaging "Productive Thinking"

1. (Ash, 1998; Külpe, 1909; Stumpf, 2019; Von Ehrenfels, 1937)

2. (Myers, 1907, p. 249)

3. (Wertheimer, 2017)

4. (Wertheimer, 1938, p. 2)

5. (Köhler, 1925, pp. 238, 255–56, 258). Emphasis in original.

6. (Wertheimer, 1959[1945], p. 63)

7. (ibid., p. 64)

8. (ibid., p. 191)

9. (ibid., p. 136)

10. (Geertz 1973; Turner 1967)

11. (Miller et al., 1960, p. 113)

12. (ibid., pp. 103–4). All emphases in original

13. (ibid., p. 105)

14. (Green & Swets, 1966)

15. (Wittgenstein, 1980, para. 118). "Here it all depends on *what we want to know* when we ask someone what he sees."

16. (Gibson, 1986)

17. (Bates, 2007, p. 239)

18. (ibid., p. 250)

19. (ibid.)

Chapter 10: Moving beyond the Lab

1. This is the context for his remark: "However, the reconciliation of irrational forms in which certain economic relations appear and assert themselves in practice does not concern the active agents of these relations in their everyday life. And since they are accustomed to move about in such relations, they find nothing strange therein. A complete contradiction offers not the least mystery to them. They feel as much at home as a fish in water among manifestations which are separated from their internal connections and absurd when isolated by themselves" (Marx, 2006[1867], p. 779).

2. Dr. B had already acted as an ethnographer of his discipline by conducting a series of experiments without brief reaction times, allowing subjects as much time to respond as they liked. He repeated a series of classic experiments about the "word-superiority effect," which had shown that subjects' responses were more accurate when the stimulus was a word rather than a nonword. The main results of previous experiments using brief reaction times controlled by a tachistoscope were replicated in his new experiments without brief reaction times. He concluded that the word-superiority effect was a more general phenomenon that previously realized and did not depend on brief reactions timed by the tachistoscope (Prinzmetal, 1992).

3. (Mackenzie, 2008, p. 12)

4. See (Rabinbach, 1990, p. 265ff) for how ergonomics during the war built on earlier studies of human energy and fatigue.

5. (Fitts, 1947, p. 8)

6. (ibid., p. 2)

7. In those early years, psychological experiments were used alongside extensive interviews with pilots and engineers to understand how and when human capacities did not match well with technological devices. Psychologists even did a sort of participant observation by learning to use the problematic equipment themselves (Fitts, 1947, p. 11).

8. (Grether, 1968)

9. (Kroemer-Elbert, 2018)

10. (Norman, 1988, 2013)

11. (Kuang & Fabricant, 2019, pp. 10, 22)

12. (ibid., p. 87)

13. (Irani, 2018) makes the important point that the recent hype around the history of "design thinking" also carries racialized assumptions about the preeminence of North American design faced with global competition from Asia.

14. (Murayama et al., 2010)

15. (Allen, 2017)

16. (Public Broadcasting Service, 2018)

17. (Wong, 2017)

18. (Lewis, 2017a; Lewis, 2017b). Facebook designers probably did not intend to produce the effect, demonstrated by experimental psychologists, that passive viewing of Facebook reduces affective well-being, in part because of envy at the positive posts of friends. (Kross et al., 2013; Ryan et al., 2014; Verduyn et al., 2015) explore the studies on addiction and Facebook.

19. (Barry, 2018)

20. (Schüll, 2014)

21. (ibid., p. 18)

22. (Busby, 2018)

23. (Skinner, 1953)

24. (Berns et al., 2001)

25. (Alter, 2017, pp. 127–28)

26. (Lewis, 2017a)

27. (Eyal, 2014; see also Alter, 2017).

28. (Jensen, 2010; Turkle, 2015) provide some access to both sides of the debate.

29. (Mullings, 2005, p. 679)

30. (Boellstorff & Mauer, 2015) provides insights about how to understand data and big data.

31. (Benjamin 2019)

32. (Eubanks, 2018)

33. See (Broussard, 2019, p. 179) on the binary foundations of computing and how poorly a simple binary system—"which is what computers are"—can represent human expertise.

34. (Lupton, 2018) explores the active ways people amplify, cull, contextualize, build on, or ignore personal digital data.

35. (Suchman, 2020)

36. (Copeland, 2019)

37. (Sayer, 1990, pp. 129–30)

38. (Christian & Griffiths, 2016, p. 3; Moschovakis, 2001; Mueller & Massaron, 2017, p.11)

39. Such labor is arduous because it is punishingly repetitive and tedious, though in some cases it can provide a living (Gray & Suri, 2019; Metz, 2019a).

40. (Edmonds, 2019)

41. (Zuboff, 2019, p. 300)

42. (ibid.)

43. (ibid.)

44. (ibid., p. 279)

45. (Kosner, 2012)

46. (Helft, 2011)

47. (Stolzoff, 2018)

48. (Fogg, 2003)

49. (ibid., p. 185)

50. (ibid., pp. 219–20)

51. (Cadwalladr, 2018; "Cambridge Analytica files," 2018)

52. (Wylie, 2018, pp. 10–11)

53. (Hill, 2019)

54. (Hill, 2021)

55. (Weise & Singer, 2020)

56. (Rainie & Anderson, 2017, p. 19)

57. (Bond et al., 2012)

58. (Heidegger, 1977, p. 14)

59. (Hacking, 1982, p. 280)

60. (Kurita, et al., 2019)

61. (Rainie & Anderson, 2017)

62. (Levendowski, 2017)

63. (Noble, 2018, p. 171). In her book, *Algorithms of Oppression: How Search Engines Reinforce Racism*, Safiya Noble details the ways algorithms behind search engines enact racialized and gendered content. Other sources agree. *Frontline*'s "The Facebook Dilemma" quotes Rand Waltzman, Program Manager at DARPA, who feared as early as 2010 that social media could be used for nefarious manipulative purposes.

64. (Bogen, 2019; Metz, 2019b; Obermeyer et al., 2019; Singer, 2019; Stout 2019)

65. (Broussard, 2019, pp. 92–119) provides a detailed demonstration of how training sets are used to evaluate algorithms in machine learning.

66. Efforts to do ethnographic research using online material include (Bjork-James 2020; Haynes 2016; Hine 2017; Procter et al. 2013; Utekhin, 2017).

67. (Fisher & Taub, 2018)

68. (Menczer & Hills, 2020)

69. (Roose et al., 2020)

70. (Wittgenstein, 1953, para. 132)

71. (L. A. Suchman, 2007, p. 11)

Chapter 11: Entering Social and Digital Media

1. (Lambek, 2010, p. 2)

2. (Keane, 2016)

3. (Scism, 2019)

4. (Marx, 2006[1867], p. 171)

5. (ibid., p. 229)

6. (Algorithmic Justice League, 2020)

7. ("Sign the petition: Amazon, Stop powering ICE's deportation machine" n.d.)

8. (Daniels, 2018)

9. (Lapore, 2018)

10. (Manjoo, 2019)

REFERENCES CITED

Adair, J. G., & Spinner, B. 1983. Task perceptions and behavioural expectations: A process-oriented approach to subject behaviour in experiments. *Canadian Journal of Behavioral Sciences*, 15(2), 131–41.

Alač, M. 2020a. Beyond intersubjectivity in olfactory psychophysics I: Troubles with the Subject. *Social Studies of Science*, 50(3), 440–73. https://doi.org/10.1177/0306312720915645

——— 2020b. Beyond intersubjectivity in olfactory psychophysics II: Troubles with the Object. *Social Studies of Science*, 50(3), 474–502. https://doi.org/10.1177/0306312720915646

Algorithmic Justice League. 2020. Our mission. https://www.ajl.org/about

Allen, M. 2017, November 9. Sean Parker unloads on Facebook: "God only knows what it's doing to our children's brains.". *Axios*. https://www.axios.com/sean-parker-unloads-on-facebook-god-only-knows-what-its-doing-to-our-childrens-brains-1513306792-f855e7b4-4e99-4d60-8d51-2775559c2671.html

Alter, A. L. 2017. *Irresistible: The Rise of Addictive Technology and the Business of Keeping Us Hooked*. Penguin.

American Psychological Association. 2018, August 8. APA Rejects Proposal Expanding Role of Military Psychologists to Treat Detainees in All Settings [Press release]. https://www.apa.org/news/press/releases/2018/08/military-psychologists-detainees

Anderson, A. 2018. *Psyche and Ethos: Moral Life after Psychology*. Oxford University Press.

Angell, J. R., Moore, A. W., & Jegi, J. J. 1896. Studies from the psychological laboratory of the University of Chicago: I. Reaction-time: A study in attention and habit. *Psychological Review*, 3(3), 245–58. https://doi.org/10.1037/h0069918

Asad, T. 1973. *Anthropology & the Colonial Encounter*. Ithaca Press.

Ash, M. G. 1998. *Gestalt Psychology in German Culture, 1890–1967: Holism and the Quest for Objectivity*. Cambridge University Press.

Baker, L. D. 1998. *From Savage to Negro: Anthropology and the Construction of Race, 1896–1954*. University of California Press.

——— 2010. *Anthropology and the Racial Politics of Culture*. Duke University Press.

Baldwin, J. M. 1895. Types of reaction. *Psychological Review*, 2(3), 259–73. https://dx.doi.org/10.1037/h0068783

———. 1901. Historical and Educational Report on Psychology. In M. Shore (Ed.), *Psychology and Memory in the Midst of Change: The Social Concerns of Late–19th-century North American Psychologists* (Vol. 1, pp. 357–404). American Psychological Society.

Banister, H. 1927. Block capital letters as tests of visual acuity. *British Journal of Ophthalmology*, 11(2), 49–62.

Barkan, E. 1992. *The Retreat of Scientific Racism: Changing Concepts of Race in Britain and the United States between the World Wars*. Cambridge University Press.

Barry, E. 2018, March 28. Data-mining swung election on Brexit, says a witness. *New York Times*, A4.

Bartlett, F. C. 1936. Frederic Charles Bartlett [autobiography]. In C. Murchison (Ed.), *A History of Psychology in Biography* (Vol. 3, pp. 39–52). Clark University Press.

Bates, D. 2007. Creating Insight: Gestalt Theory and the Early Computer. In J. Riskin (Ed.), *Genesis Redux: Essays in the History and Philosophy of Artificial Life* (pp. 237–59). University of Chicago Press.

Bayer, B. M. 1998. Between Apparatuses and Apparitions: Phantoms of the Laboratory. In B. M. Bayer & J. Shotter (Eds.), *Reconstructing the Psychological Subject* (pp. 187–213). Sage.

BBC (Producer). 2011. *The Mysteries of the Human Brain*. https://www.bbc.co.uk/programmes/p009vmsq

Behar, R., & D. A. Gordon. 1995. *Women Writing Culture*. University of California Press.

Benjamin, L. T. 2014. *A Brief History of Modern Psychology*. Wiley.

Benjamin, R. 2019. *Race after Technology: Abolitionist Tools for the New Jim Code*. Wiley.

Bennett, C. M., Baird, A. A., Miller, M. B., & Wolford, G. L. 2009. Neural Correlates of Interspecies Perspective Taking in the Post-mortem Atlantic Salmon: An Argument for Multiple Comparisons Correction. http://users.stat.umn.edu/~corbett/classes/5303/Bennett-Salmon-2009.pdf

Benschop, R. 1998. What is a tachistoscope? Historical explorations of an instrument. *Science in Context*, 11(1), 23–50.

Benschop, R., & Draaisma, D. 2000. In pursuit of precision: The calibration of minds and machines in late nineteenth-century psychology. *Annals of Science*, 57(1), 1–25. http://www.informaworld.com/10.1080/000337900296281

Berns, G. S., McClure, S. M., Pagnoni, G., & Montague, P. R. 2001. Predictability modulates human brain response to reward. *Journal of Neuroscience*, 21(8), 2793–98.

Bjork-James, S. 2020. Racializing misogyny: Sexuality and gender in the new online white nationalism. *Feminist Anthropology*. https://doi.org/10.1002/fea2.12011

Bloch, M. (2009). Claude Lévi-Strauss obituary. *Guardian*. https://www.theguardian.com/science/2009/nov/03/claude-levi-strauss-obituary

Blumenthal, A. 2001. A Wundt Primer: The Operating Characteristics of Consciousness. In R. W. Rieber & D. K. Robinson (Eds.), *Wilhelm Wundt in History: The Making of a Scientific Psychology* (pp. 121–44). Kluwer Academic.

Boellstorff, T. 2013, October. Making big data, in theory. *First Monday*. https://doi.org/10.5210/fm.v18i10.4869

Boellstorff, T., & Maurer, B. 2015. *Data, Now Bigger and Better!* Prickly Paradigm Press.

Bogen, M. 2019. All the ways hiring algorithms can introduce bias. *Harvard Business Review*. https://hbr.org/2019/05/all-the-ways-hiring-algorithms-can-introduce-bias

Bond, R. M., Fariss, C. J., Jones, J. J., Kramer, A.D.I., Marlow, C., Settle, J. E., & Fowler, J. H. 2012. A 61-million-person experiment in social influence and political mobilization. *Nature*, 489(7415), 295–98. https://doi.org/10.1038/nature11421

Boring, E. G. 1950. *A History of Experimental Psychology* (2d ed.). Appleton-Century-Crofts.

———. 1953. A history of introspection. *Psychological Bulletin*, 50(3), 169–86.

Bourg, A. & Jacoby, J. (Writers and Directors). 2018, October 29. The Facebook Dilemma, Part 1, (Season 37, Episode 8) [TV series episode]. In R. Aronson-Rath (Producer), *Frontline*. Public Broadcasting Service.

Bowen, E. S. 1964. *Return to Laughter*. Anchor Books.

Bradley, M. M., & Lang P. J. 1994. Measuring emotion: The Self-Assessment Manikin and the semantic differential. *Journal of Behavioral Therapy and Experimental Psychology*, 25(1), 49–59.

———. 2007. The International Affective Picture System (IAPS) in the Study of Emotion and Attention. In *Handbook of Emotion Elicitation and Assessment* (pp. 29–46). Oxford University Press.

Braun, L. 2014. *Breathing Race into the Machine: The Surprising Career of the Spirometer from Plantation to Genetics*. University of Minnesota Press.

Breakwell, G. M., Smith, J. A., & Wright, D. B. 2012. *Research Methods in Psychology*. Sage Publications.

Brenneis, D. 2008. Telling theories. *Ethos*, 36(1), 155–69.

Brigham, C. C., & Yerkes, R. M. 1922. *A Study of American Intelligence*. Princeton University Press.

Brooks, D. 2018, January 1. The retreat to tribalism. *New York Times*. https://search.proquest.com /docview/1983153995?accountid=12768

Broussard, M. 2019. *Artificial Unintelligence: How Computers Misunderstand the World*. MIT Press.

Bruner, J. S. 1986. *Actual Minds, Possible Worlds*. Harvard University Press.

Buckley, K. W. 1989. *Mechanical Man: John Broadus Watson and the Beginnings of Behaviorism*. Guilford Press.

Busby, M. 2018, May 8. Social media copies gambling methods "to create psychological cravings." *Guardian*. https://www.theguardian.com/technology/2018/may/08/social-media -copies-gambling-methods-to-create-psychological-cravings

Cadwalladr, C. 2018, March 17. I created Steve Bannon's psychological warfare tool: Meet the data war whistleblower. *Guardian*. http://www.theguardian.com/news/2018/mar/17/data -war-whistleblower-christopherwylie-faceook-nix-bannon-trump

Cahan, D. (1993). *Hermann Von Helmholtz and the Foundations of Nineteenth-century Science*. University of California Press.

Callon, M. 1998. *Laws of the Markets*. Wiley.

Cambridge Analytica Files, The: A year-long investigation into Facebook, data, and influencing elections in the digital age. 2018. *Guardian*. https://www.theguardian.com/news/series /cambridge-analytica-files

Canguilhem, G. 2016. Qu'est-ce que la psychologie? [What is psychology?] (D. Peña-Guzmán, Trans.). *Foucault Studies*, 21(June), 200–13.

Carp, J. 2012. On the plurality of (methodological) worlds: estimating the analytic flexibility of fMRI experiments. *Frontiers In Neuroscience*, 6(149). https://doi.org/10.3389/fnins.2012 .00149

Carson, J. 1999. Minding matter/mattering mind: Knowledge and the subject in nineteenth-century psychology. *Studies in History and Philosophy of Science, Part C: Studies in History and Philosophy of Biological and Biomedical Sciences*, 30(3), 345–76.

Cattell, J. M. K. 1886. The time taken up by cerebral operations. *Mind*, 11, 220–42.

———. 1897. Note on "reaction types." *Psychological Review*, 4(3), 298-99.

———. 1898. Mrs. Piper, the medium. *Science*, 7(172), 534–35. http://www.jstor.org.proxy.library .nyu.edu/stable/1624885

———. 1904. The conceptions and methods of psychology. *Popular Science Monthly*, 66 (November), 176–86.

———. 1947. *James McKeen Cattell, 1860–1944: Man of Science. Part 2: Addresses and formal papers*. (A. T. Poffenberger, Ed.). Science Press.

Cattell, J.M.K., & Sokal, M. M. 1981. *An Education in Psychology: James McKeen Cattell's Journal and Letters from Germany and England, 1880–1888*. MIT Press.

Christian, B., & Griffiths, T. 2016. *Algorithms to Live by: The Computer Science of Human Decisions*. Henry Holt and Company.

Cohn, S. 2008. Making objective facts from intimate relations: The case of neuroscience and its entanglements with volunteers. *History of the Human Sciences*, 21(4), 86–103.

Collins, H. 2001. What Is Tacit Knowledge? In K. Knorr Cetina, T. R. Schatzki, & E. von Savigny (Eds.), *The Practice Turn in Contemporary Theory* (pp. 115–28). Routledge.

Comaroff, J., & Comaroff, J. 2003. Ethnography on an awkward scale: Postcolonial anthropology and the violence of abstraction. *Ethnography*, 4(2), 147–79.

Coon, D. J. 1992. *Testing the Limits of Sense and Science: American Experimental Psychologists Combat Spiritualism, 1880–1920* (Vol. 47). American Psychological Association.

———. 1993. Standardizing the subject: Experimental psychologists, introspection, and the quest for a technoscientific ideal. *Technology and Culture*, 34(4), 757–83.

Copeland, R. 2019, November 12. Google amasses personal medical records—company teams up with one of the U.S.'s largest health systems in "Project Nightingale." *Wall Street Journal*. http://proxy.library.nyu.edu/login?url=https://search-proquest-com.proxy.library.nyu.edu /docview/2313481203?accountid=12768

Dallenbach, K. M. 2013. *The Measurement of Attention*. Hardpress. (Original work published 1913)

Daniels, J. 2018. The algorithmic rise of the "Alt-Right." *Contexts*, 17(1), 60–65. https://doi.org /10.1177/1536504218766547

Danziger, K. 1985. The origins of the psychological experiment as a social institution. *American Psychologist* 40(2), 133–40.

———. 1990. *Constructing the Subject: Historical Origins of Psychological Research*. Cambridge University Press.

———. 2001. The Unknown Wundt. In R. W. Rieber & D. K. Robinson (Eds.), *Wilhelm Wundt in History: The Making of a Scientific Psychology* (pp. 95–120). Springer US.

Daston, L., & Galison, P. 2007. *Objectivity*. Zone Books.

de Waal, F. 2019. *Mama's Last Hug: Animal Emotions and What They Tell Us about Ourselves*. W. W. Norton.

Despret, V. 2017. *What Would Animals Say If We Asked the Right Questions?* University of Minnesota Press.

Diriwächter, R. 2004. Völkerpsychologie: The synthesis that never was. *Culture & Psychology*, 10(1), 85–109. https://doi.org/10.1177/1354067X04040930

Downing, P. E., Jiang, Y., Shuman, M., & Kanwisher, N. 2001. A cortical area selective for visual processing of the human body. *Science*, 293(5539), 2470–73.

Dror, O. Y. 1999. The scientific image of emotion: Experience and technologies of inscription. *Configurations*, 7(3), 355–401.

———. 2001. Counting the affects: Discoursing in numbers. *Social Research*, 68(2), 357–78.

Dumit, J. 2004. *Picturing Personhood: Brain Scans and Biomedical Identity*. Princeton University Press.

Dwyer, C. 2020, April 23. Coronavirus has infected a 5th of New York City, testing suggests. NPR. https://www.npr.org/sections/coronavirus-live-updates/2020/04/23/842818125 /coronavirus-has-infected-a-fifth-of-new-york-city-testing-suggests

Edmonds, R. 2019, April 10. The New York Times sells premium ads based on how an article makes you feel. *Poynter*. https://www.poynter.org/business-work/2019/the-new-york-times -sells-premium-ads-based-on-how-an-article-makes-you-feel

Edwards, E. 1998. Performing Science: Still Photography and the Torres Strait Expedition. In A. Herle & S. Rouse (Eds.), *Cambridge and the Torres Strait: Centenary Essays on the 1898 Anthropological Expedition* (pp. 106–35). Cambridge University Press.

Ekman, P., & Friesen, W. V. 1971. Constants across cultures in the face and emotion. *Journal of Personality and Social Psychology*, 17(2), 124.

Eubanks, V. 2018. *Automating Inequality: How High-Tech Tools Profile, Police, and Punish the Poor*. St. Martin's Publishing Group.

Experimental Psychology at the Fair. 1893, November 5. *Chicago Daily Tribune*, p. 28.

Eyal, N. 2014. *Hooked: How to Build Habit-Forming Products*. Penguin.

Fanon, F., Sartre, J. P., & Farrington, C. 1963. *The Wretched of the Earth*. Grove Press.

Feeley-Harnik, G. 2001. The Mystery of Life in All Its Forms: Religious Dimensions of Culture in Early American Anthropology. In S. L. Mizruchi (Ed.), *Religion and Cultural Studies* (pp. 140–91). Princeton University Press.

Fisher, D. F., Monty, R. A., & Glucksberg, S. 1969. Visual Confusion matrices: Fact or artifact? *Journal of Psychology*, 71(1), 111–25.

Fisher, M., & Taub, A. 2018, April 26. Does Facebook just harbor extremists? Or does it create them? *New York Times*, A11.

Fitts, P. M. 1947. Psychological Research on Equipment Design. *Army Air Forces Aviation Psychology Program Research Reports*, Report 19.

Fogg, B. J. 2003. *Persuasive Technology: Using Computers to Change What We Think and Do*. Kaufmann.

Forte, M. C. 2011. The Human Terrain System and anthropology: A review of ongoing public debates. *American Anthropologist*, 113(1), 149–53.

Fourtané, S. 2018, August 31. The Turk: Wolfgang von Kempelen's Fake Automaton Chess Player. https://interestingengineering.com/the-turk-fake-automaton-chess-player

Frankenberg, R. 1997. Introduction: Local Whitenesses, Localizing Whiteness. In R. Frankenberg (Ed.), *Displacing Whiteness: Essays in Social and Cultural Criticism* (pp. 1–34). Duke University Press.

Freire-Marreco, B. W., & Myres, J. L. 1912. *Notes and Queries on Anthropology*. The Royal Anthropological Institute.

Galton, F. 1891. *Hereditary Genius: An Inquiry into its Laws and Consequences*. D. Appleton.

Geertz, C. 1973. Deep Play: Notes on the Balinese Cockfight. In *The Interpretation of Cultures: Selected Essays* (pp. 41–44). Basic Books.

Gell, A. 1996. Vogel's net. *Journal of Material Culture*, 1(1), 15–38.

Gibson, J. J. 1986. *The Ecological Approach to Visual Perception*. Lawrence Erlbaum Associates.

Goff, P. A., Eberhardt, J. L., Williams, M. J., & Jackson, M. C. 2008. Not yet human: Implicit knowledge, historical dehumanization, and contemporary consequences. *Journal of Personality and Social Psychology*, 94(2), 292–306. https://doi.org/10.1037/0022-3514.94.2.292

Gray, M. L., & Suri, S. 2019. *Ghost Work: How to Stop Silicon Valley from Building a New Global Underclass*. Houghton Mifflin Harcourt.

Green, D. M., & Swets, J. A. 1966. *Signal Detection Theory and Psychophysics*. John Wiley & Sons Canada, Limited.

Grether, W. F. 1968. Engineering psychology in the United States. *American Psychologist*, 23(10), 743–51.

Grimshaw, A. 2009. Visual Anthropology. In H. Kuklick (Ed.), *New History of Anthropology* (pp. 293–309). Wiley.

Hacking, I. 1982. Biopower and the avalanche of printed numbers. *Humanities in Society*, 5(3–4), 279–95.

Haddon, A. C. (1891). *Reports on the Zoological Collections Made in Torres Straits*. Royal Dublin Society.

———. (1901). *Head-Hunters: Black, White, and Brown*. Methuen & Co.

Haddon, A. C., Wilkin, A., Ray, S. H., McDougall, W., Myers, C. S., Seligman, C. G., & Rivers, W.H.R. 1901. *Reports of the Cambridge Anthropological Expedition to Torres Straits* (Vol. 2, Physiology and Psychology). The Cambridge University Press.

———. 1935. *Reports of the Cambridge Anthropological Expedition to Torres Straits: Vol. 1. General Ethnography*. The Cambridge University Press.

Haxby, J. V., Gobbini, M. I., Furey, M. L., Ishai, A., Schouten, J. L., & Pietrini, P. (2001). Distributed and overlapping representations of faces and objects in ventral temporal cortex. *Science*, 293(5539), 2425–30.

Haynes, N. 2016. *Social Media in Northern Chile: Posting the Extraordinarily Ordinary*. UCL Press.

Heaven, D. 2020. Why faces don't always tell the truth about feelings. *Nature*, 578(7796), 502–4.

Heidegger, M. 1977. *The Question Concerning Technology, and Other Essays* (W. Lovitt, Trans.) Harper & Row. Original work published 1952, 1954, 1962.

Helft, M. 2011, May 7. The class that built apps, and fortunes. *New York Times*. https://www.nytimes.com/2011/05/08/technology/08class.html

Helmreich, S. 2001. After culture: Reflections on the apparition of anthropology in artificial life, a science of simulation. *Cultural Anthropology*, 16(4), 612–27.

Hering, E. 1868. *The Theory of Binocular Vision*. Springer.

Hill, K. 2020, January 19. Face scan app inches toward end of privacy. *New York Times*.

———. 2021, February 4. Facial recognition app ruled illegal in Canada. *New York Times*, 3.

Hine, C. 2017. Ethnographies of Online Communities and Social Media: Modes, Varieties, Affordances. In N. Fielding, R. Lee, & G. Blank (Eds.), *The Sage Handbook of Online Research Methods* (pp. 401). Sage Publications Ltd.

Hopkirk, P. 2006. *The Great Game*. Hodder & Stoughton.

Howitt, D., Owusu-Bempah, J., & Owusu-Bempah, K. 1994. *The Racism of Psychology: Time for Change*. Prentice Hall.

Ingold, T. 2013. *Making: Anthropology, Archaeology, Art and Architecture*. Routledge.

Irani, L. 2015. Difference and dependence among digital workers: The case of Amazon Mechanical Turk. *South Atlantic Quarterly*, 114(1), 225–34. https://doi.org/10.1215/00382876-2831665

———. 2018. "Design thinking": Defending Silicon Valley at the apex of global labor hierarchies. *Catalyst: Feminism, Theory, Technoscience*, 4(1), 1–19.

Jack, A., & Roepstorff, A. 2003. *Trusting the Subject?: The Use of Introspective Evidence in Cognitive Science*. Imprint Academic.

Jacobs, A. M., Nazir, T. A., & Heller, O. 1989. Perception of lowercase letters in peripheral vision: A discrimination matrix based on saccade latencies. *Perception & Psychophysics*, 46(1), 95–102. http://proxy.library.nyu.edu/login?url=http://search.ebscohost.com/login.aspx?direct=true&db=mnh&AN=2755768&site=ehost-live

James, W. 1909. Report on Mrs. Piper's Hodgson-control. *Proceedings of the Society for Psychical Research*, 23, 2–121.

———. 1918. *The Principles of Psychology*. H. Holt. (Original work published 1890)

James, W., & Cattell, J. M. (1898). Mrs. Piper, "The medium." *Science*, 7(175), 640–42. http://www.jstor.org.proxy.library.nyu.edu/stable/1624522

Jarrett, C. 2017. These nine cognitive psychology findings all passed a stringent test of their replicability. *Research Digest, The British Psychological Society*. https://digest.bps.org.uk/2017/06/05/these-nine-cognitive-psychology-findings-all-passed-a-stringent-test-of-their-replicability/

Jastrow, J. 1890. *The Time-Relations of Mental Phenomena*. N.D.C. Hodges.

———. 1893. The Section of Psychology. In W. A. Smith (Ed.), *Official catalogue: World's Columbian Exposition* (Vol. Part VII, pp. 50–60). W. B. Conkey.

———. 1930. Joseph Jastrow. In C. Murchison (Ed.), *A History of Psychology in Autobiography* (Vol. 1, pp. 135–62). Russell & Russell.

Jensen, K. B. 2010. *Media Convergence: The Three Degrees of Network, Mass and Interpersonal Communication*. Taylor & Francis.

Jukes, J. B., & Browne, C. A. 1871. *Letters and Extracts from the Addresses and Occasional Writings of J. Beete Jukes*. Chapman and Hall.

Kantowitz, B., Roediger, H., & Elmes, D. 2014. *Experimental Psychology*. Cengage Learning.

Kaplan, A. 2017. *The Conduct of Inquiry: Methodology for Behavioural Science*. Taylor & Francis.

Keane, W. 2016. *Ethical Life: Its Natural and Social Histories*. Princeton University Press.

Kevles, D. J. 1968. Testing the Army's intelligence: Psychologists and the military in World War I. *Journal of American History*, 55(3), 565–81. https://doi.org/10.2307/1891014

Kim, A. 2016. Wilhelm Maximilian Wundt. In E. N. Zalta (Ed.), *Stanford Encyclopedia of Philosophy*. https://plato.stanford.edu/entries/wilhelm-wundt/

Klagge, J. C., & Nordmann, A. 2003. *Ludwig Wittgenstein: Public and Private Occasions*. Rowman and Littlefield.

Knorr-Cetina, K. 2009. *Epistemic Cultures: How the Sciences Make Knowledge*. Harvard University Press.

Köhler, W. 1925. *The Mentality of Apes* (E. Winter, Trans.). Harcourt, Brace and Company.

Kosner, A. 2012, December 4. Stanford's school of persuasion: B. J. Fogg on how to win users and influence behavior. *Forbes Tech*. https://www.forbes.com/sites/anthonykosner/2012/12/04/stanfords-school-of-persuasion-bj-fogg-on-how-to-win-users-and-influence-behavior/?sh=2a6c349d390d

Kroemer-Elbert, K. E. 2018. *Ergonomics: How to Design for Ease and Efficiency.* Academic Press.

Kross, E., Verduyn, P., Demiralp, E., Park, J., Lee, D. S., Lin, N., Shablack, H., Jonides, J., & Ybarra, O. 2013. Facebook use predicts declines in subjective well-being in young adults. *PLOS ONE,* 8(8), e69841. https://doi.org/10.1371/journal.pone.0069841

Kuang, C., & Fabricant, R. 2019. *User Friendly: How the Hidden Rules of Design Are Changing the Way We Live, Work, and Play.* Farrar, Straus and Giroux.

Kuklick, H. 1998. Fieldworkers and Physiologists. In A. Herle & S. Rouse (Eds.), *Cambridge and the Torres Strait: Centenary Essays on the 1898 Anthropological Expedition* (pp. 158–80). Cambridge University Press.

———. 2011. Personal equations: Reflections on the history of fieldwork, with special reference to sociocultural anthropology. *Isis,* 102(March), 1–33.

Külpe, O. 1909. *Outlines of Psychology: Based upon the Results of Experimental Investigation.* George Allen & Unwin.

Kupferschmidt, K. 2019, July 11. Is the Western mind too WEIRD to study? https://www .sciencemag.org/news/2019/07/western-mind-too-weird-study

Kurita, K., Vyas, N., Pareek, A., Black, A. W., & Tsvetkov, Y. 2019. Measuring bias in contextualized word representations. arXiv [preprint]. https://arxiv.org/abs/1906.07337v1

Kutas, M., & Hillyard, S. A. (1980). Event-related brain potentials to semantically inappropriate and surprisingly large words. *Biological Psychology,* 11(2), 99–116.

Laber-Warren, E. (2019, October 17). You're only as old as you feel. *New York Times.* https:// www.nytimes.com/2019/10/17/well/mind/age-subjective-feeling-old.html

Lambek, M. 2010. *Ordinary Ethics: Anthropology, Language, and Action.* Fordham University Press.

Lang, P. J. 1995. The emotion probe: Studies of motivation and attention. *American Psychologist,* 50(5), 372–85. https://doi.org/10.1037/0003-066X.50.5.372

Lang, P. J., Bradley, M.M., & Cuthbert, B.N. 2008. *International Affective Picture System (IAPS): Affective Ratings of Pictures and Instruction Manual.* University of Florida.

Lapore, J. 2018, September 16. The hacking of America. *New York Times,* SR1.

Latour, B. 1999. *Pandora's Hope: Essays on the Reality of Science Studies.* Harvard University Press.

Latour, B., & Woolgar, S. 1986. *Laboratory Life: The Construction of Scientific Facts.* Princeton University Press.

Lave, J. 1988. *Cognition in Practice: Mind, Mathematics and Culture in Everyday Life.* Cambridge University Press.

Levendowski, A. 2018, July 24. How copyright law can fix artificial intelligence's implicit bias problem. *Washington Law Review,* 579. https://ssrn.com/abstract=3024938

Lewis, P. (2017a, November 19). How Silicon Valley hooks us. *Week.* http://theweek.com /articles/737813/how-silicon-valley-hooks

———. (2017b, October 6). "Our minds can be hijacked": The tech insiders who fear a smartphone dystopia. *Guardian.* https://www.theguardian.com/technology/2017/oct/05 /smartphone-addiction-silicon-valley-dystopia

Libet, B. 1985. Unconscious cerebral initiative and the role of conscious will in voluntary action. *Behavioral and Brain Sciences,* 8(4), 529–66.

Linstead, S., & Pullen, A. 2006. Gender as multiplicity: Desire, displacement, difference and dispersion. *Human Relations,* 59(9), 1287–1310.

Liu, L., & Arditi, A. 2001. How crowding affects letter confusion. *Optometry and Vision Science*, 78(1), 50–55.

Luck, S. J. 2014. *An Introduction to the Event-Related Potential Technique*. MIT Press.

Lupton, D. 2018. How do data come to matter? Living and becoming with personal data. *Big Data & Society*. https://doi.org/10.1177/2053951718786314

Lynch, M. 1985. *Art and Artifact in Laboratory Science: A Study of Shop Work and Shop Talk in a Research Laboratory*. Routledge & Kegan Paul.

Mackenzie, D. 2008. *An Engine, Not a Camera: How Financial Models Shape Markets*. MIT Press.

Mama, A. 2002. *Beyond the Masks: Race, Gender and Subjectivity*. Routledge.

Manjoo, F. 2019, April 10. It's time to panic about privacy. *New York Times*.

Martin, D. 2007. *Doing Psychology Experiments*. Cengage Learning.

Marx, K. 2006. *Capital: A Critique of Political Economy* (Vol. 1). Penguin Books Limited. (Original work published 1867)

Mauss, M. 1954. *The Gift: Forms and Functions of Exchange in Archaic Societies*. Cohen & West.

Mcdermott, P., & Simpson, L. 2017. A note from the artistic directors (*Opening Skinner's Box* by the Improbable Theatre, July 10–12, 2017). *Playbill*, 21.

McGuinness, B. 1988. *Wittgenstein: A Life. Young Ludwig (1889–1921)*. University of California Press.

Menczer, F., & Hills, T. 2020. The attention economy. *Scientific American*, 323(6), 54–61.

Metz, C. (2019a, August 18). Oh, the monotony of shifting the tedium to A.I. *New York Times*, BU1.

———. (2019b, November 13). We teach A.I. systems everything, including our biases. *International New York Times*. https://link.gale.com/apps/doc/A605550862/STND?u=nysl_me_newyorku&sid=STND&xid=2d841f58

Miller, G.A., E. Galaanter, and K.H. Pribram. 1960. *Plans and the Structure of Behavior*. Holt.

Miller, G. A. 1962. *Psychology: The Science of Mental Life*. Harper & Row.

Monk, R. 1991. *Ludwig Wittgenstein: The Duty of Genius*. Vintage London.

Morawski, J. G. 1988. Impossible Experiments and Practical Constructions: The Social Bases of Psychologists' Work. In J. G. Morawski (Ed.), *The Rise of Experimentation in American Psychology* (pp. 72–93). Yale University Press.

———. 1994. *Practicing Feminisms, Reconstructing Psychology: Notes on a Liminal Science*. University of Michigan Press.

———. 1998. The Return of Phantom Subjects? In B. M. Bayer & J. Shotter (Eds.), *Reconstructing the Psychological Subject: Bodies, Practices and Technologies*. Sage.

———. 2015. Epistemological dizziness in the psychology laboratory: Lively subjects, anxious experimenters, and experimental relations, 1950–1970. *Isis: An International Review Devoted to the History of Science and its Cultural Influences*, 106(3), 567–97.

Morgan, L. H. 1868. *The American Beaver and His Works*. Lippincott.

Morrison, H., S. McBriar, H. Powell, J. Proudfoot, S. Stanley, D. Fitzgerald, and F. Callard. 2019. What Is a psychological task? The operational pliability of "task" in psychological laboratory experimentation. *Engaging Science, Technology, and Society*, 5, 61-85.

Moschovakis, Y. N. 2001. What Is an Algorithm? In *Mathematics Unlimited—2001 and Beyond* (pp. 919–36). Springer.

Mueller, J. P., & Massaron, L. 2017. *Algorithms for Dummies*. Wiley.

Mullings, L. 2005. Interrogating racism: Toward an antiracist anthropology. *Annual Review of Anthropology*, 34, 667–93.

Murayama, K., Matsumoto, M., Izuma, K., & Matsumoto, K. 2010. Neural basis of the undermining effect of monetary reward on intrinsic motivation. *Proceedings of the National Academy of Sciences*, 107(49), 20911–16.

Myers, C. S. 1907. The Ethnological Study of Music. In H. Balfour, et al. (Ed.), *Anthropological Essays Presented to Edward Burnett Tylor in Honour of His 75th Birthday, Oct. 2, 1907* (pp. 235–54). Clarendon Press.

———. 1909. *A Text-Book of Experimental Psychology*. Cambridge University Press.

———. 1913. The Beginnings of Music. In E. C. Quiggin (Ed.), *Essays and Studies Presented to William Ridgeway on His 60th Birthday* (pp. 560–82). Cambridge University Press.

Newman, A. 2019, November 18. I found work on an Amazon website. I made 97 cents an hour. *New York Times*. http://proxy.library.nyu.edu/login?url=https://search-proquest-com.proxy.library.nyu.edu/docview/2315011371?accountid=12768

Noble, S. U. 2018. *Algorithms of Oppression: How Search Engines Reinforce Racism*. New York University Press.

Norman, D. A. 1988. *The Psychology of Everyday Things*. Basic Books.

———. 2013. *The Design of Everyday Things* (Revised and Expanded Edition). Basic Books.

North, M. 2002. *Reading 1922: A Return to the Scene of the Modern*. Oxford University Press.

O'Donnell, J. M. 1985. *The Origins of Behaviorism: American Psychology, 1870–1920*. New York University Press.

Obermeyer, Z., Powers, B., Vogeli, C., & Mullainathan, S. 2019. Dissecting racial bias in an algorithm used to manage the health of populations. *Science*, 366(6464), 447–53. https://doi.org/10.1126/science.aax2342

Open Science Collaboration. 2015. Estimating the reproducibility of psychological science. *Science*, 349(6251).

Orne, M. 1969. Demand Characteristics and the Concept of Quasi-Controls. In R. Rosenthal & R. L. Rosnow (Eds.), *Artifact in behavioral research* (pp. 143). Academic Press.

Paolacci, G., Chandler, J., & Ipeirotis, P. G. 2010. Running experiments on Amazon Mechanical Turk. *Judgment and Decision making*, 5(5), 411–19.

Parker, I. 2007. Critical psychology: What it is and what it is not. *Social and Personality Psychology Compass*, 1(1), 1–15.

Pettit, M. 2007. Joseph Jastrow, the psychology of deception, and the racial economy of observation. *Journal of the History of Behavioral Sciences*, 43(2), 159–75.

Plato. 2016. *The Republic* (B. Jowett, Trans.). Digireads.com.

Price, D. H. 2011. How the CIA and Pentagon harnessed anthropological research during the Second World War and Cold War with little critical notice. *Journal of Anthropological Research*, 67(3), 333–56. http://www.jstor.org/stable/41303322

———. 2016. *Cold War Anthropology: The CIA, the Pentagon, and the Growth of Dual Use Anthropology*. Duke University Press.

Prinzmetal, W. 1992. The word-superiority effect does not require a T-scope. *Perception & Psychophysics*, 51(5), 473–84.

Prochnik, G. 2012. *Putnam Camp: Sigmund Freud, James Jackson Putnam and the Purpose of American Psychology*. Other Press.

Procter, R., Vis, F., & Voss, A. 2013. Reading the riots on Twitter: methodological innovation for the analysis of big data. *International Journal of Social Research Methodology*, 16(3), 197–214. https://doi.org/10.1080/13645579.2013.774172

Project Implicit. 2011. https://implicit.harvard.edu/implicit/index.jsp

Public Broadcasting Service. 2018. WATCH: Cambridge Analytica whistleblower testifies before Senate. https://www.pbs.org/newshour/politics/watch-live-cambridge-analytica-whistleblower-testifies-before-senate

Rabinbach, A. 1990. *The Human Motor: Energy, Fatigue, and the Origins of Modernity*. Basic Books.

Rainie, L., & Anderson, J. 2017. *Code-Dependent: Pros and Cons of the Algorithm Age*. http://www.pewinternet.org/2017/02/08/code-dependent-pros-and-cons-of-the-algorithm-age

Renkl, M. 2018, July 31. The way to talk to a racist. *New York Times*. https://www.nytimes.com/2018/07/30/opinion/how-to-talk-to-a-racist.html

Rhees, R. 1970. *Discussions of Wittgenstein*. Schocken.

Richards, G. 1997. *Race, Racism, and Psychology: Towards a Reflexive History*. Routledge.

———. 1998. Getting a Result: The Expedition's Psychological Research, 1898–1913. In A. Herle & S. Rouse (Eds.), *Cambridge and the Torres Strait: Centenary Essays on the 1898 Anthropological Expedition* (pp. 136–57). Cambridge University Press.

———. 2002. The psychology of psychology: A historically grounded sketch. *Theory & Psychology*, 12(1), 7–36.

———. 2012. *Race, Racism and Psychology: Towards a Reflexive History*. (2nd edition). Taylor & Francis.

Roose, K., Isaac, M., & Frenkel, S. 2020. Facebook struggles to balance civility and growth. *New York Times*. https://www.nytimes.com/2020/11/24/technology/facebook-election-misinformation.html

Rose, N. S. 1985. *The Psychological Complex: Psychology, Politics and Society in England, 1869–1939*. Routledge Kegan & Paul.

———. 1998. *Inventing Our Selves: Psychology, Power and Personhood*. Cambridge University Press.

Ryan, T., Chester, A., Reece, J., & Xenos, S. 2014. The uses and abuses of Facebook: A review of Facebook addiction. *Journal of Behavioral Addictions*, 3(3), 133–48. https://doi.org/10.1556/JBA.3.2014.016

Sanford, E. C. 1888. The relative legibility of the small letters. *American Journal of Psychology*, 1(3), 402–35. https://doi.org/10.2307/1411012

Saunders, B. F. 2008. *CT Suite: The Work of Diagnosis in the Age of Noninvasive Cutting*. Duke University Press.

Sayer, D. 1990. *Violence of Abstraction: The Analytical Foundations of Historical Materialism*. Wiley-Blackwell.

Schüll, N. D. 2014. *Addiction by Design: Machine Gambling in Las Vegas*. Princeton University Press.

Schulz, A. J., & Mullings, L. 2005. *Gender, Race, Class and Health: Intersectional Approaches*. Wiley.

Scism, L. 2019, January 30. New York insurers can evaluate your social media use—if they can prove why it's needed. *Wall Street Journal*. https://www.wsj.com/articles/new-york-insurers-can-evaluate-your-social-media-useif-they-can-prove-why-its-needed-11548856802

Shapin, S. 2012. The sciences of subjectivity. *Social Studies of Science*, 42(2), 170–84. https://doi .org/10.1177/0306312711435375

Shore, M. 2001. Psychology and Memory in the Midst of Change: The Social Concerns of Late–19th-century North American Psychologists. In C. D. Green, M. Shore, & T. E. Teo (Eds.), *Influences of 19th Century Philosophy, Technology, and Natural Science* (pp. 63–86).

Sidowski, J. B., J. H. Johnson, & T. A. Williams (Eds.). 1980. *Technology in Mental Health Care Delivery Systems*. Ablex Publishing.

Sign the Petition: Amazon, Stop powering ICE's deportation machine. n.d. https://www .dailykos.com/campaigns/petitions/sign-the-petition-amazon-stop-powering-ices -deportation-machine

Singer, N. 2019, November 15. Apple adds its muscle to medicine. *New York Times*, B1(L). https://link.gale.com/apps/doc/A605808023/STND?u=nysl_me_newyorku&sid =STND&xid=cc3680d9

Skinner, B. F. 1953. *Science and Human Behavior*. Free Press.

Slater, L. 2005. *Opening Skinner's Box: Great Psychological Experiments of the Twentieth Century*. W. W. Norton.

Smith, D., Schlaepfer, P., Major, K., Dyble, M., Page, A. E., Thompson, J., . . . Migliano, A. B. 2017. Cooperation and the evolution of hunter-gatherer storytelling. *Nature Communications*, 8(1), 1853. https://doi.org/10.1038/s41467-017-02036-8

Smith, E. E. 2014, June 12. Masters of love. *Atlantic*. https://www.theatlantic.com/health/archive /2014/06/happily-ever-after/372573/

Sparks, O. (Producer). 2013. Oxford Sparks: A spin around the brain. https://www.youtube.com /watch?v=ouSYLy9itgg

Spiro, J. P. 2009. *Defending the Master Race: Conservation, Eugenics, and the Legacy of Madison Grant*. University of Vermont Press.

Stam, H. J., Radtke, H. L., & Lubek, I. 2000. Strains in experimental social psychology: A textual anaylsis of the development of experimentation in social psychology. *Journal of the History of the Behavioral Sciences*, 36(4), 365–82.

Stanley, T., Carter, E. C., & Doucouliagos, H. 2018. What meta-analyses reveal about the replicability of psychological research. *Psychological Bulletin*, 144(12), 1325.

Stark, L. 2012. *Behind Closed Doors: IRBs and the Making of Ethical Research*. University of Chicago Press.

Sternberg, S. 1966. High-speed scanning in human memory. *Science*, 153(3736), 652–54.

———. (2016). In defence of high-speed memory scanning. *Quarterly Journal of Experimental Psychology*, 69(10), 2020–75. https://doi.org/10.1080/17470218.2016.1198820

Stocking, G. W. 1968. *Race, Culture, and Evolution: Essays in the History of Anthropology*. Free Press.

Stolzoff, S. 2018. The formula for phone addiction might double as a cure. *Wired*. https://www .wired.com/story/phone-addiction-formula/

Stout, N. 2019. Automated Expulsion in the U.S. Foreclosure Epidemic. In C. Besteman & H. Gusterson (Eds.), *Life by Algorithms: How Roboprocesses Are Remaking Our World* (pp. 31–43). University of Chicago Press.

Stumpf, C. 2019. *Tone Psychology: Vol. 1. The Sensation of Successive Single Tones*. Routledge.

Suchman, L. 2020. Algorithmic warfare and the reinvention of accuracy. *Critical Studies on Security*, 1–13. https://doi.org/10.1080/21624887.2020.1760587

Suchman, L., & Jordan, B. (1990). Interactional troubles in face-to-face survey interviews. *Journal of the American Statistical Association*, 85(409), 232–41. https://doi.org/10.2307/2289550

Suchman, L. A. 2007. *Human-Machine Reconfigurations: Plans and Situated Actions.* Cambridge University Press.

Taussig, M. 1993. *Mimesis and Alterity: A Particular History of the Senses.* Routledge.

Teo, T. 2015. Critical psychology: A geography of intellectual engagement and resistance. *American Psychologist*, 70(3), 243.

Tinker, M. A. 1928. The relative legibility of the letters, the digits, and of certain mathematical signs. *Journal of General Psychology*, 1, 472–96.

Titchener, E. B. 1901. *Experimental Psychology: A Manual of Laboratory Practice.* Microform. Macmillan.

——— 1908. *Lectures on the Elementary Psychology of Feeling and Attention.* Macmillan.

Traweek, S. 1992. *Beamtimes and Lifetimes: The World of High Energy Physicists.* Harvard University Press.

Turkle, S. 2015. *Reclaiming Conversation: The Power of Talk in a Digital Age.* Penguin Publishing Group.

Turner, V. W. 1967. *The Forest of Symbols: Aspects of Ndembu Ritual.* Cornell University Press.

Tversky, A., & Kahneman, D. 1974. Judgment under uncertainty: Heuristics and biases. *Science*, 185(4157), 1124. https://doi.org/10.1126/science.185.4157.1124

Utekhin, I. (2017). Small data first: pictures from Instagram as an ethnographic source. *Russian Journal of Communication*, 9(2), 185–200. https://doi.org/10.1080/19409419.2017.1327328

Verduyn, P., Lee, D. S., Park, J., Shablack, H., Orvell, A., Bayer, J., . . . Kross, E. 2015. Passive Facebook usage undermines affective well-being: Experimental and longitudinal evidence. *Journal of Experimental Psychology: General*, 144(2), 480–88.

Von Ehrenfels, C. 1937. On Gestalt-qualities. *Psychological Review*, 44(6), 521–24.

Von Helmholtz, Hermann. 1867. *Handbuch der physiologischen Optik.* Leopold Voss, p. 517, fig. 167.

Walkerdine, V. (Ed.). 2002. *Challenging Subjects: Critical Psychology for a New Millennium.* Macmillan International Higher Education.

Watson, J. B. (1913). Psychology as the behaviorist views it. *Psychological Review*, 20(2), 169.

———. 1919. *Psychology from the Standpoint of a Behaviorist.* J. B. Lippincott Company.

Weber, M. 1958. *The Protestant Ethic and the Spirit of Capitalism* (T. Parsons, Trans.). Scribner. (Original work published 1904-5.)

Weise, K., & Singer, N. 2020, June 11. Amazon stops letting police use its software for facial recognition. *New York Times*, B3.

Wertheimer, M. 1938. Gestalt Theory. In W. D. Ellis (Ed.), *A Source Book of Gestalt Psychology* (pp. 1–11). Routledge.

———. (1959). *Productive Thinking* (M. Wertheimer, Ed.). Harper and Row. (Original work published in 1945)

———. 2017. *Max Wertheimer and Gestalt Theory.* Taylor & Francis.

Where men's senses are tested. 1893, September 10. *Chicago Daily Tribune.*

Whipple, G. E. 1921. *Manual of mental and physical tests in two parts: A book of directions compiled with special reference to the experimental study of children in the laboratory or classroom.* Warwick & York. https://www.flickr.com/photos/internetarchivebookimages/14597524180/

Williams, M. 2002. *Wittgenstein, Mind and Meaning: Towards a Social Conception of Mind*. Taylor & Francis.

Winston, A. S., & Blais, D. J. 1996. What counts as an experiment? A transdisciplinary analysis of textbooks, 1930–1970. *American Journal of Psychology*, 109(4), 599–616. https://doi.org/10.2307/1423397

Wise, M. N. 1997. *The Values of Precision*. Princeton University Press.

Wittgenstein, L. 1953. *Philosophical Investigations*. Basil Blackwell.

———. 1980. *Remarks on the Philosophy of Psychology*. (Vol. 1; G.E.M. Anscombe, Trans.; G.E.M. Anscombe & G. H. von Wright, Eds.). Basil Blackwell.

Wittgenstein, L. 2014. *Remarks on the Foundation of Mathematics*. (G.E.M. Anscombe, Trans.; G.H. von Wright and R. Rhees, Eds.). Martino Fine Books. (Original work published 1956)

Wittgenstein, L., & Muscio, B. 1912. Experiments on rhythm (Demonstration). *British Journal of Psychology, including Proceedings of the British Psychological Society*, 5, 356.

Wittgenstein, L., Anscombe, G. E. M., & Wright, G. H. 1969. *On Certainty*. Harper.

Wong, J. C. 2017. Former Facebook executive: Social media is ripping society apart. *Guardian*. https://www.theguardian.com/technology/2017/dec/11/facebook-former-executive-ripping-society-apart

Wong, W.C. 2009. Retracing the footsteps of Wilhelm Wundt: Explorations in the disciplinary frontiers of psychology and in Völkerpsychologie. *History of Psychology*, 12(4), 229–65.

Wylie, C. 2018, May 16. *Written statement in the matter of Cambridge Analytica and other related issues, United States Senate Committee on the Judiciary*, 115th Cong.

Zuboff, S. 2019. *The Age of Surveillance Capitalism: The Fight for a Human Future at the New Frontier of Power*. PublicAffairs.

INDEX

Aberdeenshire, Scotland, 37
ein Abrichten, 182–83
abstraction, 219–20
activation, pattern of, 135
Adair, John, 179
Addiction by Design (Schüll), 215
aesthetics, measurement of, 154–55
Affect-Behavior Checklist, 179
affordance, 203–4
African Americans, 224, 225
After Tylor (Stocking), 38
Age of Surveillance Capitalism, The (Shoshana), 221, 230
AggregateIQ, 227
Alač, Morana, 249n5
algorithms, 218–22; training of, 227–29
Amazon Mechanical Turk, 89–92
Amazon, 2, 225
American Beaver, The (Morgan), 27
American Psychological Association, 50
analog clock, effect of, 67
Anderson, Amanda, 8, 237
Angell, J. R., 47–48
apperception, 45
Ascension (system), 219
"attention and impulsivity" experiment, 128–29
averaging: definition of, 99; of ERP signals, 94–97; of fMRI signals, 97–101

Baldwin, Mark, 45; on introspection, 46–47
Banister, H., 151–52
Banks, Bill, 67

Barkan, Elazar, 38
basic science, 224–25
Bates, David, 204
Bayer, Betty, 56
beavers, 26–27
Beck, Diane, 192
Beck Depression Inventory (BDI), 61
behavioral technologies, 125–29
Benschop, Ruth, 30, 146
bias: algorithms and, 218, 219, 228–29, 243; in data, 228, 244; in databases, 85; implicit, 6–7; perceptual, 67; racial/gender, 89, 219, 243, 229, 243; in subjects, 133
Bidirectional Encoder Representations from Transformer (BERT), 227
bite board, 139, 144–45
black box, 153, 189; in eye tracking, 166–67
blind spot, 75
Boas, Franz, 27
Bohannan, Laura, 159
Boring, Edwin, 30
Brenneis, Don, 82, 176
British India Survey, 174
British Psychological Society, 183
Brooks, David, 7
Bruner, Jerome, 32, 81
Buckley, Kerry, 48

Cambridge Analytica, 214, 224
Cambridge Anthropological Expedition, 17, 35–44, 243. See also *Reports of the Cambridge Anthropological Expedition to the Torres Straits*; Torres Straits Islanders

A NOTE ON THE TYPE

This book has been composed in Arno, an Old-style serif typeface in the
classic Venetian tradition, designed by Robert Slimbach at Adobe.